INTERNATIONAL COMMERCIAL
BANKING MANAGEMENT

JAMES L. KAMMERT

International Commercial Banking Management

A Division of
American Management Associations

To my wife, Marly,
and my sons,
Mark and Jim

Library of Congress Cataloging in Publication Data

Kammert, James L.
   International commercial banking management.

   Includes index.
   1. Banks and banking, International. 2. Bank
management.   I. Title.
HG3881.K27   332.1'5'068   80-69688
ISBN 0-8144-5680-4   AACR2

© 1981 AMACOM

A division of American Management Associations, New York.
All rights reserved.
Printed in the United States of America.

FIRST PRINTING

Preface

B efore the American Management Associations requested a book on the management aspects of international commercial banking, the need for such a book already was obvious. For the last twenty-five years the international commercial banking industry has grown faster and produced more profits than at any time in history. Moreover, in spite of difficult economic conditions and sweeping political changes throughout much of the world for most of the last decade, the industry continued to grow and attract new entrants of all sizes each year.

During the 1980s it seems certain that international banking activity will continue to expand. More corporations will trade internationally to increase revenues and obtain needed raw materials. In addition, the government policies of most nations will promote increased exports in order to pay for energy imports. At the same time foreign investment will be encouraged in order to create jobs and provide higher living standards. Furthermore, this increased activity will require higher levels of international banking services in the face of perhaps the most challenging economic and political environment since the end of World War II. Accordingly, more people involved in international banking will need ideas and guidance to cope successfully under these circumstances.

A significant body of literature now exists on the various specialized techniques of international banking, ranging from letters of credit and trade financing to foreign exchange and cross-border lending. However, little has been written to date about international commercial banking from the management viewpoint. The purpose of this book is to help fill that void.

This book deals with planning, people, procedures, and problems from the management viewpoint for the members of the international commercial banking team and various specialists who work with that team. This includes not only those within the various international units of banks but also members of the board of directors and senior management who are responsible for directing the international banking function and domestic bankers, lawyers, accountants, and others from inside and outside the commercial banks who have dealings with the international division. Government banking regulators and corporate treasury department personnel also should find this book useful.

Surely, greater understanding of international commercial banking from the management perspective will help all international bankers and those who work with them to become more effective in the conduct of their work, especially during the dynamic decade of the 1980s, for success in international banking, as in any other form of organized activity, depends upon good management.

Finally, of course, the views and ideas expressed in this book are based solely on the author's concept of international commercial banking management and do not necessarily reflect the practices or positions of the author's employer, past employers, or any other organization or institution with which the author is or has been associated.

J. L. Kammert

Contents

PART II PEOPLE

6 Direction Function Personnel 115

7 International Division Personnel 136

8 Support Function Personnel 157

9 Control Function Personnel 179

10 Correspondent Bank Personnel 200

PART III PROCEDURES

PART IV PROBLEMS

16 Handling Problem and Workout Credits   326

Origins and Early Warning Signals / Definitions and Collection Responsibility / Information Gathering and Fact Finding / Foreign Counsel and Asset Searches / Study of Possible Solutions / Nonaccrual, Recovery, or Write-Off

APPENDIXES

1

International Banking Organization

International Commercial Banking / International Banking Units / Merchant Banks, Eurobanks, and Export Finance Agencies / The IMF, World Bank, and Development Finance / Profit and International Division Organization / Bank-Within-a-Bank Concept

B efore dealing with planning, people, and procedures, which form the core of our study, this chapter establishes basic definitions and provides general background for better understanding of the subject. International commercial banking activities must be defined and understood within the overall context of commercial banking in general. This is especially important with regard to money center and regional banking organizations, since the approach to international banking usually differs noticeably between these two types of commercial banks. Also, the different parts of the banking organization that provide international services — including the head-office international unit, foreign branches, representative offices, and subsidiaries and affiliates — must be identified and described.

In addition, international commercial banking must be differentiated from several related international financial functions, which are conducted by various specialized institutions. On the

1

surface the activities of these institutions may seem similar to the work of international commercial banking organizations. Closer examination, however, shows that most of these other institutions and their purposes are quite different from the subject of our study. The purpose of such institutions also raises the issue of the profit motive, because many do not exist for profit.

There can be no doubt that the profit motive and modern management methods apply to international commercial banking. All international commercial banking units are organized to compete worldwide, and success is measured, with few exceptions, by profit levels. To maximize the chances for success, modern management methods must be followed by each international unit within the commercial banking organization.

It is important to keep in mind that in most situations in international commercial banking the individual unit exists almost as a bank within a bank. Each separate unit thus has many, if not all, of the broad range of management functions in connection with the services it provides and the work it performs. This is not generally true of many other business organizations, where separate units may conduct different specialized activities. The concept of a bank within a bank has important consequences for the management function and will be discussed in future chapters.

INTERNATIONAL COMMERCIAL BANKING

International commercial banking as used in this study deals with the planning, people, procedures, and problems involved in providing a range of international banking services within the context of a commercial banking organization. In the United States, for example, such an organization is often called a full service bank. Commercial banks in all nations, in contrast to various types of specialized banks, serve wide varieties of customers with broad ranges of different services.

The focus of this book is on international services provided to corporate or wholesale customers, although some retail services to individuals will be mentioned for the sake of completeness in certain areas. Corporate or wholesale customers include other banks and financial institutions, governments, and related organizations, as well as businesses and corporations, which may be privately owned, publicly owned, or government owned and may or may not operate primarily for profit.

The range of international services varies considerably from bank to bank around the world, depending upon location, size, market area, and fields of special expertise. However, as a general rule certain minimum basic international services tend to be available at almost all commercial banks that provide international services. These basic services will be described further in the next chapter, but usually they include taking deposits, granting loans and extending other forms of credit, and handling international payments, collections, letters of credit, and foreign exchange.

Although each international banking service has a separate income, cost, and profit structure, it is important that one organization provide all of these basic services and often many others as well. Single organizations generally achieve considerable economies of scale in international activity. Therefore, the primary goal for conducting international commercial banking is to provide as many services as possible, both domestically and internationally, to any one customer so as to maximize profits by customer and line of activity.

The commercial banking organization often has been compared to a modern department store or supermarket, which sells full ranges of merchandise and even services of all types under one roof. Each time the commercial banking customer steps through the door, an effort should be made to sell every available service. Thus, the expression "one-stop banking" is most appropriate.

To this concept of one-stop banking, another dimension must be added on the international scene. This is the general rule that each time a financial transaction crosses a national boundary, either physically or by currency change, the opportunity arises to provide an additional service. To pursue the analogy, it is almost as if the international customer must stop at the banking department store or supermarket at each boundary and purchase some service so as to be equipped to continue business in the next country. This circumstance arises not only because of different currencies in almost every nation of the world but also because of different financial techniques required to cope with longer times and distances and various risks — political and otherwise — associated with each separate nation or region. The opportunity to supply needed services through one organization profitably under these circustances is obvious. This basic concept forms the foundation of modern international commercial banking.

Although all banks that provide minimum international service compete with each other to some extent, the difference of approach between money center banks and regional banks has important management consequences. *Money center bank* is a phrase commonly applied to the largest banks in the world's leading financial capitals. These banks generally carry on their domestic business throughout the entire nations of their home offices and, as a rule, have numerous offices and activities overseas. For example, Citibank, Deutsche Bank, and Bank of Tokyo in New York, Frankfurt, and Tokyo, respectively, are considered to be money center banks. *Regional bank* is a term used to identify smaller banks in locations not considered to be major financial centers.

Generally, the domestic activities of regional banks are more concentrated in their local areas, although some may have a few national and international offices. Some examples of regional banks are U.S. National Bank of Oregon in Portland, Bayerische Vereinsbank in Munich, and Bank of Yokohama in Yokohama. A useful rule of thumb for sorting out regional from money center banks, at least in the United States, most of Western Europe, and Japan, is that regional banks tend to be characterized by strong, easily identifiable deposit bases. Most of the deposits from regional banks come from particular cities, areas, states, or other readily definable geographic areas. Deposits of money center banks, on the other hand, are not so concentrated in any particular geographic area and in fact may be gathered from across entire nations and the entire world on quite a diversified basis.

This terminology often is useful as shorthand to characterize a particular bank's approach to international activity, but it is not always helpful since it has obvious limitations. For instance, the largest bank in the United States, Bank of America, is often identified in banking literature as a regional bank because of its high percentage of business from the State of California. For this reason, a combination of absolute size of international business (usually measured by loans) and the percentage of total business is usually more helpful in identifying regional banks.

In a bank where international business forms a relatively significant absolute level and a reasonably large percentage of the bank's overall business, the views of management tend to become more universalist and similar to those in other banks whose international business is important, especially the further one goes up the chain of command. At the true regional bank, on the other hand, management goals and attitudes must of necessity be more provincial and weighted toward domestic business considerations. For this reason, regional banks tend to follow their customers abroad and attempt to relate their international business closely to their domestic activities. Money center banks, however, tend to regard the entire world as their market and to build their activities around customers regardless of the home-office location of these customers. Other examples of differences between regional and money banks will be seen in our study.

INTERNATIONAL BANKING UNITS

For the sake of consistency in this book, the phrase *international division* is used to refer to the part of the commercial bank that provides international banking services. Some banking organizations may use the term *department,* or *group,* or some other name to designate the international part of the bank. Furthermore, it is assumed that departments are subunits of divisions in most banks. On this basis, money center banks tend to have international banking divisions and regional banks have international departments.

The older term for the international part of the commercial bank, *foreign deparment,* still survives in many banks today, especially outside the United States. Some banks apply the term *overseas* to their international banking department, but that description is not always accurate, such as in dealings between the United States and either Canada or Mexico.

Although use of *international division* may simplify our terminology, it should be observed that in some banks, especially United States money center banks, extensive international activities may be broken into other categories and placed under departments, divisions, or groups dealing with retail banking, wholesale or corporate banking, lease financing, or trust, investment, and other financial services, for example.

Several aspects of our working definition for international commercial banking should be emphasized. Our definition does not require that international services be provided within or by the commercial bank itself. The broad phrase "within the context of a commercial banking organization" is used to allow for services being provided by not only the head office and branch offices of a commercial bank but also by subsidiaries, affiliates, and sister companies or organizations, such as entities owned parallel to commercial banks by the one-bank holding companies, which are possible under United States banking laws. Also, although our frame of reference for this book will be weighted in favor of the United States commercial bank, most of the issues covered in this book seem to have substantial application to banks in most of the other countries of the world.

In a sense, the United States banking system is one of the most complex in the world, mainly because of peculiar historical factors, such as distrust of financial institutions and suspicion of large concentrations of power, which have greatly influenced the content of American banking laws. The dual banking system permits national or state chartering of banks and, in addition to state banking authorities, three different regulatory bodies at the federal level are involved in supervising banks. However, by working mainly from the U.S frame of reference and by understanding this heavily regulated industry, perhaps more issues relating to management will be brought into focus for closer examination.

At the same time, non-American readers should be aware that the U.S. banking system has many pitfalls and is badly in need of reform. The United States may have some banking management techniques worth emulating, but not many U.S. bank regulatory concepts, especially in the international area, are worth repeating. With regard to bank regulation, the United States may have a great deal to learn from other nations. Study of selected non-U.S. banking systems might prove extremely useful as the United States Congress considers further banking reforms in this country.

As a result of the dual banking system in the United States, banks usually are not allowed to establish branches or another bank in states outside their home state, and branches within their home state may operate only where permitted by state laws, even if they are national banks. Without such rules the dual banking system would not survive, although there are certain historical exceptions to these rules, mainly in western states, to permit banks with operations in several states to continue operating after the rules were changed.

In addition, decades ago it was recognized that in order to adequately serve the international needs of domestic customers, U.S. banks should have the ability to establish entities (Edge Act banks) for the conduct of international business outside their normal boundaries for branching. Although the original intent might have been to permit landlocked banks to reach the key coastal cities where most international banking business was conducted, over the years Edge Act banking subsidiaries also have been established by the largest U.S. banks in important cities in many parts of the country.

This historical background and the rules for Edge Act banks are most confusing to foreign bankers establishing operations in the United States. In an attempt to make uniform rules for U.S. and foreign-owned banks, which previously enjoyed certain advantages with regard to branching among other matters, the International Banking Act of 1978 was passed by the United States Congress. In most developed nations outside the United States, no distinction is made between domestic and international business when establishing branches or new banking entities inside the home country. To better serve their customers' needs, many non-U.S. banks conduct international business from any domestic branch or office, as well as from the head-office international division.

On the other hand, to provide economies of scale for better use of skilled international personnel, some foreign banks, especially in Western European countries, have selected certain regional domestic offices for handling international transactions for numerous domestic branches in the nearby area. Banks within the United States also may do this within the areas generally prescribed by law for branching and may use Edge Act banks to go outside these boundaries and out of state for conducting strictly international banking activities.

The first step for many banks going to foreign countries for the first time is establishment of *representative offices*. All banks must follow not only the laws of their home country, of course, but also the rules of any other country where they do business. Generally, however, representative offices are permitted in most nations of the world, since these offices consist merely of a place where business meetings and communications can take place. No loans are granted, deposits accepted, or transactions handled at representative offices of banks. Often these offices have only one or a few employees, and usually one officer. These offices maintain no general banking accounts and books, but they provide a useful base for keeping in permanent contact with customers and expediting transactions for other units of the bank that can conduct actual business over their own books. Establishment of a representative office usually involves only a minimum investment for office space, furniture, and equipment and entails little risk since all business generated and decisions recommended on credit extension will be handled elsewhere, usually at the head office.

Because a representative office involves limited risk, investment, and personnel, many banks test the business conditions and market in new countries in this way before opening branches, establishing subsidiaries, or investing in affiliates. Some banks, on the other hand, make investments in affiliates in foreign nations new to them, and still others make such investments and simultaneously establish a representative office, perhaps on the premises of the new affiliate. An intermediate level between a representative office and a branch may exist under the laws of some countries and is know as an *agency*. Under the International Banking Act of 1978, an agency in the United States is an office or place of business for a foreign bank "at which credit balances are maintained . . . but at which deposits may not be accepted from citizens or residents of the United States."

Foreign branches, as opposed to representative offices, generally take deposits, extend credit, conduct other transactions, and maintain books and records. In short, a foreign branch is generally a complete bank within a bank and carries on domestic and international business in the host country in competition with host country domestic banks, other foreign branches, and subsidiaries and affiliates of foreign banks. In accordance with the laws of some nations, foreign branches are required to have certain amounts of capital, although the better view is that the entire capital of the foreign bank stands behind any of its branches anywhere in the world.

Since branches are an integral part of the foreign bank and have the total backing of the head office, they usually require a substantial commitment of trained and experienced personnel. Investments in subsidiaries and affiliates, on the other hand, might be made in order to acquire qualified indigenous personnel in an existing operation and established market. Also, for certain types of transactions, such as leasing, merchant banking, or consumer financing, it may be advantageous or even necessary by law to have a separate limited liability corporation, regardless of whether adequate personnel are available or a branch already exists in a foreign country.

MERCHANT BANKS, EUROBANKS, AND EXPORT FINANCE AGENCIES

This chapter has developed several aspects of our definition by describing a few basic attributes of international commercial banking. Perhaps additional light can be shed on the subject by discussing what it does not include. *Merchant banking,* for example, involves mainly the arranging of loans and the underwriting and sale of loan and nonloan securities, which are funded by others, as well as providing various specialized corporate financial services. Merchant banking services can be among the many services provided by some office or unit in the international commercial banking organization. Most of the larger international commercial banks engage in merchant banking, most often from London-based units. However, unless some other part of the organization funds international loans, issues letters of credit, handles foreign exchange, and provides other basic international services, then the bank in question, as a merchant bank standing alone, is outside our definition, no matter how far flung its activities may be around the world.

Recent trends in the merchant banking business tend to validate the fundamental rule that international commercial banking involves providing as many services as possible to each customer. Over the last several years several important merchant banks have been partially or totally acquired by commercial banks. Additionally, some commercial banks have started *de novo* their own international merchant banking arms. These developments seem to indicate that merchant banking units may have difficulty standing alone, at least in some cases.

One possible explanation might be that without the capability to supply international commercial banking services, these institutions must continuously give up to others the lucrative collateral business, which is generated by their customers, such as letters of credit, foreign exchange, and even deposit accounts. Another problem with pure merchant banking is the cyclical nature of this specialized activity. During times of recession and low levels of economic activity and new investment, large financings are less frequent. Under these circumstances, competition increases and fees are lower, whereas underwriting risks are increased, since many providers of funds stay out of the market.

Eurobanks may be viewed to some extent as specialized merchant banks. Merchant banking grew up in London and other European cities long before the advent of the Eurodollar market and spread to a degree, especially to parts of the British Empire, where large, free money markets developed. In the United States, because of the legal separation between investment banking and commercial banking — and other laws — no institutions of size evolved exactly like the merchant banks. With the rapid growth of the Eurodollar and Eurocurrency market starting in the 1950s, long-established London merchant banks and newly formed entities began to conduct increasing amounts of business in Eurocurrencies, the most important of which was and remains to this day the Eurodollar.

In addition to originating and syndicating Eurocurrency loans and bonds, these specialized, largely London-based banks began conducting an active market in the taking and placing of interest-bearing Eurocurrency deposits. Commercial banks also became part of this market, but because such Eurodeposits formed a significant part of the total liabilities of these specialized banks as opposed to sterling or other local currency deposits, the term Eurobanks came into existence.

It is not within the scope of this book to deal in any depth with the Eurocurrency market or the Eurobank, since these topics have been well developed by other authors. However, for the purpose of this study it should be noted that currencies deposited or loaned outside the home nations of such currencies are defined as *Eurocurrencies* and the market for these currencies has become large in volume and worldwide in extent. Thus, dollars loaned by a London bank or deposited in Paris, as well as yen deposited in Frankfurt or loaned in Singapore, are known as *Eurodollars* or *Euroyen*.

The Eurocurrency markets have grown because they serve needs for vast sums of capital economically and conveniently and provide an opportunity for earnings on idle funds at agreed upon rates free from government price limits and controls. This vast free market is one of the greatest financial developments since the end of World War II, and to date no government has taken steps to interfere with its workings. Various U.S. banking organizations have been working to change U.S. banking regulations to allow for the creation of U.S.-based entities known as *international banking facilities* that could receive and loan Eurocurrencies free of excessive taxes, reserve requirements, and interest rate ceilings in the United States. If such facilities were permitted in the United States, many large U.S. cities could become more important international financial centers, and U.S.-based banks could serve their customers more effectively.

In contrast to merchant banks, Eurobanks, and the proposed U.S. international banking facilities, which are or would be privately owned and which operate at free market rates for interest and charges, government-subsidized *export finance agencies* have been started by most developed and many developing nations of the world. Most of these entities are patterned after the Export-Import Bank of the United States (usually referred to as Eximbank) and should not be confused with international commercial banks. These export finance agencies, many of which, including the U.S. Eximbank, earn some profit, lend at low rates of interest to encourage exports from each entity's country. Rates of interest on export loans are fixed for the period of the loan in many cases, as opposed to rates that float over or are periodically adjusted in relationship to a base rate or cost of funds, as is the practice in the Eurocurrency market and in pricing domestic commercial bank loans.

Export finance agencies generally lend for longer periods of time than commercial banks, but often international commercial banks and government export finance entities work together to provide the total package of funds needed for specific projects. Since many nations compete to export the same products, equipment, and services, representatives of government export agencies from around the world meet from time to time to agree upon the ground rules for their activities, including minimum lending rates and maximum maturity schedules. Some of these entities, such as the Export-Import Bank of Japan, have foreign representative offices, and most state in their rules that they are to complement or extend the services of commercial banks and not compete with them.

International project finance is a form of lending activity in which international commercial banks, Eurobanks, and export finance agencies engage. Sometimes two or all three types of institutions will be involved in the same large project. Project finance involves lending on the basis of the technical and commercial success of some income-producing activity. Mining, transportation, energy production, and manufacturing activities that involve extensive new or expanded process plant facilities are typical examples. Many of these projects are so large and complex that no group of sponsors is capable of guaranteeing the loans or arranging adequate security in the form of physical assets. Accordingly, in project finance, study is made of all aspects of the projects, and all participants — including the lenders, sponsors, suppliers, contractors, customers, and governments — are so tightly bound together by contractual arrangements that all parties become partners in the broadest sense, with carefully limited rights and duties to insure the success of the project, which will generate the funds to repay the participants.

THE IMF, WORLD BANK, AND DEVELOPMENT FINANCE

Similar to the specialized merchant banks, Eurobanks, and export finance agencies, another grouping of specialized institutions is extensively involved in international financial activities but also falls outside the scope of our study. The broad purpose of entities in this grouping is to help entire nations with financial problems, and especially to encourage the development process. The organizations in this grouping are usually created by treaty or international agreement and owned by a government, several governments, or even many governments. However, a few institutions in the development finance area are privately owned. The largest and best known government-owned institutions in this general category are the International Monetary Fund (IMF) and the International Bank for Reconstruction and Development, or the World Bank, for short. Both the IMF and the World Bank were created by treaty under international law, and the World Bank is owned by about 140 shareholder nations throughout the world.

The IMF exists to coordinate the efforts of all member nations to maintain a sound and effectively functioning international monetary system and to help each other in times of special financial needs. The IMF and the World Bank were both founded at the Bretton Woods Conference after World War II, and since its founding the IMF has been involved in the gradual evolution of the international monetary system. The Bretton Woods Agreement established a system of par values or fixed values for each major currency in the world. Over time, a system based on floating or free market exchange rates has developed.

In less than thirty years the world has moved from a system of currency prices fixed by agreement among governments to one determined by supply and demand forces in a free market, in which governments through their central banks also participate. Since its creation, the IMF has made loans to various member countries from funds provided by its members. Since 1973 most of its efforts have centered on providing funds to developing nations, which are in financial difficulties mainly because of the increase in oil prices and the low level of current economic activity in some parts of the world.

The World Bank and its subsidiaries, the International Development Association and the International Finance Corporation, are collectively referred to as the World Bank Group. These entities are involved extensively in planning and financing hundreds of projects in the developing nations of the world, including the creation and start-up of numerous other development finance institutions. The World Bank concentrates on infrastructure projects involving loans to governments and government agencies. Included in this category are highways, dams, and irrigation projects. International Development Association (IDA) projects also involve lending to governments, but at lower rates of interest for relatively longer terms than are available from the World Bank. The International Finance Corporation operates mainly in the private sector by granting loans and supplying equity to corporate ventures that speed development. Once a nation reaches a determined stage of development, based upon per capita income, it is no longer eligible for World Bank Group assistance.

In addition to the World Bank Group, various regional and national development banks have been created, following the general pattern of the World Bank. The Asian Development Bank, the Inter-American Development Bank, the African Development Bank, and similar regional organizations and numerous nationally owned development banks are examples of this type of institution. These entities fall outside our definition of international commercial banking, because they exist for entirely different purposes than commercial banks and do not provide the full range of commercial banking services, including taking deposit accounts. Some of these development finance organizations are extensive users of international commercial banking services because, although their activities might be worldwide, they provide no international commercial services.

In addition to indigenous national development institutions in developing countries, many developed nations have government-owned entities, funds, or agencies to assist less developed countries. The U.S. Agency for International Development and Kreditanstalt für Wiederaufbau in West Germany are well-known examples of this type of entity. Furthermore, some developed nations operate government-related agencies that encourage private foreign investment by insuring equity and loan investments by their nationals in selected developing countries. The risks insured, for example, by the U.S. Overseas Private Investment Corporation, which also provides loan funds in certain cases, include war, revolution, nationalization, expropriation, and inconvertability, or the absence of foreign exchange at the host country's central bank after the host country borrower has tendered its country's national currency to make a loan repayment. Private organizations also insure against international credit risks in some countries. In the United States, a group of private insurance companies work together as the Foreign Credit Insurance Association (FCIA), for example.

Examples of privately owned development institutions include, among others, the Private Investment Corporation for Asia (PICA), and ADELA, which operates in Latin America. In both of these examples the ownership is spread widely among banks, other financial institutions, and private corporations from diverse fields of commerce and industry. Shareholders in both come from numerous developed countries, mainly in North America, Western Europe, and Japan. These organizations work with investor-owned corporations in their geographical areas of operation, especially to encourage new projects and expansion of existing companies in industries that will speed up and encourage the development process in the private sector as opposed to the government sector.

Space does not permit a listing of the numerous private, government, and mixed ownership institutions that have been started during the last few years mainly in the Middle Eastern OPEC countries. Many of these new institutions generally are limited to operating in selected Arab or Islamic countries. However, their efforts undoubtedly will become more noticeable with the passage of time and the development of their capabilities. Although organizations such as PICA, ADELA, and those in the Middle East make loans and may invest equity usually in more than one county, they are specialized lending or investment entities and not commercial banks that take deposits and perform numerous services in addition to lending.

It is not unusual for commercial banks, Eurobanks, and export finance agencies to be involved with international, regional, or national development banks in the same projects. These joint activities are challenging, not only because of the complex and difficult nature of dealing with the risks involved in project finance, but also because of the need to harmonize the sometimes diverse objectives, working methods, and management styles of the different financial institutions. Accordingly, a clear understanding of the motives and management objectives of each entity by all other parties is necessary for the success of these projects. Not only must international commercial banks understand the other participants, but these others must understand the international bankers and how they contribute and seek to benefit from their participation in the project.

PROFIT AND INTERNATIONAL DIVISION ORGANIZATION

As part of our discussion of defining international commercial banking and especially after reviewing the many specialized institutions whose main goal is not profit, the role of maximizing profits must be emphasized further. Most entities with international commercial banking divisions are engaged in business primarily for profit, but not all fit within this category. Some commercial banks with extensive international activities are cooperative institutions with a primary objective of serving their members rather than paying dividends to shareholders. Other entities that operate as and on the surface might appear to be international commercial banks are in reality government-owned organizations, created to carry out specific political aims in a manner not always consistent with maximizing earnings or obtaining any profit at all.

The Export-Import Bank of the United States is not an international commercial bank, for example, because, although it grants direct loans, guarantees commercial bank loans in many countries of the world, and provides many special international services, it does not provide a full range of the usual international services. In fact, this U.S. government-owned institution earns a substantial profit each year, which is paid to the U.S. Treasury, but it exists primarily to encourage U.S. exports by providing attractive financing for this purpose, not to maximize profits. Banco Exterior de Espana, on the other hand, should be considered an international commercial bank, although in addition to a full range of international commercial banking service it is also responsible for certain Spanish government export finance functions, which in the United States probably would be carried out by the Export-Import Bank.

For the purposes of this book, however, it will be assumed that the international commercial banking function and the international division are always managed as a business for profit. In order to achieve political aims, government regulations may control or forbid certain activities, set prices below cost or maximum profits, or require that certain additional duties be assumed such as exchange control or export promotion, for example. Basically, all international divisions in commercial banking organizations of all types around the world are competing within the same arena for efficient delivery of similar or identical services. Hence, there can be no doubt that modern management methods are applicable to them.

Therefore, the international division and the entire commercial bank must be organized to facilitate the delivery of as many different services to each customer as possible.

Having established what is and is not considered part of the usual international commercial banking function and its primary motives and operating methods, it is now time to turn to the organization of the international division. Although no two international departments anywhere in the world are identical, certain general patterns prevail. As a rule, at least two or three main areas of activity are found in all international divisions. We shall refer to these different parts of the divisions as lending, operations, and administration.

Some part of the division must be responsible for administering account and credit relationships and making credit decisions or recommendations. Usually this part of the division is referred to as the *lending* area, since credit extension is one of its most significant functions. Most banks tend to carve up responsibility for these functions by geographic areas. In smaller and regional banks, the geographic areas tend to be quite large, such as North America, Europe, Middle East, Africa, Asia, and Latin America, or even combinations of these continental areas. As the international division becomes larger, more specialization develops and thus ten or twelve or more geographic units are not uncommon in the international divisions of the largest banks.

The geographic units are assigned responsibility for serving customers in specific, usually neighboring, countries. If a country is large, active internationally, and important to the particular bank, one-country units might exist. In addition to regional geographic groupings to create more efficient travel patterns, language influences the division of labor in some banks or departments. For example, responsibility for Spain might be assigned to Spanish-speaking bankers responsible for Latin America, and responsibility for Portugal might be assigned to officers handling Brazil. European and Asian banks often combine responsibility for Canada and the United States, as another example of language specialization.

A newer trend in some banks is to provide separate units for the conduct of certain forms of specialized or corporate financing services, such as lease financing, project financing, export financing, or merchant banking. Such specialized functional units tend to have worldwide authority but, because of the difficulty in becoming experts in every part of the world, officers in these functional areas tend to work closely with the bankers in the geographic units. Moreover, hybrid organizations that combine geographic and a few specialized financing functions are not uncommon. One of the more recent trends is to create worldwide industrial groupings. Most banks still have branches, offices, or operations outside the head office that report through the head-office international department geographic regions. However, exceptions may exist again for specialized units such as merchant banking operations, where the importance of their activity overrides the need for geographic expertise or convenience.

In most banks another part of the division is responsible for specialized functions such as handling letters of credit, collections, international payments, and foreign exchange. Again, as in specialized types of financing, the importance of technique and common procedures in these functions overrides the need for geographic specialization. With the addition of certain bookkeeping and control duties, all these functions are referred to as *operations*, in contrast to the geographic or specialized account and credit units, which are usually labeled lending areas.

Some banks create another broad division for *administration* or even other separate sections to handle certain administrative duties such as study of economic, political, and social conditions in borrowing countries, analysis of financial statements of international customers, requests for credit information on international entities, handling of personnel matters for international employees, supervision of buildings and housing at foreign offices, and worldwide telex and cable communications, or other operations. As would be expected, these administrative or housekeeping sections are more numerous in the banks with larger international divisions. The larger the division, the more economies of scale can be obtained from specialization. Almost all the activities of any international division can be grouped into lending, operations, and administration.

BANK-WITHIN-A-BANK CONCEPT

Because of this comprehensive range of international activities conducted within the international division, the division of the commercial bank sometimes may be considered as "a bank within a bank." By way of further specific example, the operations section dealing with international payments is often compared to the teller's function in a domestic office. In fact, at one time many banks called such units foreign tellers. As a further example, the specialized bookkeeping and control functions are roughly similar to the controllership function of the entire bank. If functions for personnel matters, buildings overseas, and other specialized activities from the administrative function are added, the analogy becomes more apparent.

Moreover, the bank-within-a-bank concept is a useful management device, not only for the international division itself, but also for the individual units that report to it, such as international branches and other overseas units and, for U.S. banks, the Edge Act entities operating elsewhere in the United States. This idea will be referred to occasionally elsewhere in this book since the concept has many management applications. For example, completely separate procedures and audit routines are indispensable for successfully managing the international division or other overseas units. Although basic bankwide concepts in these areas may be followed or adapted for international use, bankwide routine is usually not sufficient. Furthermore, several specialized international functions do not exist in domestic banking, and most international transactions involve more than one unit of the international division. Such circumstances require a broad, integrated, independent management approach. Mere extending or tacking on modifications to domestic approaches here and there will not do the job internationally.

Although domestic branches in some commercial banks also may operate as a bank within a bank, that usually is not the case. Domestic branches usually have specialized functions to gather deposits and handle certain types of loans and other transactions, whereas the head office is responsible for most, if not all, staff functions, check clearing and other operations, funding, policy making, major credit decisions, and similar matters. Foreign branches of international banks are quite different in this regard because of the time and distance factor, among other considerations.

Foreign branches may do almost all their own planning, especially for marketing, and may hire personnel, modify their own organizational structure as required, own or lease premises, deal with their own funding, handle all their own operations, and in many cases make their own policy and credit decisions within the framework of head-office ground rules. Since they exist within the legal regime of their host countries, foreign branches also deal with host country central bankers, bank supervisors, and other government officials, as well as customers and other commercial banks. Foreign branches generally engage in domestic banking in their host countries and, although international banking may represent a large proportion of their business, in some foreign branches international functions are separated from other functions, analogous to the relationship of the head-office international division within the rest of the headquarters banking organization.

Finally, it should not be overlooked that international divisions and their units are producing increasing numbers of senior executives in commercial banks around the world. The international division has become an ideal training ground for top management personnel, not only because international business is a growing percentage of the total activity in many banks, but also because of the broad experience available from working with lending, operations, and administrative matters as well as all management functions.

2

International Banking Services

Credit Approval Procedure / Departmental Jurisdiction / Deposit-Taking Services / Eurodollar and Eurocurrency Deposits / Loans and Other Credit Extensions / International Payments / International Collections / Letters of Credit / Foreign Exchange / Other Services

The planning, people, procedures, and problems in our study of international commercial banking all focus upon providing services. This chapter first considers several basic concepts that apply to all international services. Then it examines the most common of these services and concludes with a brief, representative sampling of some newer services that are now being provided by some banks.

In international banking services, an unusual feature of the risk element within service industries and particularly in commercial banking should be kept in mind. Whereas most businesses usually transfer the largest part, if not all, of the risks associated with their line of activity at the time of sale, that is not the case with the majority of banking functions. In banking, risk usually begins at the time the transaction or function starts. That is true both for extensions of credit and most fee-producing services.

21

In addition to all the normal risks of domestic commercial banking, international commercial banking also involves country risk, which is the risk of doing business within different countries, and foreign exchange risk, which arises from conducting transactions in different currencies. Excessive or unreasonable risk of all kinds, as determined by each commercial bank, obviously must be avoided in order to minimize the likelihood of loss to the bank. In international as well as in domestic commercial banking, therefore, all business development or marketing effort must be carefully balanced against the risks involved in each transaction. When business is sought, it is likely to be obtained.

Because of the higher costs, usually greater lengths of time, and other complexities involved in developing international markets, the most effective marketing effort for international services involves a division of labor. Such division of labor encourages international personnel to specialize in delivering services in foreign nations and domestic personnel to concentrate on selling services in the home market. In our study this division of labor is referred to as departmental jurisdiction.

Following from the concept of departmental jurisdiction, credit decisions in connection with international services should be made only by credit or lending specialists. These specialists are trained for and entrusted with the responsibility for extending credit in accordance with the bank's rules and procedures. However, sometimes credit decisions can be made inadvertently by nonlenders, unless proper credit controls are in place to prevent this.

Most deposit-taking activities in international banking are quite similar to those activities in domestic banking. However, functions involving the Eurodollar market, more properly called the Eurocurrency market, involve important distinctions. Furthermore, lending and other extensions of credit tend to be somewhat different in international banking, because the greater variety of transactions encountered involves various degrees of risk. International movement of funds and collections, in contrast, provide fee income with relatively little risk. Finally, letters of credit, foreign exchange, and other services involve unique situations with risks and opportunities seldom seen in purely domestic transactions.

CREDIT APPROVAL PROCEDURE

Several international services involve obvious extensions of credit, such as term loans. An example would be the granting of a five-year term loan in U.S. dollars to a public utility in Costa Rica for the purchase of U.S. generating equipment to produce electrical power. For other services, the extension of credit is not so obvious. Let us assume that the Costa Rican utility requests that its U.S. dollar demand deposit account be charged for the cost of Swiss francs needed to pay the expenses of the Swiss power plant contractor that is installing some items related to the generators.

In the first example, the money for the term loan is literally going out the door of the bank for five years. Study of the economy and politics of Costa Rica, analysis of the electrical utility and other power-producing entities in the country, and examination of the details of the particular project all would be in order before authorization is given to sign loan documentation and disburse loan proceeds.

The second case is not quite so clear. Swiss francs are going out the door of the bank, but an account on the books of the bank is being charged at the same time. The bank makes money selling Swiss francs and the customer is a term loan borrower. Yet, if the foreign exchange trader carries out the foreign exchange transaction without an approved foreign exchange line and the U.S. dollar account is overdrawn after the U.S. dollar equivalent of the Swiss franc is charged to the account, some embarrassment and heated discussion could occur within the bank.

Let us assume for the sake of further example that the term loan was made under a guarantee of the Export-Import Bank of the United States, which specifically required that the loan proceeds be used only to pay exporters of U.S. electrical equipment. Assume further that the contract and the loan agreement are canceled. The company never uses the loan as a result and, for sake of further example, the overdraft is still not covered. At this point under the circumstances described, there is clearly an unauthorized extension of credit.

This example illustrates that almost every transaction performed in the international division involves extension of credit. The account officer in charge of credit extension and the deposit accounts for the Costa Rican utility must follow the bank's rules for obtaining credit approvals for every type of credit extension that the Costa Rican customer might use. In addition to approval of the term loan, a line of some amount for foreign exchange, and an authorization for temporary overdrafts pending receipt of funds, a facility may be required for opening letters of credit in favor of the U.S. supplier of generators, since this is the normal method of disbursing loan proceeds in connection with loans guaranteed by the U.S. Export-Import Bank.

All of these credit extensions in total represent the bank's maximum exposure to the utility. Upon obtaining the required approvals according to the bank's internal rules, each section of the international division should be advised in writing of the amount and conditions of the facility for use in each section. The foreign exchange traders and letter of credit section will be advised, for example, that foreign exchange contracts up to a certain amount may be entered into on behalf of the customer and that letters of credit up to a set limit may be issued for the account of the customer. The loan control department will be advised that the term loan proceeds may be disbursed and the officer in charge of overdrafts will have knowledge of the limits for this purpose.

This is a relatively simple example, but more complex situations are neither difficult to imagine nor hard to find in international banking. A large money center bank with numerous overseas branches, subsidiaries, and affiliates may extend credit to the dozens of units of a multinational corporation around the world under 100 or more separate facilities. Each facility extended by every unit of the bank must be identified clearly with the name of the borrowing entity or user of the facility, the amount, purpose, terms, conditions, and expiry date of the facility. Each unit of the bank then must forward this information periodically to some part of the international division or bank, which is in charge of obtaining the necessary approvals for all of the facilities.

For a large multinational corporation, the summary of its facilities from the bank may require dozens of pages, and the total exposure of the bank easily could amount to more than $100 million. To control such vast extension of credit over wide geographic areas, literally around the globe, it is necessary to strike a grand total of all facilities and obtain approvals according to the bank's rules for extension of credit. Usually this is done at least once a year, as soon as possible after receipt of the customer's audited financial statements. This process usually is referred to as *annual review*.

Upon completing the approval process, each unit of the bank and each section within any unit that deals with the customer must be advised of the approval of the facilities related to it and the conditions, including expiry date, of such approved facilities. Only in this way can the customer's account officer know the total of all credit extensions to the multinational customer and each unit of the bank know that its activities with the multinational corporation are authorized.

DEPARTMENTAL JURISDICTION

In defining many of the basic international services from a management viewpoint, a perspective on the basis of jurisdiction or domicile of account is useful. For example, in deposit taking, all accounts with foreign addresses should be supervised by some international division department, as opposed to a domestic department. The reverse of this rule generally seems to make sense also; namely, all accounts with domestic addresses should be handled by domestic units of the commercial bank and not by the international division. Of course, there are always good reasons for exceptions to almost any rule. However, more often than not, if clear jurisdictional lines are not drawn early and repeatedly from time to time, service suffers.

For example, in some banks the officer responsible for obtaining the account may domicile the account wherever he pleases, in which case it will usually end up in his department. By way of further illustration, let us assume that an international officer, as part of a loan transaction to finance an export by a domestic company to a foreign purchaser, opens the first demand deposit account in the bank for the domestic company. The loan is made directly to the foreign importer on the basis of the foreign company's credit standing, and the importer also opens a demand deposit account. With freedom of choice, both accounts end up in the international division, but it is doubtful that the international officer can effectively service both the foreign and the domestic companies to maximum effect. For the sake of efficiency, international officers will usually be responsible for account and loan relationships in foreign nations, and domestic officers serve the needs of domestic customers.

To carry the example another step, let us next consider who should be responsible for calling on the domestic company to obtain additional business and sell new services. Obviously, if further international sales financing or other international services are contemplated, the international officer is a candidate for the job. But the next question that arises is whether the international officer should call to discuss domestic cash management or corporate trust services, assuming he is familiar with these services. If the international officer travels frequently to visit foreign customers, speaks a foreign language, or is a specialist in the economics and politics of several geographically related countries, it does not make sense for this officer also to have sole or primary responsibility for domestic customers.

Obviously, this arrangement would provide variety, good training, and job enrichment for the international officer, but it does not serve the domestic customer in the best manner, provide the bank with the maximum chance to sell the greatest number of services from throughout all parts of the bank, and use its specialized personnel in the most efficient manner. Although this rule seems so simple as to be obvious, many banks do not follow the guidelines of having domestic officers handle domestic customers and international division officers handle foreign customers. As a general rule, therefore, every deposit account should be assigned to the appropriate division or department, namely, the area best able to serve the customer.

Next, the same rule should be applied to all loans and other extensions of credit. International officers should administer credit in foreign countries, and domestic officers should handle credit extended to domestic companies. This is not so say that in complicated transactions both divisions should not be involved or that domestic and international officers should not call together on multinational customers if no specialized multinational department exists. However, clear and consistent guidelines should establish ultimate account and credit responsibility for both potential and existing customers. In some cases, such as the multinational corporate customer, which was discussed in the earlier example, it may be necessary for a domestic officer to handle approval of a credit facility that will be administered in the international division. Therefore, the responsibility for particular transactions may seem to shift from one division or department to another, but problems will be minimized if rules are clear.

If one unit of the bank is responsible for obtaining approval of credit extension to be administered in another unit and this situation occurs frequently enough, it may be useful to have both of these units within the same grouping. Assuming most of a bank's international business is corporate related, then the international division perhaps should be grouped with the domestic corporate banking units. Yet, in some banks with predominantly corporate international activity, the international division or department sometimes may be grouped with investment, trust, or even operations units. For the best administration the international division or department belongs in a grouping with those units with which it has most frequent contact from the standpoint of customer dealings, business development, and account and loan administration. Recently, for example, Citibank reorganized to form two large divisions, one for handling personal banking or individual customers, and the other for handling all nonindividuals, including businesses, corporations, and governments.

DEPOSIT-TAKING SERVICES

With these organizational and jurisdictional questions now settled, we can explore briefly some of the different types of specific services provided by the international department, starting with the liability side of the bank's balance sheet. Generally, all types of deposits that can be accepted from domestic depositors may be accepted from international customers. This, of course, would include demand deposits, time deposits, and certificates of deposit. Outside the deposit category, international customers may also purchase commercial paper. For our purposes, the distinction between commercial paper and deposits can be defined as the difference between an unsecured general creditor-debtor relationship and a special bank-depositor relationship. Depositors in a bank under most legal systems outrank other creditors of the bank and hence in a bankruptcy or bank failure are the first creditors to be paid. In many countries depositors also have certain insurance protection. The Federal Deposit Insurance Corporation in the United States, which generally insures accounts up to $100,000, is an example.

Demand deposits usually earn no interest or else only low rates of interest, depending upon the national laws of the country in which the bank is operating. Historically, in the United States banks have been prohibited from paying interest on demand deposits, although the law in this area is now changing rapidly. The theory behind this prohibition apparently is that banks would be more likely to fail as a result of ruinous competition from interest rate wars to attract deposits. Since bankers must be presumed to be at least as prudent as other businessmen and do carefully watch their cost of funds, which is the raw material for their lending activities, such reasoning seems questionable.

In any event, money can be placed in foreign offices or converted from interest-earning accounts to demand deposits as checks are presented. Only a bit more work by both the bank and the customer is required to accomplish this. Occasionally, in some countries banks are required to charge interest on demand deposits as a penalty to discourage inflow of funds, which could upset the nation's economy by causing inflation or creating unwanted balance of payments flows. Such charges are referred to as *negative interest.* Negative interest, of course, must be distinguished from an interest or loan charge for overdrawing an account, which generally is called *overdraft interest.*

Time deposits earn interest, when yield curves are normal, at increasing per annum rates, as a rule, the longer a deposit is placed with the bank. Usually time deposits may not be withdrawn prior to the end of the contractual period, and if this is permitted, then some or all of the interest that has accrued is forfeited by the customer. Certificates of deposit evidence a time deposit and generally are negotiable, which facilitates sale of the deposit to another depositor before the end of the period for which the deposit was placed with the bank. Usually in cases of bank insolvency, after payment of all deposits, funds left over pay general creditors, including holders of commercial paper, which represents an unsecured promise to pay.

Up to this point deposit services provided in the international division to international customers are virtually identical to those provided in the bank's domestic departments to domestic customers. Perhaps the only difference is that statements for accounts of international customers should be sent by international airmail, whereas domestic customers receive their statements by regular mail. With the cost of postage increasing in most countries of the world, the cost of airmail is not insignificant. Accordingly, small international accounts are not encouraged.

Finally, another reason for grouping all international accounts together is to speed handling and delivery to the post office. Account numbering systems in most banks automatically sort out the statements by country grouping for mailing. However, this will not happen automatically unless an account numbering system by countries is established for all newly opened accounts and clear rules for departmental jurisdiction spell out which unit of the bank should have responsibility for foreign-domiciled accounts, so that proper account numbers are assigned.

EURODOLLAR AND EUROCURRENCY DEPOSITS

One form of deposit that is peculiar to international banking units is the *foreign currency deposit.* Any currency other than that of the nation where a banking office is located is referred to as foreign currency or foreign exchange. Keeping records for deposits in foreign currencies involves debit, credit, and balance columns in both the local currency and the foreign currency equivalents, since records must be kept for all of the bank's assets and liabilities for each location in local currency. Eurocurrencies or Eurodollars identify currencies located in nations outside the country of that denomination. For example, a U.S. dollar deposited in an account in a bank in a European country or anywhere else outside the United States is called a *Eurodollar.* A French franc deposited in a French franc account in Germany or in any country other than France is a *Eurocurrency,* or, more specifically, a Eurofranc.

The prefix *Euro* has come to be applied to all currencies outside their home country anywhere in the world, because after World War II free markets for depositing and lending foreign currencies grew up in Europe, starting mainly in London. Today, a Eurodollar or even Euroyen may be found in Singapore, Hong Kong, or Bahrain, among other locations, but the *Euro* prefix has remained. After World War II, the U.S. dollar became the most frequently used currency for conducting international transactions for trade and investment. Other currencies were largely suspect because of the weakened economies of most European nations and Japan, the small size of money markets for other nations such as Switzerland which escaped war damage, and the fear of government controls on the free movement of money as the Cold War developed.

The Soviet Union, for example, conducted most of its foreign trade in U.S. dollars, but kept excess dollars on deposit in London or other European banks to be outside the reach of U.S. laws, which could freeze its assets, as happened with enemy property during the war. This fear of seizure or sequestration is not groundless, since the United States froze Iranian bank deposits as recently as late 1979 in connection with Iranian nationals holding American hostages in Teheran.

Russians and others who held dollars in Europe and elsewhere outside the United States soon began lending the funds in dollars in order to earn interest on their deposits and avoid exchange risks and expenses of converting the dollars to other currencies. With time, the market for Eurodollars grew as commercial banks and Eurobanks placed and accepted deposits between banks. Multinational corporations, other businesses, and governments placed excess funds on deposit with the banks and in turn borrowed funds in Eurodollars from the banks when needed.

The Eurocurrency market operates, therefore, on two levels, between customers and banks, and between banks. Because of the close communication links among all international banks around the world, the interest rates paid for Eurocurrency deposits remain quite uniform at any one time throughout the world. However, there is an element of slight tiering in the rates on the basis of the credit standing and size of each bank. Thus, at any time the largest and strongest banks in the market tend to pay slightly less then do other banks for Eurodeposits offered to them.

The rate at which deposits are offered to each bank by other banks has come to be called the *London InterBank Offered Rate (LIBOR* or the

LIBO rate). LIBOR is the base rate for pricing Eurocurrency loans with an added margin or percentage over LIBOR for three- or six-month deposits on the basis of the credit standing of the borrower to cover risk and other expenses for the lenders. Eurocurrency rates are quotes by banks for daily and monthly periods, usually for up to one year in most currencies. This is an over-the-counter market carried on by telephone and telex either directly between banks or through brokers. Each bank is free to pay what it wishes for deposits and to establish its relationship by verbal or telex contract, confirmed by telex or mail.

With regard to placing deposits with other banks, since credit is being extended, the personnel handling Eurocurrency funds should have established lines approved for each bank receiving deposits. The Eurocurrency placement lines should be set up and advised to the appropriate international division person in the same manner in which other facilities are set up and advised, as explained in the first section of this chapter.

As a rule, only the international division maintains the subsidiary accounting ledgers for foreign currency accounts both in foreign currency units and in their local currency equivalents. Therefore, all foreign currency deposits are maintained in the international division. In the U.S. banking system, since a U.S. dollar by definition cannot be a Eurodollar if it is on deposit in the United States, all Eurodollars held by U.S. banks must be deposited at or loaned from a branch or entity outside the United States. Most U.S. banks accept Eurodollar deposits at their London, Nassau, or other foreign branches. Again, since supervision of these branches generally falls under the responsibility of the international division, all these deposits are within the division.

LOANS AND OTHER CREDIT EXTENSIONS

International lending and extensions of credit in forms other than loans fall into several readily identifiable categories. In our discussion of credit approval procedures, for example, we referred to term loans and the credit extension involved in handling letters of credit, foreign exchange transactions, and temporary overdrafts in current accounts. Under Eurocurrency deposits we mentioned the need for approved lines to place deposits with other banks.

Perhaps one of the most useful methods for categorizing all credit extension is by degree of credit risk. Another method involves division by use of bank funds versus use of bank credit or the bank's name, and still another approach uses the concepts of direct and contingent risk, the latter risk sometimes being referred to as "below the line." "Below the line" means the transaction is not recorded in accounts that are included in the assets and liabilities of the bank, at least in most nations. Items such as guarantees, which U.S. banks generally are not allowed to issue, and future foreign exchange contracts are examples of contingent or below-the-line items. In some nations banks roll these items up in their total assets and liabilities; however, this practice tends to overinflate balance sheets.

In the final analysis, however, all credit risk involves the risk of loss, and loss involves the payment of the bank's money. Thus, although degrees of credit risk and the other categories of credit may be useful in distinguishing between different types of credit extension and in making credit decisions, all forms of credit extension to a customer ultimately must be added together to determine total exposure. A chart of degrees of risk for international credit extension, moving from the lowest degree of risk to the highest risk, is shown in Appendix A.

Loans are usually evidenced by promissory notes. Medium- or long-term loans require extensive loan agreements and various other legal documents tailored to each situation. In addition to the maturity categories long-term (five or more years), medium-term (more than one but less than five years), and short-term (one year or less) loans are also labeled by other identifying characteristics. They include the purpose of the loan, the source of funding, or means for pricing the loan. For example, loans financing exports, especially under government programs that have certain routine requirements such as the Export-Import Bank in the United States, might be referred to as export loans. Term loans to projects, where the repayment risk centers largely on the success of the project in generating adequate cash flow rather than payments from guarantors or other sources, are often called project loans.

International term loans, whether for export or project financing, are often, but need not necessarily be, Eurodollar or Eurocurrency loans, meaning that the loans are funded by Eurocurrencies as opposed to domestic funds. Eurocurrency lending started when bankers began to take deposits in these currencies and the Euromarket grew up, as we discussed under deposit taking. Thus, Euroloans have their own peculiar rate structure on the basis of the London InterBank Offered Rate. Most loans in the United States are priced equal to or at increments over (or percentages of) the U.S. *prime rate*, which is the rate charged by each bank for loans to its best customers. Outside the United States, similar concepts exist, such as the *base rate* in the United Kingdom. The LIBO rate, as previously mentioned, is a different rate determined for each bank by its credit standing and importance in the market as determined by other banks. The prime rate or base rate, on the other hand, is a rate determined internally and announced by each bank to its borrowing customers.

Financing by means of *bankers' acceptances* utilizes bills of exchange rather than promissory notes. The bill of exchange is drawn by the customer to whom credit is extended and who is known legally as the drawer. This customer may be another bank. The bank that is extending credit and upon which the draft is drawn is called the drawee. The drawee bank then accepts the bill by having one of its authorized personnel sign the bank's name on the draft to indicate its agreement to become an additional obligor. This accepted bill of exchange or banker's acceptance then may be held by the bank in its portfolio as evidence of the credit extended to the drawer. Should the bank need funds or find interest rate variations favorable, it may sell the acceptance in a highly developed and active market to investors who have excess short-term funds. The rates for bankers' acceptances generally are in line with commercial paper rates. At maturity of the acceptance, the bank pays the holder of the acceptance, who presents it for payment and charges the account of its customer, the drawer.

The banking laws in each jurisdiction prescribe precise requirements for the creation of bankers' acceptances. Most bankers' acceptances finance short-term, self-liquidating trade transactions of readily salable commodities. In the United States, the maturities for most acceptance financing do not exceed 180 days. Since each banker's acceptance contains a bank's obligation to pay, as well as the obligation of a bank's customer, bankers' acceptances are referred to as two-name paper. For these reasons, bankers' acceptances are considered an ideal short-term money market investment vehicle. Before the invention of the negotiable certificate of deposit, bankers' acceptances were one of the most important short-term investment instruments provided by commerical banks.

Time deposits placed with other banks as international division assets usually are in the form of short-term Eurocurrency placements. Demand deposits, also called *due-from accounts, our accounts, or nostro accounts* by those who prefer Latin, represent the working account balances, usually in foreign currencies, held by banks in other banks, referred to as their correspondents. As explained in the next section on international payments services, these working balances are used to transfer funds overseas to foreign countries. If each of two banks maintains an account with the other, the correspondent relationship is said to be reciprocal. The account of Bank A with Bank B is called a due-from account by Bank A and represents an asset to Bank A, but to Bank B the same account is a liability and is called a *due-to account, their account,* or *vostro account.* The account of Bank B with Bank A likewise is called a due-to account by Bank A, but represents a due-from account or asset to the personnel at Bank B.

INTERNATIONAL PAYMENTS

International payments services involve sending customer funds outside the commercial bank's country and receiving customer funds from outside the country. Payments may be accomplished by means of *mail* instructions, *telex* or *cable* instructions, and bank *drafts.* Payments and receipts are accomplished through the use of accounts maintained by the bank with foreign banks, called correspondent banks, and accounts that the correspondents keep with the other banks, mentioned above.

For example, to make payment to a company in France from the United States, the U.S. customer would instruct its U.S. bank to charge its account with the U.S. bank and pay French francs to the French company's account with a bank in France. The U.S. bank carries out this instruction by ordering its French correspondent, the French bank with which it maintains a French franc account, to charge the French franc account of the U.S. bank and pay the amount to the French bank of the French company for credit to the French company's account. On its records the U.S. bank simultaneously decreases the balance in its French franc account with its French correspondent and charges the equivalent amount plus its costs and commission for the transaction to the account of the U.S. customer.

In carrying out its customer's instructions, the U.S. bank also has entered into a foreign exchange contract with its U.S. customer. Usually, a brief telephone call between the U.S. bank and an authorized employee of its customer establishes the rate of exchange between French francs and U.S. dollars, which the U.S. customer includes in a subsequent confirming letter or other signed instruction to the bank, authorizing the U.S. dollar charge to its account. The U.S. bank sends its instructions to its French correspondent either by airmail or telex, according to its customer's instructions. Upon receipt of the U.S. bank's instructions, the French correspondent bank charges the U.S. bank's French franc account and pays the French bank of the French company, whose account is credited by that bank.

The same process in reverse accomplishes an incoming payment from France. Each day the international divisions of banks throughout the world not only send payment instructions by airmail and telex machines but also receive instructions from their correspondents from around the globe to charge their correspondent accounts and pay beneficiaries, which may be corporations, other entities, or individuals. A small bank might have only one or a few telex machines in its international department for payments messages, but a large bank might have a large room full of machines for this purpose in its international division or in a separate communications department.

In most banks these incoming and outgoing payments are handled by the international payments department, or, as it is sometimes called, the paying and receiving section, which is usually part of the operations unit of the international division. Foreign exchange traders help to expedite the transaction by establishing the rate of exchange whenever two different currencies are involved.

It is not necessary for the U.S. customer to make a foreign exchange contract with the U.S. bank to accomplish the payment in the previous example. The U.S. customer may instruct that the payment be made in U.S. dollars. Then the U.S. bank, with notification to its French correspondent, would decrease the balance in the U.S. dollar account that the French correspondent maintains with the U.S. bank. Upon receipt of notification through its French bank, the French company would enter into a foreign exchange contract with its bank in France to sell the U.S. dollars for French francs, unless it had a use for the U.S. dollars.

Customers also may transfer funds internationally by purchase of bank drafts, which are checks drawn by one bank on another bank. The drawing bank then sells the draft to its customer for a commission and the customer can mail the draft to the payee. In our example, the U.S. bank would draw a French franc draft on its French correspondent, which upon presentation by the French company would charge the U.S. bank's French franc account.

Use of drafts and bank-to-bank airmail instructions takes more time than telex or cable transfers, but the latter cost more since the bank must recoup its expenses of internal telex or outside cable company transmission. Most larger transactions are made by telex, and drafts are used for smaller amounts when the sender is not certain of the location of the beneficiary's bank account.

In addition to charging for its services, whether payment is made by telex transfer, airmail advice, or draft, the bank also earns profits on its foreign exchange activity, assuming that it is selling foreign exchange in small lots at higher rates than its cost for bulk purchases and buying at lower rates for small amounts than it is selling for. If the bank can match buyers and sellers for the same currencies, profits increase further, since foreign exchange is one of the oldest recycling businesses.

Beyond these tangible income streams from foreign exchange and service fee income or commissions, the activity of the paying and receiving area also builds account balances. To the extent that the bank is a prompt and efficient receiving bank, foreign correspondent account balances will be increased to cover the greater volume of payments they initiate, which creates a source of funds for the receiving bank. In the event that foreign correspondents do not maintain sufficient funds in their accounts, banks of deposit may levy overdraft charges calculated at some rate of interest, which also produces additional income.

These factors are sometimes overlooked by analysts who attempt to allocate income and expenses for international funds transfer services. Foreign exchange earnings, income from incidental overdrafts of correspondents, and earnings from correspondents' accounts must be taken into account along with direct commissions and fee income from international payments services to obtain the true balance of income and expense in this area.

Risk of loss to the bank generally is slight in handling international payments. Losses usually result from making payments to wrong beneficiaries or overpaying beneficiaries. Sometimes wrong or overpaid beneficiaries are difficult, if not impossible, to locate after they have received funds. Furthermore, in accordance with sound procedures for credit extension, it is necessary to obtain proper internal approvals for correspondent account overdrafts of a temporary nature, pending receipt of incoming funds after payments have been ordered by the correspondent.

INTERNATIONAL COLLECTIONS

International collection activity is related to foreign exchange and funds transfer activities, but it is usually considered a separate function in most banks' international operations. Basically, collections can be of two types, known as clean and documentary. *Clean collections* include checks, notes, drafts, and other bills of exchange that must be sent to a foreign bank in order to be paid or collected and that are unaccompanied by any other documents except a cover letter or form of instruction.

Documentary collections consist of payment instruments plus any of the usual shipping documents, such as invoices, bills of lading, packing lists, insurance certificates, inspection certificates, and similar items related to export or import of goods. A seller sends payment instruments plus title documents through banking channels, consisting of his bank, its foreign correspondent overseas, and perhaps the buyer's bank, in order to require the buyer to pay or make payment arrangements before receiving the bill of lading or other title document that permits him to obtain possession of the goods being purchased.

Collections, both clean and documentary, come into the bank from foreign correspondents for delivery in accordance with instructions to the receiving bank's customers and go out from the sending bank to its correspondents for delivery to the correspondents' customers. Thus, collection activity represents an opportunity to earn fees for foreign exchange and international payments services in connection with their settlement. The collection activity generates a special commission in addition to income streams from the payment or settlement mechanism fees that involves international payments, because the bank has the responsibility to handle all items promptly and properly in accordance with instructions.

There is usually little risk of loss to banks handling collections, provided that outgoing items are routed with correct addresses and instructions as soon as they are received and that title documents with incoming items are released only in accordance with instructions. Instructions on incoming collections may require actual payment or obtaining a written obligation to pay, generally in the form of signing a bill of exchange drawn by the seller on the buyer. After signature this instrument is called a *trade acceptance* as distinguished from a banker's acceptance, which, as previously explained, is a bill of exchange accepted by a bank. The trade acceptance belongs to the drawer, usually the seller of goods, but when the seller has extended credit terms, the bank in the buyer's country usually holds the trade acceptance until the due date in accordance with instructions from the seller's bank. Upon the obligation's maturity, the bank presents the acceptance to the buyer for payment and then remits payment in accordance with the international funds transfer process.

If the buyer does not remit for sight payment items (those items for which no credit is being extended) or create an acceptance when credit terms are being extended, the bank is not permitted to deliver the documents, which usually include the title document, to the buyer. If the buyer does not pay accepted items when due, the seller may sue the buyer for nonpayment, since the buyer obtained the goods when he signed or created the trade acceptance. Provided the bank has acted in accordance with instructions, it has no liability. But it is possible that the bank may incur losses in handling collections.

For example, by issuing a *guaranty for a missing bill of lading* or *airway bill* before a collection arrives, the bank may expose itself to risk if the buyer subsequently does not pay. This situation is becoming more common with the increase of air shipments. Often, the airplane has unloaded the goods, and the airline has asked the buyer to clear the goods before the collection documents have made their way through the seller's bank and arrived in the buyer's bank. The buyer then requests the bank, which is to receive the collection, to issue a guaranty to the airline so that the airline will release the goods in the absence of an airway bill. Usually when the bank issues such a guaranty, after receipt of the collection and payment by the buyer, the airway bill, which arrives with the other collection documents, is exchanged for the bank's guaranty, which then is surrendered by the air carrier and returned to the bank. However, if the buyer refuses to pay the collection after the bank issues its guaranty and the buyer obtains the goods, the buyer's bank may owe the foreign bank for the amount of the collection. The buyer's bank could sue the buyer on the basis of his obligation to reimburse it, but this is time-consuming and expensive.

To protect itself in this situation, the buyer's bank should issue the guaranty for the missing title document only against the buyer's signed application and only after the authorized lending officer for the buyer has approved an extension of credit for the amount of the shipment. The amount of this credit extension, of course, would be over and beyond any other amounts of credit that might be extended to the buyer in connection with other transactions.

LETTERS OF CREDIT

Letters of credit are written instruments issued by banks stating that payments will be made on behalf of persons arranging the credit, called *account parties,* to certain persons described in the instrument, called *beneficiaries,* provided that all conditions described in the instrument are fulfilled. The effect of a letter of credit is to substitute the credit of a bank, which generally is well known, for the credit of the account party, which is either not so well known or not considered to be adequate by the beneficiary.

It is important to remember that the account party and the beneficiary in each letter of credit transaction have a direct contractual relationship outside the letter of credit arrangement. Generally, the letter of credit contains only part of the terms of the contract between the parties; thus, bankers involved with letters of credit usually do not see all of the contractual arrangements and the communications between the parties. As is the case with collections, the role of the bank is to follow instructions exactly as given in the instrument to the bank. The bank should not become involved in the contract between the parties.

Letters of credit are classified into two broad categories known as *commercial letters of credit* and *standby letters of credit*. In earlier times *travelers' letters of credit* were used to provide funds for individuals traveling to foreign countries. *Clean letters of credit* sometimes are used to make periodic or predetermined payments over a period of time. However, this section will be concerned only with commercial and standby letters of credit.

Letters of credit were first used most extensively in connection with financing international trade and other foreign transactions, although there is no restriction against using letters of credit in domestic transactions. During recent years domestic uses for letters of credit have increased. Since international division personnel are trained to work with the mechanics of these instruments and maintain the records and subsidiary accounts for them, all letters of credit, whether foreign or domestic, usually are handled in the international division at most banks.

If sellers will not supply buyers on open account and mail documents directly to them or if sellers do not wish to send documentary collections to the buyer through banking channels, commercial letters of credit may be used. Sellers often require a letter of credit when extensive preparation, manufacturing, or special order work is involved. Under these circumstances sellers often incur risk of substantial loss if buyers refuse to accept delivery or make payment after completion of work by the sellers.

To avoid this risk a seller may require in its contract with a buyer that the buyer establish at a bank a letter of credit in favor of the seller. By means of the letter of credit, the bank signifies that it will honor drafts drawn on it by the buyer up to a certain amount of money until a specified expiry date, provided that certain specified documents in good order accompany the draft. These documents generally include the usual shipping documents, mentioned in connection with documentary collections, such as commercial invoices describing certain merchandise or services, packing lists, marine bills of lading or equivalent items, certificates of origin, certificates of inspection, evidence of insurance coverage, and similar documents.

If the credit standing of the *opening bank*, usually in the country of the account party, will not be satisfactory to the beneficiary, the latter can provide by contract provisions for the addition of the obligation of a bank satisfactory to him. This second bank is known as the *confirming bank* and generally it is also the *advising bank* that informs the beneficiary the letter of credit has been established. Often this same bank is the *negotiating bank* where the beneficiary may deliver his draft and documents and receive payment.

When the seller has been advised that the letter of credit has been established or opened and when the seller has examined the details of the advice and is satisfied with the terms of the letter of credit, he may then prepare goods for shipment. With a satisfactory letter of credit in hand, the seller knows that should the buyer default on the contract between them he still has a method to obtain payment in his own country. He need not sue in a foreign court to enforce his contract. If the buyer believes that the seller has breached their contract, the buyer then has the burden of suing the seller in the courts of the seller's country, if a mutually agreeable settlement to the dispute cannot be reached.

For these reasons beneficiaries of letters of credit usually require that letters be irrevocable and confirmed by banks satisfactory to the beneficiary in the beneficiary's country. The terms of *irrevocable letters of credit* cannot be changed without the consent of all the parties, including the beneficiary, the account party who requested that the letter of credit be opened or established, and the opening bank, and, if confirmed, the confirming bank.

From this brief description of the commercial letter of credit it should be obvious that several banks in different countries may be involved in various capacities in any single letter of credit transaction. Naturally, each bank will incur certain risks and each will earn certain fees for doing so. The opening bank must know the credit standing of the party requesting that the letter of credit be established. The appropriate lending officer in the opening bank must obtain the necessary approvals and be certain that the letter of credit section of the operating part of the international division has been informed of the credit approval.

As discussed earlier under the topic of departmental jurisdiction, this lending officer might be from the domestic side of the bank, assuming that the party which requested opening of the letter of credit is a local importer. On the other hand, the account party also could just as easily be a foreign customer, which imports goods from the bank's country or even a third country. Then, one of the international division lending officers from the headquarters or some foreign location would be in charge of obtaining the appropriate approvals.

A confirming bank, usually in the seller's country, assumes quite a different risk. Whereas the opening bank must know the importer's business, which might be large or small, the confirming bank is assuming a risk of another bank. Banks, too, can be large or small, but generally most banks are considered to be a better risk than most private companies. In any event, banks should be better able to assess the creditworthiness of other banks since both are operating in the same line of business. Moreover, in most cases banks are regulated by well-defined legal systems in their home nations; international bankers tend to study and understand these systems. Furthermore, correspondent banks visit each other periodically and are informed of each other's activities, sometimes including the activities of major customers and any problem situations within the bank.

For these reasons the risk and fees for confirming a letter of credit tend to be less than the risk and fees obtained for opening a letter of credit. Also, the confirming bank usually has the opportunity to be the negotiating bank and to earn a fee for paying the beneficiary and for examining the documents to verify that they conform to the conditions in the letter of credit before such payment. This often gives the bank a chance to handle foreign exchange transactions or even obtain a deposit account from the beneficiary. Further, when the negotiating bank pays the beneficiary it will usually charge the account of the opening bank on its books, assuming the two banks are correspondents. If not, there is another chance to obtain an account when there is sufficient volume to warrant one, and when accounts are opened, additional transaction-related deposit balances are generated.

The concept of the letter of credit is remarkably flexible and in the United States has been used to overcome the peculiar legislative proscription that national banks cannot, as a rule, issue guarantees. For this reason, in the United States noncommercial letters of credit usually are called standby letters of credit to indicate that they are merely standing by and probably will not be utilized. A commercial letter of credit, however, as we have seen, is to be utilized, generally to carry out a specific export or import transaction.

Documents accompanying a draft under a standby letter of credit are not the usual shipping documents, but often a mere letter signed by an authorized signatory and stating that some specified event has occurred or not occurred. Accordingly, standby letters of credit have been used in lieu of bid and performance bonds, to assure reclamation of mined lands, to obtain release of holdback monies under construction contracts, and for countless other purposes. Fees for standby letters of credit tend to be more negotiable between bank and customer. Although commercial letter of credit charges tend to be somewhat standard for all banks in a similar area, the risk, of course, for a standby letter of credit varies, depending upon the credit rating of the customer and the purpose for which each credit is used.

If the beneficiary makes a drawing under a standby letter, as in the case of the commercial letter of credit, the bank must either charge the demand deposit account of the customer or else immediately create a loan to its customer, because, if the draft and document are in order and in conformity with the credit, the beneficiary must be paid immediately. In the ordinary course of a commercial letter of credit transaction, the bank expects the letter to be utilized; for most standby letter of credit transactions, it is not expected that drawings will occur.

FOREIGN EXCHANGE

Throughout this chapter foreign exchange transactions have been discussed mainly in connection with other transactions. Although separate credit facilities must be established, as noted earlier, for each customer, including other banks with which the bank contracts, foreign exchange transactions generally result from some other service that the international division provides. Loan transactions in foreign currencies, Eurocurrency deposits and placements, international payments, settlements for collection, and letter of credit transactions all generate foreign exchange business. The purchase and sale of foreign bank notes and coins are also foreign exchange transactions.

Every foreign exchange transaction involves entering into a contract, and the bank documents generated by entering into these contracts are also called contracts or confirmations. Each of these documents carries the name of the party the bank is dealing with, the amounts of the two currencies involved, and the rate of exchange for determining the relationship between the two currencies. Additional information includes the settlement or value date, which is the date when immediately available funds are received and delivered by the parties, the date of the contract, and the locations and account numbers for receipt and delivery of funds.

Foreign exchange contracts are made for *spot* or immediate settlement, which for most currencies in most markets means two days after the date the contract was made unless agreed otherwise, or for *future* or forward delivery, which involves any date after the spot delivery date as agreed between the parties. All foreign exchange contracts involve credit risk, because the bank may deliver funds before it learns that the other party is unable to do so because of lack of funds, government intervention, or other causes. When this occurs, the bank obviously must try to recover the funds paid out. If the other party to a future contract is declared bankrupt or is known to be otherwise unable to perform its part of the contract before the settlement date, the bank may minimize its loss or even make a profit by entering into a similar contract with another party that will be able to fulfill its obligations.

Foreign exchange dealers, the employees of the international division who buy and sell foreign currency, work mainly with inventories of foreign currency held in the bank's due-from accounts maintained with foreign branches and correspondents. The more quickly and accurately the dealers can know the balances and historical cost of the bank's inventories, the better their chances to maximize exchange profits or minimize losses for the bank. For this reason, most modern banks use mechanized or computerized bookkeeping systems for foreign exchange accounting. Of course, with a steady stream of transactions that constantly increase and reduce the due-from account balances, it is difficult to maintain any prescribed target account balance. Excessive balances or temporary overdrafts occur, but in controlling foreign exchange risk, as opposed to credit risk, it is also necessary for the dealers to stay within limits prescribed by management that are called *net oversold* and *net overbought* limits.

The total foreign currency condition of a bank at any given time for any foreign currency is called its *net position*. This is determined for each foreign currency by assuming that all assets and liabilities in that currency would be liquidated at the same time. Because the bank may have numerous foreign currency assets and liabilities in addition to the balances in its due-from accounts, it is obvious that due-from balances are only part of the bank's total foreign exchange condition at any one time. If, upon the liquidation calculation for all assets and liabilities in a particular foreign currency, excess foreign currency liabilities exist, then the bank or unit is *oversold*. If the calculation produces excess foreign currency assets, then the unit's or bank's position is net *overbought* in the currency.

Foreign exchange profits are calculated by *revaluing* all the foreign currency accounts to bring the foreign currency and local currency relationships in line with current foreign exchange rates. After repeated buying and selling at different rates, the foreign currency and local currency balance columns in each foreign currency account soon bear no realistic relationship to each other. As local currency carrying values are adjusted, local currency amounts over or under the local currency value necessary to equal the foreign currency balance at the current rate are carried to foreign exchange profit or loss accounts. In most banks this calculation is made at least monthly and is governed by local accounting requirements.

OTHER SERVICES

In addition to the basic international services that have been discussed to this point according to broad categories, there are numerous other activities in which international banks engage. Some of these services represent refinements or specialized aspects of the basic services, whereas others involve a substantial departure from the concepts behind the basic services. Although each bank is limited by the banking laws in its own nation as to the services it can provide, four broad areas of other services deserve some mention in our study, because all probably are open to most, if not all, international banks. Further, many banks now seem to be moving to expand their services in one or some of these areas.

The areas are (1) dealing in gold, silver, and other precious metals; (2) working with customers to identify specific opportunities for increasing trade or direct investment; (3) providing other banks and nonbank customers with training in various aspects of international banking, trade financing, export documentation, or related areas; and (4) serving as advisors or consultants for international activities ranging from general topics such as political risk and foreign exchange management to specific work on individual transactions involving such matters as project and export financing and the full scope of corporate financial services, which blend into the activities of merchant or investment banks.

Dealing in gold, silver, and other precious metals. Some international banks, especially in Europe, Asia, and the Middle East, have bought, sold, and maintained inventories of gold, silver, and other precious metals for years. Banking originated in many nations with gold, since it was one of the earliest forms of money. With increasing inflation, many customers prefer to own precious metals instead of bank deposits that may earn interest but depreciate in value. Because the techniques for buying, selling, and controlling precious metals, some of which are in monetary form, are closely related to handling foreign exchange, international divisions of commercial banks are often responsible for these services. Some banks take positions in precious metals, and some act as agents on behalf of others to earn a commission or fee for buying and selling gold and silver coins, ingots, bars, or ownership certificates. Other banks, including Rhode Island Hospital Trust Bank in the United States, for example, handle gold to accommodate customers that are industrial users of gold, mainly in the jewelry business. Numerous banks handle gold in various fiduciary or trustee capacities.

With the increase in the price of gold during 1979– 1980 and in the number of nations issuing gold coins of various weights, it seems likely that more banks will be handling gold to accommodate their customers in the future. As significant demand develops for other precious metals, it will be only natural for banks to handle them also.

Developing trade and investment opportunities. International bankers continuously meet new organizations and ideas in their worldwide travels. New markets, new trading partners, and new activities for direct investment result both from the initiative of bankers approaching their customers and from customers seeking assistance from their banks. Many banks, especially in Europe and other countries for which exports are important, have had special trade development sections or departments for many years. Personnel from these units contact correspondent banks and other organizations in foreign countries to search for importers or users of their customers' exports. Although previously limited mainly to commodities or manufactured products, trade development departments more recently have become involved with services, especially engineering, contracting, and similar technical services.

Certain countries or regions of nations in search of direct investment to increase employment and economic activity have followed the pattern of trade development departments to use their banking contacts to find foreign investors. Generally, when banks help customers increase trade or direct investment, resulting business flows to the banks that worked to create such opportunities. However, particularly in the engineering services and direct investment areas, lead times can be long and effort expended substantial for the bank in relationship to the rewards.

Providing training and related programs. For years many international as well as domestic bankers have been exchanging personnel and conducting informal training sessions with their correspondents. Banks, especially the newer banks, in developing countries are anxious to improve ties with correspondents in developed countries and also to have their personnel learn the latest techniques in international banking. Many developing countries do not have organized study programs in their universities or banking associations.

Although direct fee arrangements for such training are not uncommon, many banks, in effect, pay for training by directing payment, collection, letter of credit, and foreign exchange business and maintaining deposit balances with their correspondents. Such personnel ties also expedite the handling of transactions and resolution of problems, which increases the efficiency and effectiveness of the banking partners. Some older bankers from developing countries have been assigned to management positions in newer banks in developing countries, where no ownership or investment ties exist. This, too, can lead to a closer working relationship between the institutions involved and to increased business volumes.

Training of staff of domestic customers in handling letters of credit and export documentation is common for many banks, and larger banks in many countries, especially money center banks, often provide extensive training for selected personnel from smaller, downstream correspondents. Although this may tend to grow competitors on one's own home ground, international business is usually expanded in the downstream correspondent's locale to the benefit of both the upstream and the smaller correspondent, which may identify customer needs it otherwise might not be able to serve without assistance.

Selling advisory and consulting services. Finally, the entire area of consulting and providing advice and information on international banking matters is becoming a lucrative specialty for many banks. Various international banks provide studies on systems for assessing country risk, advice on controlling foreign exchange risk, and newsletters on various specialized topics, such as doing business in different regions of the world.

A subsidiary of Chase Manhattan Bank is noted for its detailed studies on dealing with the People's Republic of China, Middle Eastern nations, and socialist countries in East Europe. Chemical Bank has an elaborate foreign exchange advisory service, which is developed and marketed by a staff separate from its own foreign exchange dealers. Citibank for years has prepared an extensive study of foreign exchange controls that now comprises several volumes and is revised each year.

On a fee basis the merchant banking specialists of international commercial banks may be engaged to perform specialized services in connection with large project financing, export loans, and general corporate financing. Although the largest banks tend to have more experience in these areas, several smaller banks have become experts in various financial techniques and areas of the world and supplement their income from more routine banking transactions with fees from services in these specialized areas. Equator Bank — headquartered in Hartford, Connecticut, and concentrating on services for business transactions involving selected African nations — is a good example of such a smaller, specialized institution.

PART I

Planning

3

International Planning Within the Bank

Purposes of Bank Planning / Bankwide Planning Process / International Planning Requirements / The Head-Office – Field Syndrome / Planning Up and Planning Down / Multinational Banking Units

P lanning is the foundation for every bank's international division, as well as all its other units. Although some banks, notably certain regionals, have survived without an elaborate planning process, international commercial banking requires a more sophisticated approach to planning than merely preparing an annual budget.

To improve any bank's planning process it is necessary to understand the purposes of planning. This chapter examines those purposes and discusses the bankwide planning process from a general aspect and from several detailed aspects. A several-step process is outlined, which can be adapted with modifications to almost any size bank in any stage of developing its planning process.

Within the overall planning effort, special planning needs for the international division must be considered. One significant international problem is what is called head-office – field syndrome, which sometimes develops in commercial banking organizations with over-seas offices directed from the bank headquarters. Emphasis on planning up along with planning down can often help overcome this problem.

An area of almost constant change in most commercial banks with international activity involves the method of providing banking services to the multinational corporation. All of a bank's experience and abilities in the planning field come into play in dealing with that situation. As a result of applying the planning process in this area, reorganization involving domestic units of the bank sometimes may be necessary to adequately serve multinational customers.

This chapter introduces broad planning concepts and the planning process. Chapter 4 deals with annual international planning, and Chapter 5 discusses long-range planning for international activities.

PURPOSES OF BANK PLANNING

No single definition of the planning process within the commercial banking organization is valid for all banks. Because each bank has its own method of planning, each bank in effect has its own definition for this process. For our purposes, however, it will be assumed that any bank large enough to have an international division at least has a written annual budget. If this budget with its monthly projections for asset, liability, income, and expense accounts is the only plan for the bank, then the process for developing that budget is the planning process for that bank.

In banks with such a limited planning process, some department, ad hoc committee, or special task force usually is charged with collecting from each unit the numbers for future budgets. Usually this occurs near the end of each calendar year. Often those responsible for administering the budget process provide all budget units with certain information on assumptions about common factors such as economic environment, interest rates, and guidelines for salary reviews for the next year, for example. These assumptions help to provide some uniformity for the process, especially during later stages when budget numbers are likely to be reviewed and changed by senior management after the numbers have been collected by departments and tabulated by divisions and larger groupings.

Obviously, such a narrow approach to planning has drawbacks. Therefore, most successful commercial banks go well beyond working with budget numbers in the planning process. These banks develop other written instruments or documents to guide the organization in establishing and achieving common goals. In order to improve any bank's efforts in this area and develop these other written instruments, it is necessary to understand the purposes of planning. By knowing why banks plan, any bank that wishes to improve its planning process can modify and expand its own planning activities and documents, in stages over time. In this way a bank can derive the maximum benefits from its own tailor-made planning process.

The first purpose of bank planning is to hold together the framework of the bank organization. Planning is the glue for the bank organization chart. In a military unit or a manufacturing company, the goals of the entire organization and each part of it usually are readily apparent to each member of the organization. For example, all effort focuses on maintaining readiness for military action in the peacetime army or achieving defined objectives during war; all members of the auto company concentrate on carrying out the steps for designing, producing, and selling automobiles. In such activities there is substantial investment in equipment, or capital goods. Distinctions between workers and management or officers and nonofficers are clear, and personnel are arranged in a heirarchy.

In the banking service organization, on the other hand, the objectives and related duties of each member and unit are not always so obvious to the other participants. Most of the bank's real investment and greatest expense relates to its people, although buildings and equipment, including computers, are carried as assets on the balance sheet. Moreover, large numbers of the bank's personnel are knowledge workers, as defined by Peter Drucker. These people seem more equal to each other in skills and responsibility. The organizational pyramid is less steep. Even after giving title, location, department, and division, further discussion with the bank employee is often required to pinpoint the actual customers who are served directly or indirectly or the types of services or staff support provided.

Many members of the bank provide entirely different services or support for various services to the same customers. Others specialize in only one service or support function. Some deal directly with the customers constantly day in and day out. Others seldom, if ever, see the customer. To function effectively in relation to the others in the bank, each key member of the organization must have more than budget numbers to serve as benchmarks. Knowledge of marketing plans or strategies and which people in the organization have close contacts with specific customers is indispensable to reach the desired customers in the right industries or lines of activity with the proper services or support functions that contribute to profit. Without a detailed plan that ties together incurring expense with creating new assets, liabilities, income, or all three, the forest cannot be seen for the trees. Without knowing who is calling on which customers, many economies of scale and follow-up sales opportunities will be lost.

The second purpose of bank planning is to measure performance against objective standards. Budget numbers together with actual results produce a final summary but seldom provide a detailed explanation of why the budget was exceeded or not met, or how the budget was achieved in some area. To answer these questions, words must be put together with the numbers in the planning process, in maintaining the plan, and in making progress reports from time to time. For example, detailed listings by customer and service are required in many cases, and summaries of all income and expense related to each major individual customer are indispensable to determine profitability in other cases.

The third purpose of bank planning is to maintain the order of priorities and be able to adjust quickly throughout the entire organization to new orders of priorities. When dealing with many services and multiple relationships, it is easy to become bogged down in low-profit activities. Excessive time and effort expended on low-profit activities usually detract from developing higher-profit-margin services and dealing with more profitable customers.

Throughout modern history new industries and services have emerged, while others mature, become less important, or even pass out of existence. In the free market economies, excessive government regulation or supposedly helpful assistance often imperils one industry, whereas decreasing regulation frees up another. Recent examples in the United States of such historical development include the basic steel and automotive industries, which are facing difficulties while the domestic airlines, trucking, and railroads (and, to some extent, banking) are being freed from some government regulations. Steel, shipbuilding, chemicals, and synthetic fibers in Western Europe since the mid-1970s provide other examples of possibly declining industries.

Changes in the long-term outlook for individual customers or entire industries require that the bank's resources and efforts be shifted smoothly to avoid loss or low-profit situations while gaining competitive advantage by increasing business with growing names in new fields. Without sufficient detail in the planning process, entire areas of the bank still can be dealing with "old losers," while other parts have moved on to "new winners," in the sense of services or even individual customer names.

The fourth purpose of planning is to bring to bear the best information and ideas for the benefit of the entire bank. Because large numbers of highly skilled specialists throughout the bank serve diverse markets and provide so many different services, it is difficult, if not impossible, for any one person or small group of planners to become expert in all the bank's markets and services. In fact, generally the higher the level of management, the less detailed is their knowledge of particular markets and services.

For this reason, the process of "planning up" is more important for the international bank than for many other kinds of organized activity. Later in this chapter we shall deal with this process of "planning up" in greater detail. However, it should be emphasized that if marshaling the information and ideas of the bank's various experts to the greatest extent possible is not one of the goals of the planning process, then the entire organization risks having key decisions made without the benefit of the maximum knowledge available.

The fifth purpose of bank planning is to commit all personnel in the bank to using their best efforts toward achieving the plan. Each employee in the bank must realize that the others in the organization are committed to the plan — in fact, bound together by it. Each person also should know that results will be measured against the plan and that priorities will be arranged in accordance with it. Further, if each employee knows that planning up has occurred, then an opportunity has been provided for hearing his or her views or perhaps incorporating those views into the final plan.

Under these circumstances there should be less reason for criticizing or withholding wholehearted support for the plan. If during the planning process the reasons for including or excluding various suggestions for each part of the plan are carefully explained at various levels throughout the organization, then the possibility for maximum understanding and support of the plan by all members of the organization has been increased significantly. When such explanations take place during the planning process, the plan is well on its way toward achievement before formal implementation has even started.

BANKWIDE PLANNING PROCESS

Planning for the international department cannot take place in a vacuum. International planning must relate directly to the goals of the entire bank. Therefore, before considering special needs of the international division in the planning process, we must briefly survey the operation of the bankwide planning process. We have observed already that a minimum planning process for a bank involves working with *budget numbers*. In order to grow beyond this level of planning, it is necessary to work with budget numbers plus detailed written plans, including market strategies for each of the bank's markets and services.

This process involves defining markets, determining services for such markets, and weighing costs against benefits. The tasks required for development of budget numbers and market strategies must be done in stages and involve many different areas of the bank working together. The first stages of this process involve fact-finding and making assumptions. Then alternatives must be set forth with ranges of expense and income for reaching different markets with different services according to various strategies. Next, facts, assumptions, and alternatives must be blended to make decisions.

Then the detailed budget and written strategies must be developed. Finally, in many cases, the organization of the bank must be modified to implement these decisions, carry out the strategies, and achieve the budget. The remainder of this section describes a seven-step planning process that could be partially or totally adopted by most banks.

1. *Bank description.* In the fact-finding stage of the planning process, the characteristics of the bank must be described. Emphasis should be placed upon the strengths of the organization, its basic units, and key personnel. Existing markets and services should be cataloged thoroughly, and competitive positions enumerated. We shall refer to the document produced at this stage as the *bank description.*

This document may be prepared by a specialized planning department in the larger banks or by an ad hoc committee in the smaller bank or the bank less experienced in detailed planning beyond budgeting. Often personnel skilled in collecting and working with budget numbers are not the best qualified to write verbal descriptions. Therefore, in moving from budgeting to market strategy planning, it is generally necessary to consider carefully the persons who will be assigned to this job. A combination of personnel experienced in working with past budgets, some good writers, and a few sound, creative thinkers is perhaps the best combination for this assignment.

Throughout this first fact-finding stage it is necessary for the planning department or planners to maintain contact with the division and group executives, president, and chairman of the bank, who will be working with the board of directors in the planning process. Also, the full-time planners must forge effective links down through the bank so that the "planning up" process will occur. Preparation of first drafts of various parts of the bank description should be assigned to the relevant areas of the bank. These drafts should then be combined by the planners into a complete draft of the entire description.

Next, the entire draft should be referred again down the organization to the appropriate staff and line units for their comments and suggestions. It is important that each unit see the entire draft document so that comments on the relevant parts can be made in proper context. Also, this early view of the basic facts tends to inform the various areas of the bank about other parts of the organization, which may not be so well known to them.

2. *World outlook.* Simultaneously, with the creation of the bank description, the economics department, bank economist, or outside economic consultant should be compiling certain basic materials. These should include, at a minimum, a general forecast of worldwide economic and political conditions for the next year and for the next three- to five-year period. This document shall be referred to hereafter as the *world outlook*. To obtain ideas for the political aspects of the world outlook document and join together different political and economic factors in a U.S. bank, public policy papers prepared by foreign affairs advisors to the president of the United States may be helpful. Although such documents tend to paint each current administration in the best possible light, they usually highlight critical issues and the connections between different world developments. Hence, they are often a good starting point for this document.

In the present age, emphasis in the world outlook obviously should be placed on dynamic and strategic factors such as energy sources and pricing, opening up of new markets, and possible actions of major world powers. Specifically, this would include possible actions by the Organization of Petroleum Exporting Countries (OPEC), Iran, Saudi Arabia, and other Middle Eastern nations, as well as Mexico and North Sea border states in connection with energy sources and pricing, the emergence of the People's Republic of China into worldwide relationships, and the activities of the Soviet Union in Europe, the Middle East, Africa, and elsewhere. This is not meant to be an exhaustive list by any means, but only an indication of some of the factors to be considered in this document.

In addition to the world outlook, specific studies should cover detailed economic and political surveys of major world powers and similar surveys of all other nations that are important markets for the bank. These write-ups are generally referred to as country studies and are discussed in detail in Chapter 12. At a minimum, country studies for the major world powers would cover the United States, Western Europe, Japan, Brazil, Mexico, China, and the Soviet Union.

3. *Money market developments.* For those nations with major capital markets or trading currencies, interest rates and foreign exchange rates should be considered with emphasis on the factors that will cause changes in these rates. The activities of the International Monetary Fund and developments in the European Monetary System, for example, and similar international agencies and arrangements also must be included when considering interest and exchange rates. All this material should be combined into a document on *money market developments.*

4. *Industrial surveys.* On the basis of the general world outlook, specific country studies, and probable money market developments, the economics department or bank economist should update specific studies of various commercial and industrial lines of activity. We shall call these write-ups *industrial surveys.* International division personnel obviously will be involved in assisting the economics department in the supply of information on various countries. In the same manner other lending areas of the bank and other personnel will supply information and their views about future developments in the various industries with which they work. After this collection of material has been organized into a coherent package by the planners, the line departments and divisions will be asked to pinpoint markets for the future.

5. *Market strategies.* Markets should be targeted by type of business, geographic area, and customer name. Potential activity should be identified by type and volume of service, including but not limited to loans and deposits. Various new and existing fee-producing services should be considered also. Combinations of income and expense and the number and salary level of personnel required to provide different ranges of services should be set forth. Staff departments should be alerted to changes in volume levels, and cost estimates should be revised on the basis of those inputs. Hereafter, this output will be identified as market strategy alternatives or *market strategies.*

At this point the planners will again attempt to organize the results of their collection efforts, taking care to bring any conflicts to the attention of division heads, group executives, and even the president, as well as the chairman, who should submit periodic revisions of the plan to the board for its information. After final market strategies have been selected and harmonized, the entire plan should go back down through the organization for a last checking and clearance. Staff and operations units as well as line units at this time should take care to fine tune staff and line costs and all other expenses. Final budget numbers then should flow together with detailed verbal plans.

6. *Management objectives.* During this stage of the planning process, if not earlier, expecially in the staff departments, write-ups under the heading of market strategies may become inadequate to contain the verbal goals and objectives of the plan. Ultimately, every unit of the bank is engaged in some phase of delivering services to execute the market strategies. However, some of the development work or staff support to produce these services may be of sufficient size and complexity to become individual projects in their own right. In addition, feedback from the auditing process, whether internal or external, will highlight other new tasks, perhaps also of project scale, as described in Chapter 9. To accommodate the verbal goals for these projects, an additional document called *management objectives* is required.

7. *Budget numbers.* In reality, the final market strategies, the management objectives, and the *budget numbers* form one integrated document. All three parts of the document are consistent with one another. Goals related to marketing strategies are found in the first part under that title. Other verbal goals are expressed in the section on management objectives. These two sets of goals may be referred to generally as qualitative goals. All budget numbers or quantitative goals are found in the last section of the plan.

Appendix B illustrates the sequences of this bankwide planning process and identifies the preliminary planning and final plan documents. International components of the final plan documents will be discussed in greater detail in Chapter 4. Before ending this description of the bankwide planning process, however, it should be noted that each of the board members and key managers of the bank should have a complete copy of the entire plan, with the bank descriptions, money market assumptions, world outlook, industrial surveys, and country studies, as well as market strategies, management objectives, and budget numbers. In this way each key unit and its members on a need-to-know basis can see exactly how they fit into the total plan and what they must do in order to accomplish it.

INTERNATIONAL PLANNING REQUIREMENTS

Throughout the description of the seven-step bankwide planning process, the areas where the internatonal division will be supplying input and feedback are obvious. From the international division viewpoint, management's overriding objective should be to develop realistic market strategies and sufficient management objectives to adequately support these strategies. These international market strategies should involve supplying service from throughout the bank to the corporations and other customers targeted by the international division as dynamic, growing, and successful industries, lines of activity, and nations within the bank's worldwide market areas.

Several special needs of the international division become apparent as the division carries out its role in this planning process. Most revolve around the time factor and some around the distance factor. In international commercial banking there is seldom, if ever, the chance for a "quick kill." Preparation, development, patience, and consistency are required to bring rewards.

International market strategies usually require several years to implement, especially if a bank is entering a new geographic market, as contrasted to providing a new service in an existing market. When a bank enters a new geographic area, a period of personnel training may be necessary, if other than the people who investigated the potential market are involved. If new hiring is involved to staff the new marketing function, this could slow implementation more than if existing personnel were used. New personnel usually require a minimum of orientation to their new environment, as well as time for the other personnel in the organization to learn about them. If existing personnel will be handling a new geographic area, time for study of new languages, cultures, histories, and political, economic, and business conditions also may be required.

The opening of a new office overseas will require more time. If a branch or other banking operation is being established, as opposed to a representative office, local staff must be hired, premises, furniture, and equipment obtained, and systems and procedures established. Opening even a modest representative office may take the better part of a year before all housekeeping details are completed. After this, it may take one or two years for the officers of the bank to become well known and accepted in the new location.

For these reasons new markets should be entered carefully and only after long study. And then entry should be made only on a permanent basis, not as an experiment. Potential customers, including other bankers, carefully note the openings and closings of offices and inquire as to the reasons for each action. Many banks open representative offices before establishing full branches or other operations, even when their market research shows that the larger unit may be justified. Such a cautious approach initially often avoids costly long-run mistakes, since more on-the-scene experience is gained before making key decisions on customers, staff, and premises.

Extensive visiting over a period of time is an important step in learning details about potential customers in a new area before actually starting to do business, especially business involving the extension of credit. A full range of potential customers and other institutions should be visited before a bank extends any credit, as those entities not considered creditworthy by other banks always seem swift in finding new bankers before the bankers find them. Credit files should be established for each new name visited, and information should be collected to continually process up-to-date country reports on the new areas being covered.

Obviously, in many ways selling a new service within an existing area is easier than opening up new geographic markets. Personnel training may be required, but the new service may have been test marketed with some of the existing customers. Mailing campaigns or frequent telephone calls may be all that is required to move a new service into such a market. Such devices should not be ruled out automatically for selected overseas markets, where the bank's reputation is already well established in connection with one or more services.

With long lead times for developing markets overseas, personnel ultimately destined for overseas offices must know that the bank is making a permanent commitment to a new market. Personnel typically commit for no less than two years when moving to an overseas location, and often entire families must be relocated in the process. If most of the first year is used in getting established, especially when a new office is to be set up, the overseas banker on an assignment of less than two years may be ready for his next post almost before he can make an effective contribution in his existing job.

Large banks seem particularly inclined to move personnel quickly on the assumption that their existing offices are highly standardized and the office routines uniform. The hardship, of course, often falls upon the local customers, who barely get to know one account officer before a replacement has arrived and been introduced. With long construction periods for complicated process plants and large projects, one officer often recommends or extends credit, another handles disbursement, and the replacement's replacement collects the repayments.

It is one of the ironies in today's fast-moving international banking scene that a regional bank's head-office calling officer, who has been visiting an area on a continual basis for as short a period as only a few years, can sometimes know more about a foreign market than his newly arrived counterpart at the local office of a long-established major bank. This situation alone explains why many smaller banks have done business successfully in foreign markets for years without local offices.

All these matters must be taken into account during the planning process both by international division personnel and by the planning unit. Several money center banks have established separate staff planning units for international planning. In such institutions it is then important for this special unit to work as closely with the bank's domestic planners as with international personnel. Otherwise, the possibility exists for the international division to run off in its own orbit outside the range of the total bank. This presents only minimum problems until a time of trouble, when such an international operation may have also outgrown its allies and supporters within the rest of the bank. If a separate international planning unit does not exist, another alternative is to make certain that the planning staff always contains one or more persons with at least some international perspective, if not actual international experience.

THE HEAD-OFFICE–FIELD SYNDROME

Bankers who are posted abroad on two-year-minimum assignments, with only a few weeks per year spent at the head office, quickly grow out of touch with changes and trends within the head-office organization. Credit recommendations that are curtly rejected and other unexplained developments can cut the foreign banker further adrift. In addition, almost every account officer tends at some point to become an advocate for his customers, especially when higher credit approvals must be obtained.

The time zone or travel time factor and the geographic remoteness of many overseas locations from the head office tend to isolate overseas bankers. At times these factors can build a "my customer and me" attitude, which exceeds healthy advocacy. The goal then becomes obtaining head-office or regional-office approvals or other permissions from nonlocal approving office personnel, who do not seem to understand doing business in the particular foreign country in the eyes of the overseas bankers. If head-office personnel fire back with comments and questions that evidence lack of understanding, this further complicates the problem.

This situation, which we call the *head-office – field syndrome,* can be disastrous to morale on both ends of the chain of command. Credit decisions are the most fertile area for growth of this type of disagreement, but problems can occur in many other areas. Capital appropriations, development, promotion, and benefit levels for local staff, or almost any matter where head-office authorization is required, can become a source of friction leading to development of the syndrome.

Obviously, those who have served abroad should be ideal candidates to subsequently supervise from the head office or from regional headquarters those offices where they once worked. But logic does not always prevail. Often in some of the largest banks mobile overseas managers move from one office to another, reporting to supervisors who continuously reside in the head-office country.

In those banks that apply the principle of using in the head office only officers with extensive field experience, the results can be phenomenal. Senior managers in the London head office of the British Bank of the Middle East, for example, generally have more than fifteen years of field experience within a fairly concentrated geographic area. When these veterans become head-office supervisors, there is no head-office – field syndrome, since the head-office supervisors have probably served in almost every geographic area of the bank and have personally known their bank's customers for years.

For those organizations that have a faster turnover or have tendencies toward the head-office – field syndrome, an annual planning process along the lines we have described can minimize or eliminate most problems, sometimes before they occur. By planning up, the local manager has an opportunity for maximum input before the final plan stage. Suggestions from both the field and the head office can be introduced within a routine framework of the planning process as opposed to single-issue discussions.

If disagreement exists about only the matter of timing, conditions precedent to implementation of a new project or program can be established within the planning framework. With regard to defining market opportunities, a good question and answer dialog can develop a better head-office understanding of the types of customers available locally and might lead to subsequent enlistment of greater head-office support in implementing approved marketing strategies. Disclosure of the completed final plan allows local managers and key staff to know exactly how they fit into the entire bank's effort.

PLANNING UP AND PLANNING DOWN

With this understanding of the purposes of bank planning, the bankwide planning process, and the background of several special international planning needs, it is now appropriate to explore further the concept of planning up and planning down. This approach to planning is an alternative to simple planning down, which occurs in at least two main forms: secret-session planning, where the plan is announced from on high, and end-run planning. In secret-session planning, a few key staff members or ad hoc committee members, generally at a fairly senior level, meet together, formulate a plan, and then announce it to the rest of the bank's employees. In end-run planning, staff members are selected throughout the organization at various levels to work out a plan without channeling it through their department or division heads. In general, organizations with little planning experience use one of these forms, or sometimes even a combination of the two.

Planning is sometimes viewed as a chore with which key managers should not be bothered. According to this school of thought, the most qualified and experienced persons and managers should keep working with day-to-day business while someone else deals with the planning. Planning is so important, however, that it must involve key personnel and managers most of all. Their ideas, among all others, must move up through the organization. This is the essence of *planning up.*

At the onset it should be noted that merely supplying information such as the bank description, world outlook, country studies, industrial surveys, and money market developments is not planning up. By necessity, the international division will have a significant role in the preparation of such information, because it is one of the logical sources of such data within the bank. Even if planning department personnel develop much of this information in outline or draft form, it will be necessary for international personnel to fill in or verify the details. Planning up takes place only when the international department puts forward its market strategy alternatives along with its management objectives.

Of course, preparation of market strategies and other objectives is not limited to the annual plan timetable. New ideas and proposals in these areas always should be hatching at various stages of development within the various units of the international division and throughout the entire bank. At a minimum the proposals are graded and sorted by priorities at least once a year. However, certain major developments may cause changes more often, and then the annual plan may be modified. In the absence of such major changes, various proposals can always be moving forward through the different levels of the international organization for refinement, improvement, support, approval, or rejection. This approach obviously avoids bunching at the time of the annual plan and generally provides higher-quality proposals.

Planning up in this manner should produce the benefits associated with the purposes of planning, including development of the best ideas from the experts and commitment of all parties to the final plan. Planning up obviously takes more management effort and requires more lead time than planning down. However, in the complex commercial banking organization, and especially in connection with international activities, the benefits obtained should more than offset this time and effort. A plan that is created by a few planners with minimal or no consultation, quickly blessed by management, and handed down from on high may have only the advantage of speed in creation.

Planning up should not be confused with employee democracy or other similar movements. Management still must make decisions and take responsibility for them; neither is there voting by raised hands or ballots. But planning up should bring forth new thinking, not just once, but repeatedly. With proper consideration and explanations no individual or department should be reluctant to keep pushing new proposals up the line, even when ideas are turned down, as some must be, since not every idea is worthy of implementation. This process challenges management and also creates more opportunities for communication throughout the bank and for leadership on the part of management.

Planning up is most difficult when more proposed market strategy alternatives are put forward than can be realistically implemented within a reasonable time frame. Then choices must be made within the foreign branch, subsidiary, affiliate, or head-office international division unit. Better developed proposals and those from people with a proven record of success are more likely to be accepted or approved for moving further up the line.

However, all proposals should be presented, since at this point no one within the international division knows what ideas may be moving upward through the domestic units of the bank. Early consultation with domestic commercial units is necessary for the bank with emphasis on wholesale banking activities. Much sorting and adjusting in thinking may be required at these early stages, since considerable economies of scale could be produced by combining various international market strategies with selected domestic strategies. These combinations could alter completely the cost and income projections associated with international alternatives as first proposed.

Finally, no rejected plans should ever be discarded. This year's lowest priorities may be next year's highest priorities, and any year's rejected ideas may serve as sources of future inspiration or may save investigation time in future years. In a sense, much of the work locked up in proposed market strategy alternatives is the bank's equivalent to an industrial corporation's research. Ideas for different markets and new services often rattle around the banking organization for years before they are taken up and implemented. Nowhere is this more true than in the international field of banking.

MULTINATIONAL BANKING UNITS

Earlier in this chapter we noted that organizational changes often result at the end of the planning process. Although changes can occur in any part of the international division, we shall limit our discussion here to an example in one area, namely, providing services to multinational corporations. However, this one area has far-ranging effect and has been the focus of constant attention during the last several years, especially within U.S., Japanese, Western European, Brazilian, and Mexican banks, among others. Proving that planning is a continuous process or perhaps that no plan devised to date has really worked, many banks in these countries have repeatedly changed their approach to serving the multinational corporation. Some of these changes have occurred at relatively short intervals within the same bank, and both money center and regional banks seem to be wrestling with problems in this area.

At the most elementary level, one problem might be that of having domestic lending and calling officers attempt to sell and provide international services. We touched upon one aspect of this subject briefly in Chapter 2 when discussing departmental jurisdiction in connection with international services. Often the domestic officers are inexperienced and uncomfortable in working with international services, especially those in regional or smaller money center banks.

One solution has been to rotate people trained in the international division to domestic lending divisions, especially to those units involved with corporate banking. Some banks have extended internal training programs to encompass the international division functions, and others have stepped up training by means of outside programs. A few banks have brought selected outside programs in-house for attendence only by bank employees. As yet, however, none of these efforts have stemmed the almost continuous tide of reorganizations to better serve the multinational corporate customer.

At the next level in dealing with this area, many banks, both money center and regionals, have created specialized multinational units. These units may be part of the international division, part of the domestic corporate banking group, or equal in rank to both as a separate and parallel unit. In some cases account responsibility is shared with officers in the domestic and international units; in other situations responsibility for entire multinational corporation relationships is shifted to the new unit.

Although a domestic-based multinational corporation such as General Motors may receive satisfactory service from such a specialized multinational banking unit in some banks, several of the largest money center banks have gone a step or two further. In some of these banks, for example, the contact for Volkswagen would be centered in the German office of the U.S. bank. In others, both General Motors and Volkswagen relationships would be handled by an automotive unit with worldwide responsibility.

Obviously, worldwide industrial units are most common in specialized industries, such as energy and petroleum, mining and metals, and aerospace and electronics, but more reorganization along such lines seems inevitable in many other industries. Only banking officers with a worldwide outlook and global responsibility can service such complex organizations effectively, and more banks seem to be realizing this. By now we may have gone full circle in the organizational sense and left our original international division with only limited coordination and housekeeping functions, assuming that funds transfers, collections, letters of credit, foreign exchange, and related services have been absorbed within bankwide operations or other groups.

This limited discussion is sufficient for our purposes of illustrating how planning — such as developing an effective market strategy to reach the multinational or worldwide corporation — can involve organizational change. However, this brief discussion is not meant to exhaust the substance of the topic of how to better serve the international banking needs of multinational organizations. Because of its importance, this subject will be encountered again as part of Chapter 8 in connection with the support function for the international effort performed by the domestic banking units of the bank. It will also be examined, from a different viewpoint, in Chapter 14, which deals with this topic from a matrix management perspective.

4

Annual International Planning

A nnual planning for the international division must be related to both the bankwide planning effort and a process for monitoring attempts within the international division to achieve the final international plan. One of the best ways to develop an effective link between the annual international plan and the monitoring process is by means of a series of reports, referred to in this chapter as monthly management reports.

Annual international planning is facilitated by dividing preparation of the plan into pieces for each unit of the international division and by developing qualitative and quantitative goals for each unit. Qualitative goals consist of the market strategies and management objectives. Quantitative goals are the budget numbers.

After the international division market strategies, management objectives, and budget have been harmonized with the bankwide plan and approved, the final international plan must be presented to key international staff. This clears the air, which may have been clouded by previous versions of the draft plan. Such a presentation also provides an opportunity for asking questions and giving explanations, binds all parties together to carry out the plan, and bridges the distance between bank managers in remote foreign locations and the headquarters and regional offices.

Monthly management reports are used to monitor progress in achieving the plan and to provide information to management. On the basis of this information, management makes decisions and takes corrective action, if necessary, to maximize chances for meeting the plan. Preparation of the plan and monthly progress reports also can be a useful way to train future managers. In addition, economies of scale may be obtained in some banks by grouping planning staff with personnel who design systems and prepare procedures.

LINKING PLANNING AND MONITORING

The international division participates in the bankwide planning process, as described in Chapter 3, by supplying certain information, assumptions, and proposals as requested by the unit or persons responsible for directing and coordinating the bank's planning process. Assuming adoption of some form of that process, various units from throughout the international division will contribute to the bank description, world outlook, and money market forecast. Country studies and possibly information for parts of the industry surveys also will originate within the international units of the bank. In addition, the international division head will sort through various proposed market strategies, tentative management objectives, and draft budget numbers and will move these materials up the line during the bankwide planning process.

At this point we must distinguish between the sources for the documents dealing with facts and assumptions and those materials that will contain goals and objectives. Facts and assumptions are contained in the bank description, world outlook, money market forecast, country studies, and industry surveys. These materials, or the data for most of them, will be prepared largely from daily or routine work within the division by different experts who deal with, say, countries or money markets on a continuing basis. On the other hand, the draft market strategies, management objectives, and budget involve a less routine approach. These items will be prepared mainly by area account officers in the case of market plans and usually by operations and administrative personnel with regard to projects or management objectives and budget numbers.

This chapter will not be concerned further with the documents and materials relating to facts and assumptions. Also, it will be assumed that during the bankwide planning process the strategies, objectives, and budget will be modified and approved in harmony with the other goals of the bank. Instead, this chapter will stress building or creating the original details of the strategies, objectives, and budget from the standpoint of the international division and using the final approved plan documents to guide the division during the year. Accordingly, annual international division planning consists in not only collecting and refining detailed international market strategies, management objectives, and budget numbers for a one-year future period but also monitoring the attempt to implement these strategies, objectives, and numbers during the year.

Details for the annual international plan come from numerous schedules and work papers that are prepared within the division and from general goals and feedback from the bank outside the division. Thus, detailed annual planning involves working in two directions. Under these circumstances, the earliest years of planning or expanded planning are the most difficult. With historical materials and patterns, planning as a process becomes less burdensome in most international banks, and over the years increased emphasis can be placed on the substance of each successive plan.

Although early drafts of the bankwide plan may result in general and broadly stated goals, in the final plan the annual international sections break up and develop market strategies and management objectives into segments that can be carried out by individual units within the international division during the year. Strategies and objectives are defined in more detail, and guidelines for implementing the strategies and objectives must be set forth along with a system for monitoring the progress on each aspect of the plan. Although the annual budget numbers are not usually difficult to project, refine, and compare with actual results, monitoring the qualitative goals usually requires greater effort in the form of written reports issued periodically throughout the year.

To assure that this monitoring effort occurs, a series of periodic reports or a regular collection of materials is needed. For the sake of simplicity it will be assumed hereafter that a collection of reports is contained in a document called the monthly management report. After this report is prepared, either all of the report or parts of it should be circulated to key international department managers and others outside the department, including group heads and the president and chairman of the bank. Such a collection or unified report is perhaps more common in regional or smaller banks. However, the same type of information or report is broken up to follow various separate circulation patterns throughout larger banks. Certain advantages are obtained from preparing the monthly report as one document, however. These are discussed in the last section of this charter.

Seen from the perspective of monitoring, the annual international planning process is easier to handle. With all planning effort chopped into segments, work papers for preparing the plan will not be much different in scope from the reports or materials that are used to track the results of the plan. Therefore, for those institutions that are expanding their planning efforts, many existing reports, probably some with only minor modification, can be used as a starting point for creating planning documents. Moreover, from the division-head level, the usefulness of reports on plan results should be assessed carefully. If a report is useful throughout the year, the plan should relate to the report. If information from some aspect of the plan is not needed during the rest of the year, then that related report may be unnecessary. This test between plan and report should be applied repeatedly during each annual planning process.

DEVELOPING QUALITATIVE GOALS

The buildup of detail for the qualitative goals (strategies and objectives) and the quantitative goals (budget numbers) of the annual international plan starts at the level of the various units or subsections of the international division. These units include geographic parts of the international division, such as branches, other separate offices, and regional or country groupings within the head-quarters, as well as functional components at the headquarters, such as the letter of credit, foreign exchange, and project financing sections. In branches and other offices, details from both functional and geographic units within such locations are combined to create overall strategies, objectives, and budget numbers forwarded to the headquarters by each location.

In order to develop further detail for one-year segments of the plan and to cope easily with revisions during the planning process, the format of the market strategy and management objective documents should include at least four factors for each goal or objective. First, objectives should be ranked in priority order; that is, the most important objective should be stated first, followed by other objectives in descending order of importance. Second, a clear statement of each marketing goal or objective should be set forth. Third, each objective should be followed by a clear designation of the persons who are responsible for results and by a brief outline of the means of achieving or implementing the objective. Finally, a statement of how implementation will be measured or monitored should be provided.

One page or less is generally sufficient to encompass these four items for each task or objective. Tables or customer listings are often helpful for the market strategy objectives, whereas a simple outline style is generally best for other management objectives. By way of further examples, lists could cover specific pending projects involving sale of a major bank's services (1) within a particular country or region, (2) to offices, subsidiaries, and affiliates of new domestic customers, or (3) to prospects that will be contacted during sales calls. Management objectives, as opposed to market strategies, might include such items as design and implementation of a new foreign exchange accounting system or study and purchase and installation of a new computer system to automate a clerical operation being performed manually.

The goals or objectives may be stated in one or a few lines each, but more explanation is required for the implementation section. The purpose of this section, however, is not to describe in exact detail how the goal will be achieved but merely to give some ground rules or directional pointers. Actual development of the method for implementation of a particular project is part of implementation of the plan, not the planning process. In many cases, especially for more complicated tasks of a project nature, other detailed documents must be prepared in the process of achieving the objective. However, again, it must be emphasized that these documents are not part of the plan. To include these documents would delay preparation of the final plan and make it too large to be easily controlled.

Most monitoring or follow-up for qualitative goals will be accomplished by means of reports, especially some part of the monthly management report, which will be prepared for use not only by the international department management but also by others in the bank, including the group heads and other senior management.

DEVELOPING QUANTITATIVE GOALS

The quantitative goals, or budget numbers, for the plan consist of sheets for assets. liabilities, income, and expenses for each unit plus detailed supporting schedules, such as salary worksheets and separate listings for travel expenses, capital expenditures, and dues, memberships, and subscriptions. The most detailed, yet perhaps the easiest, schedule to complete for international bank planning is the salary worksheet. After determining the staffing requirements for carrying out the marketing and other objectives, salary payments and other benefits for each existing or needed employee should be listed by months.

Sometimes it is helpful to work with only base salary numbers and apply a benefit factor to base salary totals. However, this is more applicable to head-office personnel than to foreign-based staff in most organizations. Foreign service usually involves various premiums, cost of living allowances, family educational payments, and other special items such as housing leases and travel. In these situations employee costs must be calculated employee by employee, depending upon the circumstances of each. Salaries, wages, and benefits are usually the largest controllable expense items for most units of the international banking division. Accordingly, careful attention to this area at the annual planning stage usually isolates this large area of controllable expense for the international bank manager and significantly increases chances for meeting the total controllable expense portion of the annual plan.

When travel and entertainment by the personnel in any particular unit are involved, special estimated cost schedules should be developed, not only for each country or city to be visited, but for each trip by each employee with the number of days and the names of customers or potential customers to be visited. Although this initially requires a great deal of time and effort, the repeat process becomes easier, as does all planning, assuming many of the same customers remain with the bank year after year. Old expense accounts contain valuable information for estimating costs of future visits, and some bankers meet with their customers during regular trips in roughly the same appointment order, whenever possible, to minimize backtracking around large cities. In some banks, increased attention might be directed to designing expense account forms which are more useful in the annual planning process and which record expenses incurred in the proper accounts.

Various other detailed schedules for capital expenditures; for newspapers, magazines, books, research materials, and other publications, especially those used for country analysis; and for associations, clubs, and organizations assist the budgeting process. Estimates for items such as rent, light, heat, depreciation, lease payments, repairs, and maintenance, and special payments such as licensing and professional fees, complete the controllable expense budget, similar to most other businesses. Whenever possible, attorneys' fees should be passed on to customers. However, legal fees related to general matters and auditing fees must be borne by the appropriate international unit. Banking differs from many other lines of business, however, because of its emphasis on salaries and wages, and international banking involves heavy outlays for travel.

Without a continuous investment of time and money in travel to maintain customer contacts, provide customer service, resolve problems, develop new business, and stay abreast of political, economic, and business conditions in each foreign market, any international banking organization will quickly contract and eventually atrophy. Great savings in travel expenses can be obtained by forsaking first-class airfares and planning routine travel far in advance to take advantage of special airfares. Accordingly, for most banks, reasonable amounts for salaries and related expenses to keep high-quality people on the move throughout the international bank's market areas should be the last to be sacrificed in any economy drive. In essence, expenditures for salaries and for carrying out carefully prepared travel schedules are a necessary investment to maintain existing business, develop new opportunities, and avoid future problems.

After controllable expenses have been worked out, other expenses, income, assets, and liabilities should be estimated on the basis of the marketing strategies and other objectives to be achieved and the total resources made available to the unit in question. In order to project annual loan and acceptance totals, maturity schedules of individual loans and acceptances by borrowers, countries, and geographic areas, showing outstandings for each month, are indispensable. Again, although much effort may be required to create such information initially, subsequent updating of monthly data takes little effort, especially if modern devices such as computers or word processing machines can be used to capture, store, and reproduce the data. Deposits often follow historical patterns, usually related to loan outstandings and volumes of other services and many other asset and liability accounts can be predicted with greater accuracy over time by saving and reworking detailed worksheets.

After dealing with controllable expenses, loans, and deposits, only interest income and expense and smaller balance sheet, income, and expense items remain to complete the budget. Interest income and interest expense result from applying projected interest rates to loan estimates and anticipated funding sources. Fee income estimates result from historical patterns coupled with projected results from new strategies. With such an approach from most certain to least certain projections, using numbers based upon market strategies and management objectives, the buildup of the budget takes place.

Revisions required for any budget item should always relate back to assumptions in marketing strategies and managment objectives. Either some market will not be reached as planned, perhaps because of political or economic conditions in a particular country or region, or some project will not be implemented, depending upon various circumstances such as technological change or new work methods. Or else some previously overlooked area will be uncovered during the bankwide planning process, perhaps as a result of some related development in another part of the world or the activities of some individual or group of customers. Energy, mining, and other extractive industry ventures and process plant projects are examples of this type of development. Changes in transportation patterns and methods also can cause sudden expansions or contractions.

The items in the international banking budget, as in most businesses, are interrelated. Only if a realizable, concrete plan exists will more money in some area produce greater income or reduced expense. This is the discipline of working with the written assumptions of marketing strategies, management objectives, and the budget. Working with budget numbers alone does not pinpoint trade-offs and opportunities. Nor does a budget without written assumptions allow for intelligent and systematic monitoring during the year. The raw numbers usually do not tell enough by themselves, but only point to areas for further investigation. The written goals speed up and assist that investigation.

COMPLETING THE ANNUAL PLAN

As each unit in the international division submits strategies, objectives, and related budget numbers, numerous drafts and revisions are produced. Ideas are accepted, rejected, and modified within the unit, and other drafts and proposals leave the unit to be fitted together with other international units and other parts of the bank. On the assumption that clear explanations are given for all rejections and modifications, the planning process can be a good opportunity for all international employees to learn more about the bank, its people, resources, strengths, and weaknesses. This is all valuable information to be used when implementing the final plan.

For a newer and less experienced employee, the opportunity to work with the plan in the international unit can provide an excellent chance to learn more about international banking. While learning, newer persons also can do much of the routine work, except handle the salary information, which in most cases must, of course, remain confidential with the unit manager, except for the final aggregates. The unit manager or key assistants must provide overall guidance to any person who works to prepare the plan, especially with regard to key assumptions. All work of less experienced staff must be reviewed along with relevant work papers and related materials. When the planning process has been well developed within a particular unit, the opportunity to use this type of work as a training ground for newer staff is significantly increased. When carefully used and developed, this is one of the quickest ways to develop highly qualified staff and future managers.

After the final plan emerges with appropriate management approvals, it is necessary to review the plan with all key staff involved in implementing it. Copies of the agreed upon marketing strategies, management objectives, and budget numbers should be prepared, distributed on a need-to-know basis, and then discussed in group meetings. This communicating of the final plan is one of the most important steps in the annual planning process; yet, in many banking organizations it is often largely, if not totally, overlooked.

As a result of the various drafts and proposals that are issued during the planning process, different people may have different ideas of what has been finally agreed upon. Unfortunately, some people in an organization stop listening after their ideas have been set forth. Senior management often remembers the highest income projections coupled with the lowest expense estimates. Marketing or line officers remember their most ambitious plans, including salary and staff increases. Operations personnel recall new machines or equipment, and so forth.

During a properly conducted planning process, almost everyone's ideas and original proposals are modified, at least to some extent. Some proposals are rejected or totally removed from the final plan, and entirely new thoughts and projects may be developed during the planning process. If some ideas emerge almost completely unscathed, others may be modified so severely as to be unrecognizable. For this reason it is imperative to present the final written versions of the strategies, objectives, and budget to appropriate official staff with emphasis on key areas, and then provide at these meetings an opportunity for questions and necessary clarification.

The final plan presentation meeting also represents the acceptance of the plan by all the parties in the unit involved. Obviously, if during the year circumstances change substantially or key assumptions are found to be incorrect, appropriate adjustments will be required. However, if events unfold largely as anticipated, all parties are bound by the contract. Management of the unit must do its part to request and obtain approvals needed from higher levels of the organization and provide support for achieving various goals throughout the year. Staff and line of the unit will strive to carry out objectives and meet targets.

Moreover, all agree to work together to achieve the plan and to be measured throughout the year by the standards set by the plan. The final plan meeting clears the air of what occurred earlier during the planning process and sets in motion the benefits of planning for the bank and its personnel, as described in Chapter 3. More significantly, for those in the far flung corners of the international commercial bank organization, the final plan is an important tool that spans distance and time and ties together remote units with the home country headquarters and regional centers.

Throughout the year as the monthly management reports are issued by each unit and reviewed by those in the next rung of the bank, the plan will be referred to and discussed. The plan will be the reference source for decisions on staff changes, salary increases, equipment purchases, changes in business volumes, funding sources, lines of business, and customer mix.

In some international commercial banks, monthly or quarterly ratings of units are circulated to all unit managers around the world. However, regardless of whether these ratings use criteria of absolute earnings or percentage variation from plan, it is doubtful whether such ratings or rankings improve morale or contribute positively to achieving goals in the absence of explanations about the validity of the underlying assumptions for each unit's activities. One-sheet listings seldom provide insight into that area. For these reasons it would seem better to confine downward distribution of competitive rating results to the next higher line of the organization, again applying the need-to-know criterion.

MONTHLY MANAGEMENT REPORTS

After the three-part international plan has been prepared and distributed, it is necessary to design a format for the monthly management reports on international activities. For the sake of convenience, this one document will be discussed in sections, although various sections, tables, or similar information from such a document could be distributed as separate reports to different recipients. The form, content, and order of the management report outlined here are not sacrosanct. However, this discussion is intended to review in a comprehensive manner the kinds of materials that should be considered for any international reporting system. Moreover, there are certain economies of scale and other benefits to be derived from collecting and packaging reports along the lines suggested here.

In the course of designing this report for the first time, numerous work papers and schedules that were used in the preliminary planning process will be collected. Accordingly, most of the remainder of this chapter will deal with these work papers or the corresponding monthly report sections that result from them. Once the planning process as detailed here has been under way for at least one year, many parts of the monthly report format can be used as annual planning work papers. Other work papers, especially those for the budget, will remain behind in files, but even those can be used again in future years. Naturally, the more tables, schedules, or listings that can be used throughout the report, the easier and quicker it will be to read and use, as well as to prepare, each edition of the monthly report throughout the year. Word processing equipment or computers are useful in this regard.

The first part of the monthly report should consist of an index and summary for those who may wish to read only parts of the entire report. The summary will highlight major income, expense, asset and liability accounts, significant changes or variances from budget, and significant successes or failures in carrying out market strategies or management objectives, mainly special projects. Following the summary and index, sections for assets, liabilities, income, and expenses should show actual results by individual months and year to date. Major accounts should be used for these categories. One page with the balance sheet and another with the income and expense statement usually provide the clearest presentation, and this format with columns for each month across the pages makes it easy to spot trends from month to month.

Next, these same accounts should be presented in a format to facilitate comparison between actual and budgeted results. In both the monthly comparisons of actual results and the monthly comparisons between actual and budget, these sections can divide the international activities of the bank into areas or subdivisions in a manner most convenient to management. Heads of various geographic regions, for example, might have details for every unit or officer within their region, whereas only the overall regional summaries might go into the management report directed to more senior officers.

Following the section on comparisons of budget and actual results, all major variances (generally those of 10 percent or more) from budget should be explained in a narrative that discusses assets, liabilities, income, and expense in account-by-account order. Explanations should cover both monthly and year-to-date variances with comments on likely consequences, need for action, or any actions taken. Staff increases or decreases, substantial equipment acquisitions or dispositions, or other important developments are indicated here. Large operating errors or other unusual matters should also be reported.

For those banks where money market activities, mainly Eurocurrency trading and foreign exchange, are included within the responsibility of the international division, detailed tables or schedules summarize the results of those activities. Concentrations for Eurocurrency placements and deposits accepted should be shown, as well as maturity schedules and analysis of rates. For banks that maintain Eurocurrency trading portfolios, detailed sections should pinpoint gains or losses from this activity. Foreign exchange positions, both net position limits and gap limits, should be shown by each foreign currency. Foreign exchange volumes and gains or losses can be detailed by foreign currency, and results summarized by totals. If bank notes, gold or other precious metals, or commodities are handled, detailed position and earning information should be provided on these activities.

Information on other major business activity for the month in question should be included in the next section of the report. This includes not only significant new loans and repayments but also substantial deposit activity and fees from various international services, including letters of credit, acceptances, collections, and funds transfer services. Major fees from loan syndications, commitment fees, and other activities are also included in this section.

Sources and costs of funding should be clearly presented, and significant individual, new or increased demand deposits also could be listed by name at this point in the report. Major demand depositors may be ranked by descending order of importance, and comparisons shown for current-month, past-month, or year-to-date average deposits. The same detail may be shown for time deposits, especially Eurocurrency deposits, if the unit or bank is active in taking such deposits. When such deposits fund Euroloans, the degree of matching and any unmatched funding gap should be presented. Any fees for services in which the unit or bank specializes may be shown in greater detail by customer or by size.

In the next section of the monthly management report, the loan and acceptance portfolio should be subjected to exhaustive analysis by type of asset, by maturity, by country, by type of borrower (government, bank, or private), and by industry, and with an indication of any relevant guarantees, such as governments or government agencies, especially those in the country of the bank's head office, such as the Export-Import Bank of the United States, in the case of U.S. banks. For U.S. banks also, FCIA (Foreign Credit Insurance Association) insurance, Commodity Credit Corporation, Department of Defense, or other U.S. agency guarantees are often included in this category.

Breakdowns of loans by different countries according to World Bank national classifications, based upon per capita income, also should be provided, since this information is usually included in Securities and Exchange Commission filings for U.S. banks and annual reports for most other banks. Any information regularly provided in the bank's annual report or for U.S. banks, in the 10 – K report, should be included in the monthly management report. The World Bank classifications, which are based on per capita income, are important, because risk by country usually increases as the per capita income decreases. Hence, concentrations on this chart should be compared with those on other charts that provide information on guarantees or category of borrower.

Generally, in the less developed countries, loans to the government or those guaranteed by the government or a government agency are preferable to a loan to a bank, corporation, or other private entity. Guarantees by institutions in the lending bank's home country or by special government agencies in developed countries could decrease this risk substantially, or shift the country risk to the nation of the guarantor, according to the internal rules of some banks. The better view is to consider the country risk from both perspectives, since it is sometimes difficult to separate a credit from the borrower's domicile. Footnotes or other explanations can avoid double counting and provide the most complete picture from all matrixes in these situations.

Industrial classifications for loans are useful from at least two standpoints: industry trends, that is, both weaknesses and strengths, often follow worldwide cycles, and many banks have particular strengths and weaknesses on the basis of the activities of their customers or the experience and background of their lending officers. Thus, in the United States, some Texas banks tend to concentrate overseas in the oil, gas, or related industries; Chicago or northeastern U.S. banks may specialize in steel and other heavy industries; and Midwestern and West Coast banks specialize in trade financing, agricultural exports, or business with Pacific rim nations.

Of all of the materials in this section of the management report, perhaps the most useful information relates to aging, maturity, or runoff of the loan and acceptance portfolio and to the individual and average interest rates for fixed rate, LIBO rate, and base rate loans. Most international managers usually can carry a rough notion of country distribution and the quality of individual loans in their heads. However, the aging and interest rate data are constantly changing and give valuable insight into control of net interest margin, which, along with careful foreign exchange controls, is one of the keys to successful bank management.

Finally, remaining sections of the monthly management report deal in narrative style or by use of tables with results from applying marketing strategies and executing various projects listed in the management objectives. The reports for marketing may follow customer, industry, or service lines. Fee income by services might be sufficiently developed in sections of the report already mentioned or these sections could be amplified to encompass results of the specific strategies. The management objective goals are perhaps easiest to report on, since they basically consist of a listing of specific projects; yet, a great deal of variety might go into describing progress on a wide range of activities. As one-of-a-kind projects are completed during the year, this section of the report should shrink significantly, unless, of course, the plan is modified to add new tasks to the management listings.

USING MANAGEMENT REPORTS

Our definition of annual planning at the beginning of this chapter included monitoring the progress in implementing strategies and objectives and in achieving budget targets, in addition to creating and developing these parts of the plan. In some international divisions and units, planning is treated as a one-time annual event occurring late each year when the budget is submitted. But unless all key staff are involved in formulating the plan, provided with relevant portions of the final plan, and given access to the results contained in the monthly management reports, little of significance is likely to result from the planning effort. When the type of planning process outlined here is followed faithfully to the point of distributing the monthly management reports, the planning process is complete and management is properly prepared for decision making and action, if decisions and actions are required.

In using the management reports, managers responsible for decision making and action should first study major items that show the most significant variation from plan. Most managers are quick to attack excessive expenses and take measures to improve lagging income. However, favorable results or variances also deserve serious attention in many cases. Many short-term variations from budget result from timing differences for events that were predicted. Usually, in this type of situation, adjustment occurs during the year without management intervention. Unexpected downtrends are another matter. More personnel, travel, or marketing may be required to meet competition. On the other hand, income in excess of budget may signify previously overlooked markets or opportunities, as well as the need to review quality standards and explore the exact reasons for the unanticipated business.

In addition to controlling income, expense, assets, and liabilities from the viewpoint of the bottom line, the collection of management information, as enumerated here, provides a means to work with portfolio quality and to assess foreign exchange and funding risk. These are dynamic factors that involve more than reviewing particular income sources, expenses, or balance sheet changes. Net position limits, funding gaps, loan runoff or buildup, and net interest margins often point clearly to steps that management should take to protect the bank, improve earnings, or minimize the potential for future losses. In brief, these are the most important ways in which managers can use the result of an integrated planning and reporting system. However, there also are collateral benefits from this process.

It was previously mentioned that the section of the international division or unit in charge of planning could serve as a good training ground for future managers. In addition, if the planning section is connected closely or in the same unit with those responsible for designing systems and writing procedures, economies of scale can be achieved by harnessing planning to these key tasks. In well-managed banking organizations, systems designers and procedures writers are working ahead to anticipate and prepare for new markets, new services, and new locations from which the bank's personnel will serve customers. Thus, a close connection with the planning process can save valuable time and effort for those working in this part of the bank and eliminate unnecessary work duplication. Obviously, this approach also helps to head off problems before they become crises by keeping the "back office" (operating and control capabilities) ahead of the "front office" (marketing and business development effort).

This aspect of the planning process becomes especially important in connection with long-range international planning, which goes beyond the annual plan into a three- to five-year frame of reference. Finally, preparation of monthly reports by a separate group of specialists also saves time for others in the international division, who are then more free to handle customers, make credit decisions, develop new business, and process transactions. By creating or assembling all reports, central efficiency can be improved in the use of information, and better discipline is imposed on the entire process of developing new reports and changing and eliminating existing ones. Also, when reporting is centralized, management can readily determine exactly how many people are involved in the effort, and can balance costs against benefits.

5

Long-Range
International Planning

Relating Annual and Long-Range Planning / Long-Range Planning
Process / Planning New Locations / Product Development and New Services / Developing New Customers / Contracting International Activities

After the annual planning process has taken hold firmly
within the international commercial bank, planning for
periods beyond one year may be considered. Some spillover effect from annual activities that cannot be completed in one-
year periods causes a natural flow to long-range planning. On the
other hand, if implementation of new ideas can be carried over
to future years without committing future resources, then a long-
range plan probably is not needed for channeling such an activity.

However, most ideas or activities occurring over time do not fit
this pattern. Future resources are required and must be committed
for more than a one-year period. Expenditures for salary, travel,
and buildings and equipment might accumulate for a large part of a
year or sometimes longer before deposits are received, fees earned,
or income generated in sufficient volume to earn a profit. To achieve
the maximum benefits from these ideas, a long-range plan must be

prepared and followed long enough to obtain satisfactory returns. Otherwise, all expenditures in connection with the idea will be of little or no use, except for training and experience.

To develop long-range strategic plans in the international commercial bank, various information and assumptions are required along the lines of some of the information used in the annual planning process. However, other information and projections also are needed. In this chapter we shall examine how such background is developed to be used with proposals for new locations, services, and customers.

For the sake of clarity and in order to define a process to maximize the generation of new proposals, we shall examine these lines separately. But in reality the three approaches rarely can be separated, because the interplay of these three factors creates an almost infinite variety of combinations for successful conduct of international commercial banking.

If the size of the globe limits the number of locations for providing commercial banking services, only imagination imposes restraints on inventing new services. With ingenuity, these services can be delivered anywhere they are needed. However, the large scope of this process in international banking raises the further need for careful long-range planning in order to choose the best alternatives and establish priorities. In few other fields of activity is it possible to go astray so easily and scatter limited resources with minimal lasting results. A few banks expand too rapidly at the international level, and some must retrench. Also, with difficult political and economic conditions expected to prevail in many parts of the world during the early 1980s, it seems prudent to consider at least briefly the matter of contracting international activities (in the last section of this chapter).

RELATING ANNUAL AND LONG-RANGE PLANNING

The chapters on planning in this book approach the planning process as an activity to be started and developed on an annual basis. After planning is under way on an annual schedule, longer planning periods can be selected. This approach differs from that of many planning experts who advocate, at least in theory, that long-range planning be developed either before or at least simultaneously with annual planning.

At the practical level, for most international commercial banks with little or no formal planning beyond budget preparation, and even for many banks that wish to improve existing planning techniques, an annual planning process that follows the lines discussed in the two preceding chapters is initially more than enough to handle properly. In addition to preparing market strategies and management objectives that interface with the budget, the process of circulating information, assumptions, and draft plans throughout the international banking organization requires considerable effort. Yet it is this effort that produces the benefits of planning.

Planning is a process not merely to produce immediate achievements, but to develop a method for creating a continuous stream of achievements. In the sports field, this might be stated as producing winning teams as opposed to merely winning games. Because of time, distance, and the high percentage of employees with more nearly equal skills, education, and experience who should be involved in the planning process, it may take longer in international commercial banking than in some other types of organizations to develop an adequate planning process. Working for a few years on an annual basis allows the process to take root. With shorter feedback times for annual planning in the beginning, the planning process, as well as each annual plan, can receive encouragement and fine tuning involving a maximum number of participants.

On the assumption that the annual planning process is well under way within the bank — with results for at least one or two years, for example — it is appropriate to consider longer-range planning. Long-range planning often is discussed within three- to five-year time frames. However, any planning beyond one year actually is long range; three years, five years, or other time periods are merely the monitoring points. In a sense, long-range planning deals with all of the periods after one year, and once the long-range planning process has started, the horizon then keeps moving on. For this reason, it is necessary to have a set time period for dealing with chunks of the future. Moreover, most long-range plans are reviewed annually, whether divided into two-, three-, or five-year intervals. However, annual reviews of the long-range plan are generally limited to recasting the long-range budget and to progress on carrying out the longer-term planning process.

After several years of annual planning, certain activities or projects may be identified for carryover into the next annual plan. If these carryover activities form a pattern or fall into a series, they are obviously candidates for inclusion in the first long-range plan, but long-range planning must go considerably beyond dealing with this spillover effect. As a collection of information and assumptions helps the bank deal with each annual plan, similar materials assist the long-range planning process. Some of the same materials that were used in annual planning can be used as a basis for long-range planning. However, some other ingredients also must be added.

LONG-RANGE PLANNING PROCESS

Starting with the annual planning documents dealing with world outlook, country studies, industry surveys, and money market forecasts, a hypothetical environment should be projected for the world and key regions or countries of the world. Information for longer time periods should be obtained from the various units of the bank, including the international division, to contribute to the long-range plan. Instead of money rate market forecasts, however, emphasis in this area for the long-range plan should be placed on fundamental and structural changes in major money markets, especially development of new capital markets.

For banks without the resources to gather all of this information internally, outside economic forecasting sources or economic consultants may be used. In any event, it is useful for even the largest banks to compare such outside information with internally generated materials. The important point is that a common pool of consistent data is assembled and that the key units of the bank are basically satisfied with its overall trend and conclusions. The summary document produced from this process is called the *projected market environment*.

The type of data in the projected market environment summary is easy for the planners and suppliers of information to handle, since it is basically similar to the annual planning material. The bank description from the annual planning process also is used in the long-range plan. However, the bank description must be projected forward in accordance with the long-range planning time frame and supplemented with other information to develop a document called the *hypothetical banking environment summary.*

This supplemental information will include projections of growth and development of the commercial banks' competitors, the likely legal or regulatory framework under which the bank and its competitors will be operating, and the types and estimated costs of technological innovations available to the bank and its competitors. In dealing with competitors, it is important to consider not only other commercial banks but also all other financial organizations and institutions, both public and private, which the bank will compete against, operate with, or both. A review of the types of institutions mentioned in Chapter 1 may be helpful in this regard, although for some banks other types of institutions should be added to that list.

Up to this point in the entire planning process, both annual and long range, costs for internal effort and for external consultants probably have remained within fairly reasonable bounds. Much of the information and most of the assumptions required can be either produced internally as part of normal work activities or purchased from external sources, which are used to provide this information to an established clientele in many parts of the world. It is unlikely, however, that more than a few banks will have extensive collections of data on all their competitors in readily usable form. Banks that specialize in serving financial institution customers will have a head start in this task, but even most of this data probably must be recast. Outside services for this work are available, also, and it is likely that some out-of-pocket costs must be incurred by most banks.

Information about the legal and regulatory framework affecting most banks also will be costly to forecast. House counsel might assist with some of the work, but with detailed laws to be examined in many jurisdictions and internal lawyers busy on day-to-day routine, much of this long-range legal research will require outside lawyers and corresponding out-of-pocket expense. It is for this reason that both competitive and legal research should be left for the long-range planning process, and that annual planning should be well under way before starting long-range planning. With heavy out-of-pocket costs being expended for planning at this stage, it will be necessary to use current information in a timely and proper manner to maximize return on investment.

With the construction of the projected market environment and hypothetical banking environment summaries, the background assumptions are in place to consider specific markets. At this point, the international division units can make their greatest contribution to the long-range planning process. Each international unit now should present its ideas for *new customers* by broad classifications, *new services,* and *new locations* to serve those customers.

During the annual planning process, market strategies are more than likely oriented toward individual customer or prospect names. Plans usually are geared to cross-selling services to existing customers and winning new customers with existing services. New branches or offices might be planned and opened within a total one-year period, but not in most situations, especially if new countries, laws, and environments are involved. For the long-range planning process, the rules are relaxed. Imaginations should be set free and creative thinking encouraged. However, all final proposals must contain sound cost-benefit analyses, even though long-run projections for both income and expense are likely to be less exact than one-year numbers worked by months.

Little harm can come from too many well-conceived ideas at this stage, even though similarities and trends may be detected among the many proposals. Moreover, all suggestions must be grouped as well as possible by the regional and head-office planners into logical or related combinations and passed through the double sieve formed by the projected market and hypothetical banking environments. From this process, different patterns of ideas emerge, united into possible new combinations and ranked by priorities. When these are drafted into a comprehensive document that spells out alternatives, other personnel throughout the organization should be given an opportunity to make further suggestions and comments. With time and redrafting, the *long-range plan* emerges.

As a consequence of the long-range plan, it may be necessary to reorganize various international units, other parts of the bank, or even the entire bank. An example of a change involving several units to provide better service to the multinational corporation was cited at the end of Chapter 3. More far-reaching reorganizations have resulted from the planning process, as illustrated by the major changes started at Citibank during late 1979. Accordingly, although the long-range planning process should be reviewed formally at least once a year, it may take larger banks two, three, or more years to complete such comprehensive activity. On this basis, a cycle of about two long-range plans from start to finish per decade is reasonable. The next three sections focus on how the international division creates ideas for new customers, services, and locations.

PLANNING NEW LOCATIONS

Every international commercial bank, regardless of its size or whether it has foreign offices, must carefully consider the locations where it wishes to conduct business. Country risk on the basis of local political and economic factors must be considered in addition to the usual cost-benefit analysis. A smaller or regional bank may spend proportionally as much of its budget on travel each year as the larger or money center bank invests in bricks, mortar, and equipment in order to conduct business in a particular location. Yet both the large and small bank may derive proportionate profits from their different scale activities. For the large bank with foreign offices, local deposits can offset local loans and buildings and equipment can be leased, and for U.S. banks, even capital in a foreign location can be insured against various political risks. The bank without a foreign office would not be concerned with these factors but would gain head-office deposits, of course. Accordingly, for banks with foreign locations, many risks can be hedged. Hence most banks can be compared by amounts of cross-border lending, foreign deposits, and international fee income in relation to personnel costs and travel effort expended to develop such business.

Moreover, political risk occurs not only in swift, destructive, and more obvious forms such as war, nationalization, or inconvertibility, but also as subtle and less noticeable changes in laws, especially relating to taxes, and controls of prices. Such events may arise in less developed countries, and especially in the form of legal changes in the most developed and modern countries as well. In the United States, for example, the effects of out-of-date banking laws may be difficult to assess and slow to take their toll, but the results are becoming obvious for all to see. In the United States, to continue our example into other areas, regulations on the products of automobile companies and various environmental restraints imposed on the steel, coal, and public utility industries can change the economics of entire industries within relatively short periods of time. Changes can be far-ranging in the banking industry itself. To give another example from the United States, until the International Banking Act of 1978, foreign banks enjoyed considerable competitive advantages over domestic banks, and entities outside the field of banking still do. And in Saudi Arabia, by way of further illustration, foreign banks were required by law to take on local partners. Nor is complete nationalization of banking uncommon in some countries, although some warning of such developments often is provided.

In assessing geographic or country risk, the tool of country analysis, which is used in considering foreign extensions of credit (and is discussed in more detail in Chapter 12), must be used for the bank's own investment decisions. Furthermore, in considering opening offices in other countries, it will be necessary to study not only existing laws regulating banking but also the degree of sophistication of such laws and the probability of their being changed. This is one of the main considerations for any non-U.S. bank entering the United States market. For this task of examining banking laws in other nations, in almost every case it will be necessary for the international banker to go beyond discussions with correspondent banks and to hire competent and experienced local counsel, which is dealt with in Chapter 9.

Banks that decide to operate in foreign locations generally make their long-range plans along one or another of several fairly predictable patterns. Reviewing these patterns also follows an evolutionary course. First, a bank will identify a country or city where its customers conduct a substantial volume of either investment or trading business and which is visited repeatedly by the bank's officers. The correspondent bank or banks in this location also become more important and handle increasing business volumes. Finally, the travel bill becomes so high and travel time so burdensome that it is decided to post one of the bank's own employees in the location. This employee, usually known as a representative and housed in a representative office, then typically generates more business in addition to the business he was sent abroad to handle.

After learning more about the country and measuring business volumes, the bank next might decide to open a branch or establish a subsidiary or invest in an affiliate, depending upon local laws and the type of business contemplated. Branches usually are best for handling letters of credit, collections, and foreign exchange, as well as conducting loan and deposit business. Other entities may be better suited to selected or specialized services, such as secured commercial loans, accounts receivable, or inventory financing, leasing, or merchant banking. As an alternative, the bank may skip entirely the representative office stage and open a branch or acquire an interest in a local entity.

One notion to be avoided in opening foreign offices is that such offices will develop new business where little or none previously existed. If significant business in the foreign location is not already firmly in hand or highly certain to be obtained, obviously it is risky to hang out a sign to start prospecting, especially in a location that is far from the bank's regular travel path for dealing with well-established customers. Moreover, the income allocation for representative offices generally is arbitrary. Travel expenditures may decrease more or less than the total costs for maintaining the new offices, but cost of office space and support services usually increases. One logical approach is to allocate the income from new loans and deposits to the representative office. However, the fact that the representative office has neither balance sheet nor profit-and-loss statements in the true banking sense makes all such accounting suspect. For this reason, and to be on the safe side before committing substantial new funds for capital or its equivalent, representative offices for most banks are merely way stations for larger full or specialized banking operations or significant investments in foreign banks.

A second pattern followed by many banks, after opening a first office or branch or perhaps even several offices in different countries, is to focus on a geographic region for greater specialization. A Canadian or U.S. bank might concentrate on Latin America, or a U.S. bank on the West Coast might turn its sights to Asia and nations in the Pacific area. European banks from former colonial powers have followed trade patterns from the time of colonial empires, which alone accounts for the significant presence of British and other European banks throughout the world, as well as the presence of many foreign banks in London.

Smaller or regional banks and those with newer international departments must in particular be careful to concentrate in some region that follows customer patterns and permits the development of expertise along relatively compact lines from the travel and staffing aspect. That was the historical pattern for the growth of most larger international banks, although it may have long been forgotten. The extreme to be avoided at this stage is the decision to be represented at several key locations throughout the world. If business warrants a far-flung pattern, such as Tokyo, Hong Kong, New York, London, Frankfurt, and Sao Paulo, that is one thing, but a mere desire to be represented on large patches of the globe is rooted in fantasy.

The final stage for only a few of the largest banks is to have a base in every possible major trading center. Usually, one office is opened in many countries before multiple offices appear in the same country or city. Obviously, growth may be uneven in stages or spurts; more offices will be opened in some countries where the bank has been well established, while some nations will not yet have any office, subsidiary, or affiliate. Economies of scale can be enormous for the banks that reach this level of development, since each office can handle the correspondent business of the other offices. On this basis, new locations often can become profitable on short order and literrally open their doors with assured business and resulting profits. On the other hand, the support staff at the home office to handle administration for a world empire of offices can grow significantly, as we shall examine in a future section of this chapter. One of the major challenges in such a bank is to keep the headquarters bureaucracy under control.

PRODUCT DEVELOPMENT AND NEW SERVICES

Although it is tempting to base plans for expansion on establishing locations by geographic areas, a more profit-oriented approach is based on product development or, more simply, services. In dealing with product development in any size bank, it is necessary for some unit of the bank in the international department or even outside to be assigned responsibility for defining the products or services to be developed and for continuously monitoring to assure that agreed upon sales plans are followed. Product development, which has been used for decades by some banks, started in the consumer products industry long before it was used by any bank. Yet many banks have never attempted to make use of this technique.

The advantage of the product management concept in international banking is that it cuts across all lines and units of the bank, both domestic and international. Product management involves using a separate unit of the bank to take a fresh approach to defining, describing, and preparing for the marketing of a particular service. Although all existing resources are used, entirely new ideas are developed to present the service in question and broaden the market throughout all parts of the bank. A specific example may clarify application of this concept.

In handling the creation and sale of bankers' acceptances to increase fee income in a U.S. bank, it is first necessary to clearly and concisely describe the origin, nature, legal limits, and uses of acceptances and distribute this knowledge throughout different areas of the bank. Written materials, as well as meetings or seminars, may be used for this purpose. Next, business must be solicited from customers engaged in importing and exporting through the domestic units of the bank and through the officers handling the different areas of the world where other customers, including correspondent banks, can be developed.

At the same time that business is being developed and appropriate lines of credit are being approved, the issue of selling the acceptances that will be created must be considered. The international division may be authorized to hold in portfolio and fund, up to some total amount, acceptances that it has created, pending sale of the instruments directly to customers or through brokers. Contacts must be made with acceptance dealers to prepare them for the increased volume of acceptances to be handled. Officers from the bank's domestic correspondent banking unit should contact correspondents to be certain that lines to purchase the bank acceptances are in good order and of sufficient volume to handle the projected business. Finally, arrangements must be made with the bank's investment department or other parts of the bank that also will sell the acceptances created by the international division in the bank's market area. Sale of the acceptances would occur in a manner that does not cannibalize sale of other instruments of the banking organization, such as certificates of deposit. In this regard, a special daily listing of acceptances created and for sale is indispensable to rapid movement of the merchandise.

All this effort must be coordinated and monitored for progress. Special write-ups, product descriptions, seminars, meetings, visits with domestic units, processing of lines through the credit committee, visits with acceptance dealers and correspondent bankers, and arrangements with the bank's investment department and other sales units must be coordinated and completed in accordance with an orderly timetable. Such a task may be too much for any existing line unit of the international division to tackle. Hence, a separate staff unit, specializing in product management, may be utilized, or in smaller banks the head of the international department or some other designated person may be able to apply the product management concept and cut across departments and bank lines to increase the volume and revenues from a particular product.

Let us take the bankers' acceptances product another step. During early 1980 it became widely known through the media that First National Bank of Chicago was marketing participations in bankers' acceptances to retail customers of the bank in amounts as low as $1,000. Using these relatively small participations in acceptances was a way of competing with other financial institutions, which under U.S. banking laws could pay higher amounts for funds than U.S. commercial banks. Through the product management concept, innovative use of a traditional international trade financing technique became a means for a commercial bank to maintain market share and serve its retail domestic customers. This idea followed the earlier use of bankers' acceptances as a short-term investment vehicle for corporations and other large investors before the inventions of the negotiable certificate of deposit in the early 1960s.

At least three basic directions may be taken with regard to services. Some banks emphasize nonloan fee services, others specialize in lending, sometimes export financing or merchant banking, and still others balance loan and nonloan services more or less equally.

Within these three approaches there is ample room for variation and differing emphasis.

For instance, at banks that choose to emphasize fee services, concentration could start with foreign exchange and funds transfer services and move toward collection and letter of credit activities. Or the start could be made from the letter of credit and related acceptance business with foreign exchange and funds transfer business flowing as a consequence of the letter of credit, collection, and acceptance activity. In starting with foreign exchange at the one end or letters of credit and acceptance activity at the other, it is necessary to develop personnel and procedures over more than a one-year period.

Furthermore, marketing to sell a sufficient volume of these services to sustain a corps of selected specialists usually takes longer than one year. Concentrating on building a steady volume of repeat fee business, whether foreign exchange, letters of credit, funds transfers, or collections, generally is the best course for most banks new to international business. Such repeat business can sustain a new or growing department through cyclical periods of uneven loan demand and involves credit extension on a short-term, trade-related, usually bank-to-bank basis, which avoids the relatively greater risks of term lending.

Moreover, starting in any country is usually easier on a bank-to-bank basis and permits a more gradual and systematic development of country knowledge and contacts. In addition, names introduced through repeated trade transactions become easier to know and follow. Often these trading names will be customers, dealers, agents, or suppliers of the bank's local clients and hence are tied to some extent to the bank's domestic market area. Perhaps most important, fee business generates demand deposits, which also help the growing international department pay its own way.

Some banks start their international growth or build their plans on direct term loans. This approach requires a greater commitment to country analysis and a rapid buildup of experienced international lending officers. If the bank does not have such personnel in its employ, obviously it must hire extensively from the outside. Proper country analysis and sufficient travel to identify attractive term-lending opportunities also require more than a one-year commitment. With a long-range plan heavily weighted to term lending, immediate payoff is somewhat limited.

Although some banks enter this market enthusiastically by taking loan participations from other banks and actively seeking loans with large front-end fees, this course tends to be opportunistic and potentially successful only during certain phases of the economic cycle. Obtaining permanent clients and establishing deposit relationships are seldom accomplished with such a strategy. Unfortunately, large front-end fees often signal difficulty in collecting the last repayments of loan principal.

Some banks have successfully started or expanded their international activities by becoming proficient in specialized phases of term lending, such as export financing or merchant banking. In the United States, the U.S. Export-Import Bank, by guaranteeing and providing longer-term funds for export financing packages, enlarges the resources of the commercial bank while sharing or minimizing the commercial bank's risk. However, such transactions require high-quality legal work to produce satisfactory documentation, as merely copying or joining Export-Import Bank loan agreements does not always protect the commercial bank. Moreover, the Eximbank's main aim is to increase exports and not to build a long-term, permanent client relationship, although these goals are not necessarily inconsistent. Therefore, projects are not always as thoroughly or realistically analyzed as might be required to protect the interests of the commercial bank.

Merchant banking, with emphasis on syndicating loans, requires an extremely experienced staff, not only to obtain and package business, but also to deal with prospective and actual participants. Few small banks have succeeded in this area over a long time, and even among the larger banks, which are relatively new to this activity, appetites to obtain mandates and package larger and larger transactions often outrun the ability to sell participations. In this business, unsold participations must be kept and funded by the unsuccessful seller, which puts a crimp on taking on future business.

Accordingly, in entering the merchant banking field, it is important to have adequate resources, tight limits, and the patience to start small and build a reputation slowly and carefully by conducting numerous transactions of moderate size. As in correspondent banking, reciprocity is important in merchant banking. One bank cannot always be the lead; hence, it is necessary to co-manage or take significant participations in loans led by other merchant banks so as to be able to sell future transactions. In the atmosphere of euphoria that often accompanies the heavy volumes of the up cycle, this basic concept of sharing is sometimes forgotten by the newer or more greedy entities, which then ultimately may end up with the residue of their unsuccessfully sold transactions.

The general or full-service international banks are usually among the largest banks, since they alone have the capital and personnel to provide all kinds of services and the continuous marketing effort year after year to sustain high business volumes. Yet even among the giants, many retain great flexibility, tend to shed their skins like snakes, and discontinue lines of business from time to time. The head office at a large money center bank, for example, may decide that head-office collection activity is unprofitable because of high personnel costs. By increasing its head-office fees or lowering its level of quality in handling collections, such a bank may drive away undesired business from the head office. This does not mean, however, that foreign branches of the bank will not receive the collections; branches in nations of the developing world where labor is cheap may welcome collections as profitable business on a direct basis. Or regional banks in the larger bank's country may step in and provide better quality service by using its foreign correspondents.

Merchant banking as conducted by the giant world banks may be handled through specialized entities to obtain economies of scale. Most merchant banking units are centered in London, New York, Singapore, Hong Kong, and other key financial centers in the world, and most have interconnected offices in several major money centers. Prospective transactions from the large branch network banks are fed to the headquarters or nearest regional merchant banking center, where terms and conditions are tailored to fit market requirements and the borrower's needs. Then a coordinated worldwide market effort is directed by regions, so that all potentially interested institutions are contacted almost simultaneously without duplication.

With their extensive branch networks, the largest banks in the world have tremendous opportunities for economies of scale on simple fee services, as well as in syndicating large-term credit. When all foreign exchange contracts for all branches worldwide are directed automatically through the head branches in each country, huge volumes are generated with no business development cost. For example, the London branch may handle all sterling for dozens of other branches throughout the world. When the same concentration is directed for payment orders, other funds transfers, collections, and letters of credit, it is easy to understand that huge profits can be generated from such closed circuit systems. In turn, customers of these large branch network banks usually receive better prices and more efficient service as a result of such economies of scale.

DEVELOPING NEW CUSTOMERS

In addition to developing long-range planning on the basis of geographic locations and product management, the international division may be tailored to serve various classifications of customers. Customers may be divided generally into governments, banks, and private business entities, mainly corporations, the same broad categories that are generally used for classification of credit extension. Beyond this broad classification, private entities or corporations may be further subdivided by industry grouping, by local or market-area companies where the international division supplements the efforts of the corporate treasurer, by the multinational corporations that require a wide variety of international services at numerous locations around the world, and by reverse investment opportunities for foreign entities investing or conducting business in the bank's home-office market area.

Perhaps one of the easiest groups to serve is correspondent banks; yet the opportunity for providing specialized and expert service to correspondents is often overlooked by many banks. Every international bank must have correspondents to conduct its business overseas, so the competition is heavy. However, since part of the work has already been done in most banks to establish relationships, exchange control documents, and conduct visits, modest extra attention may make the difference between some profit and large profits.

Because of their extensive branch networks, many large money center banks give minimal attention to their foreign correspondent banks. Thus, for smaller international banks or even those larger institutions without numerous overseas offices or subsidiaries, correspondent banking customers could represent a prime source of business. Although many banks deal with their overseas correspondents within national or regional geographic groupings, many others over recent years have established specialized industry groups to deal with their foreign correspondents. By frequently comparing the size of credit extensions, fee service volumes, and demand and other deposit balances on a reciprocal basis, and by making adjustments where necessary, many banks have increased significantly the profitability of their correspondent banking accounts.

Other industry groupings might be singled out for specialization according to a bank's market-area customer mix. Commodity and agricultural products lead to specialized customers in various nations, for example, which deal in certain ores, metals, coffee, sugar, bananas, or other agricultural products. Overseas customers dealing in forest products and logging, oil country equipment and services, or steel mill machinery and related technology might be the natural extension of bankers from the Oregon-Washington State area, Texas, or Pittsburgh, for example, whereas banks in Arizona, Tennessee, or Minnesota might look abroad for business related to cattle, cotton, or computers.

A variation on this theme, especially for regional banks, might be to serve as an extension of the local customer's treasury department. By a close and active working relationship, especially with smaller and medium-size corporations where specialized international staff may be limited or nonexistent in the client corporation, the international banker may provide almost every international service required, from credit checkings, money movement, and foreign exchange to trade financing, as well as personal banking services for key executives traveling abroad.

By developing comprehensive plans to serve the financial and banking needs of all creditworthy foreign dealers, agents, or distributors of a local exporter, the international banker may ease the personal staffing requirements and general workload for the corporate treasurer. Moreover, where the local client mix provides a variety of industries and countries, sufficient diversity could exist for even a relatively small international department to adequately spread risk. At the same time, any occasional overlapping country or region could provide economies of scale if foreign business development calls are properly planned.

The largest banks in the world, of course, are justified in taking a universalist approach and dealing with almost any multinational concern that is headquartered or conducts business in any country where the bank maintains an office. It is not at all unusual for a large multinational corporation to concentrate its international banking business with a bank of a nation outside its homeland, provided the bank gives the best banking service. Thus large German or Swiss concerns might deal extensively around the world with a U.S.-based international bank, and Brazilian or Argentinian concerns might deal with British or Italian banks for connections in former British areas or European nations, respectively.

Recently, U.S. banks of all sizes have been stepping up their efforts to serve foreign corporations from Europe, Asia, the Middle East, and South America that are investing substantial amounts in the United States. Banks in these areas of the world have served U.S. foreign investment especially since the postwar period, and banks in developing nations have been serving foreign investors from all parts of the world for years. Special planning and business development efforts are necessary, however, to locate prospective customers before they come into the home bank's market area. To await their arrival is to risk losing such prospects to the competition.

For this reason, close coordination is necessary with foreign correspondents, local and foreign offices of regional development organizations, and with economic officers of the home country bank's embassies. In this way companies can be contacted as soon as they have expressed any interest in the bank's market area. Also, maximum use then can be made of information and tax or other benefits and incentives that might be applicable to new businesses in the bank's area. Again, it cannot be overemphasized that this kind of business development requires especially long lead times, persistent calling, and continuous follow-up to build solid relationships. Offsetting this planning and development effort, however, are the benefits, including profits, from the establishment of permanent customer relationships with quality companies, which can be targeted and sought on a highly selective and individualized basis.

CONTRACTING INTERNATIONAL ACTIVITIES

For the last three decades the overall emphasis in international commercial banking, especially for most U.S. banks, has been on expansion. By hindsight it now appears as a golden era. Additional locations, increased services, and new customer relationships were established rapidly as international trade and investment grew and involved almost every country in the world. Perhaps the apex of this era of expansion was achieved with the rapid growth of consortium banks, banking entities with multiple shareholders, during the late 1960s and earliest years of the 1970s. Then it was discovered that consortium banking offered more disadvantages than advantages for many banks.

Usually based in London and started to engage in merchant banking, these jointly owned banks often brought together banks of different sizes, different management philosophies, and diverse national origins as shareholders. With the 1973 – 1975 recession, the strains of these sometimes quickly conceived relationships became too great for some participants. Anticipated profits failed to materialize. Syndicated loan business decreased as capital investment slumped. The effort, especially for top management, to meet, plan, and work together became disproportionate to the rewards. In some banks partners sold out to new owners or to remaining partners, which took over more of the total shareholding of the previous joint ventures.

One noteworthy exception to this pattern has been Allied Bank International in New York City, which is owned by U.S. regional banks and is the only consortium Edge Act bank now in existence. By concentrating on providing high-quality services and by avoiding forced growth for growth's sake, this bank has steadily increased profits and expanded its customer base in the face of competition from banks of all sizes in New York City and other world money centers.

Also, during the mid-1970s, some regional banks, especially in the United States, reviewed carefully the level at which they were conducting international business. Closing foreign offices was only the most visible evidence of a changed outlook, as international loan totals decreased from year to year during the late 1970s at many institutions. Eurocurrency and foreign exchange volumes, although totally recovered from the Herstatt crisis and expanding once again, did not include some of the earlier participants at their earlier levels. Repeated difficulties in extending the charters of the U.S. Export-Import Bank and Overseas Private Investment Corporation during this same period indicated that the U.S. Congress also was lessening its commitment to international activity.

At the same time, foreign banks expanded swiftly through significant acquisitions and opening of new offices in the United States. This afforded these banks diversification in a new market and placed their foreign branch networks at the disposal of new U.S. customers at the same time it provided greater competition at home and abroad for the U.S. banks. Foreign participation in the U.S. banking industry had been growing steadily for two decades. Substantial acquisitions, especially by the Hong Kong and Shanghai Bank, National Westminster, Barclay's Bank, Algemene Bank, Nederland, and others, ranging from New York to Chicago to California, focused national attention in the United States on this trend during almost the same period that Congress worked to enact the International Banking Act of 1978.

For the early 1980s the international outlook, with few exceptions, is not generally conducive to significant expansion of international banking. To the contrary, international contraction and consolidation may be the order of the day at many banks for the next few years. The intentions of the Soviet Union are becoming increasingly apparent as a result of the invasion of Afghanistan and Soviet-sponsored or -supported activities in the Middle East, Africa, and Asia, as well as in Central American and Caribbean nations. With only a slow recovery — at best — expected from the 1979 – 1980 recession, capital investment has been slowed in many industries and nations. Also, foreign investors and project sponsors have changed their perceptions of prospects in several nations after the Iranian revolution, the war between Iran and Iraq, and evidence of political and social unrest in Poland, to mention only a few nations in the news during this period. In addition, the large foreign indebtedness of certain developing countries does not augur well in the face of further oil price increases during a recessionary period when exports of traditional products and commodities from these nations to developed nations are decreasing or, at least, not increasing.

Offsetting these negative factors to some extent are expected increases in business over the next several years with various countries, including the People's Republic of China, Mexico, and Brazil, among other nations, as the United States improves relations with the People's Republic, Mexico exploits its oil and gas resources, and Brazil further develops its natural resources and technical capabilities in manufactured products of almost all types. Nigeria is becoming a significant market in Africa, and the Republic of South Africa will become increasingly important as it continues to deal with internal social problems and is recognized by more nations as a vital source of scarce raw materials, especially certain ores and minerals used in most industrialized nations.

On balance, however, until recovery from the recession that started in 1979– 1980 is strongly under way and a more stable world order results from an improved development and implementation of U.S. foreign policy toward closer and more effective relationships with its allies, the outlook for international trade and investment is not bright. Decreased world trade and investment obviously spell slower times overall for most international bankers for the near term.

Under these circumstances, total foreign term lending probably will decrease at many international banks. With decreased lending, overseas offices will be less likely to earn their way, and retreat from selected foreign outposts seems inevitable for some banks. Representative offices are the most likely candidates for early closure by some banks. Officers in charge of representative offices are usually experienced, if not senior, personnel and thus require relatively high salaries, whereas the income attributed to the activities of representative offices is quite arbitrary, as was previously discussed. If at least some of the foreign business usually conducted through the representative office can be continued in the absence of the representative office, the decision to close is relatively easy.

Foreign affiliates in many cases are not much more difficult to deal with. If no contract to supply management for the operation is involved, another passive investor may be found to replace the withdrawing bank. Foreign branches raise more difficult questions, although local or even other foreign investors may be found to purchase established operations or at least acquire leases, furniture, and equipment and sometimes even hire key local staff. In the last instance, however, closure of branches often requires as much time and effort as opening the new location. Thus, immediate savings are not likely once a decision has been made to close a branch.

Although the sale or closing of a physical location is highly visible to the international banking community, this is not the most critical factor to be considered by the bank when shrinking international activities. Banks originally open or expand to serve customers. Accordingly, the arrangements for dealing with existing customers are the most important concern of the international bank. Term loan relationships might continue with increased travel by account officers from the head office or another location. Deposit taking, foreign exchange, and money market activity also could continue from the head office or some other office, although perhaps at reduced levels. On-the-spot service, especially in connection with handling collections, letters of credit, and funds transfers, will not be possible except through correspondents which may be able to pass on parts of such transactions.

In any event, when considering any contraction that involves closing a physical location, every service used by each customer must be carefully considered and reviewed with each customer. And each customer must be contacted to assure continuation of desired business. In many cases continued service and well-established personal relationships will outweigh the convenience and proximity involved in international offices, assuming, of course, the bank wishes to maintain such relationships. Banking, especially at the wholesale international level, is founded more on trust, knowledge, and the consistency of past performance on the part of both bank and customer than on mere physical proximity.

During uncertain times banks attempt to upgrade the quality of assets. For international bankers this means avoiding or not increasing business with higher-risk nations and weaker-credit customers, regardless of domicile. At the same time, portfolio maturities are shortened. Thus, term loans lose popularity and trade financing increases in favor. A noticeable trend toward acceptance financing could be detected starting before 1979, and fee services provide a safe haven and steady, if lower, earnings as contrasted with term loan business and other credit extension involving higher degrees of risk. The problem, of course, is that as more banks move to less risky business, competition increases, and profit margins tend to decrease at the same time that there is less total business to go around.

The result of any period of contraction and consolidation, however, should be a stronger organization. During such a period the international commercial bank should prune away marginal activities, locations, and services and concentrate more than ever on the most profitable customers, markets, and services. Innovation may occur even with regard to traditional international services such as bankers' acceptances or selling gold, silver, or other precious metals. While some staff may be shifted to domestic responsibilities, the core of each vital international unit must be maintained in readiness for the next inevitable wave of general expansion.

PART II

People

6

Direction Function Personnel

Board of Directors / Chairman, President, and Senior Management / Credit Committee / Pricing Committee / International Advisory Board / Country Limit Committee

F rom previous chapters we now understand general banking organization, certain basic services, and various aspects of planning from the international standpoint. It is appropriate to consider next the different people who work together inside and outside the commercial bank to implement plans and serve customers internationally. This chapter and the following four chapters deal with these people from the viewpoint of their functional responsibilities in relationship to international activities.

As international division personnel bridge planning and procedures to deliver services, the board of directors, certain committees, and key senior officers within the bank act to direct international division personnel. Some direction comes in the form of providing ideas and consultation, both for long-range planning and for assistance on specific opportunities and problems. Other forms of direction tend to place limits on certain functions, usually by requiring

115

that approvals be obtained before carrying out certain transactions.

The board of directors, chairman, president, and senior management, and the international advisory committee, if one exists, generally are more heavily involved in planning and providing assistance in specific situations, although certain approvals also may be required by these groups or persons. The credit committee, pricing committee, and other committees usually direct to a greater degree through the approval process. Often these bodies also provide ideals and assistance in the general planning area and in individual transactions, sometimes in the course of the approval process.

Only by closely coordinating the work of all direction function personnel can the plan for the international division be achieved and its customers be served effectively. All individuals, boards, and committees within the direction function must work with complete knowledge of international goals and full understanding of the actions of all others. If some people or certain committees move away from agreed upon goals on one or more tangents, obviously the international plan will not be achieved and the work of the international division will be frustrated.

BOARD OF DIRECTORS

The board of directors of the commercial bank ultimately is responsible for the overall performance of the commercial bank, including, of course, the international division. The greatest challenge at most commercial banks is for board members, who are often occupied with other demanding and usually full-time tasks, to exercise their responsibility adequately during a few hours each month. In addition to the international functions of the bank, these same board members are charged with overseeing many other diverse activities in the bank.

Under these circumstances, the effort required for detailed study needed to understand the complexity and wide geographic range of activities of the international division often seems disproportionate to the results, in the eyes of many board members, except for those banks where international activities constitute a significant percentage of total activity, measured by assets, revenue, and income. Yet, even under the most demanding schedules, a great deal can be done to involve the board of directors in an effective manner in the international activities of the bank. Ways exist to help determine priorities, clearly frame issues, and conveniently structure alternatives for decision making at the board level. Selected materials must be carefully prepared about international plans, countries where business is conducted, and large extensions of credit.

In the first instance, however, the background and composition of the board must be considered. Most corporate business today is heavily involved with international trade and investment flows across national boundaries. Consequently, commercial banking at both money center and regional banks is either already largely international in scope or rapidly moving in that direction. During the last few decades, a global market for goods, services, and funds has been created. This market involves commercial banks in both developing countries, which finance exports or imports vital to their nations, and developed countries, where multinational corporate activities often extend into some of the smallest towns and most remote areas.

Even for many retail bankers in the United States, for example, foreign competition is not unknown. Extensive foreign-owned branch networks in some states take deposits, make personal loans, and provide the myriad other personal banking services from travelers checks to bank credit cards. With the passage of the International Banking Act of 1978, this competition in the United States has not abated. Foreign banks continue to purchase U.S. banks and to start new operations in the United States, although the rules have been made more equitable between United States and foreign banks. Furthermore, international economic consequences follow from almost every major U.S. monetary or fiscal decision, and the U.S. economy feels the impact of key decisions by leading foreign nations. Thus, a good number of the board of directors of any U.S. bank large enough to have an international division should be persons with extensive international experience. When choosing between two otherwise equally qualified people to join the board, the internationally experienced person should be preferred.

Where the local community does not offer a sufficient number of internationally experienced candidates, outsiders should be sought.

With persons of such perspective, it may be easier to teach them the local community and its needs than to try to teach a purely local person about the world. A mix of international business executives or academicians may bring a surprising dimension to an otherwise local board. Horizons may be expanded, new and different approaches considered, and new friends and contacts introduced for the benefit of all involved with the bank and board. Unfortunately, U.S. banking laws tend to put some limits on this approach by restrictions on citizenship and residency requirements for board members of national banks.

As discussed in Chapter 3, the board must be involved in planning. As part of its duty to assure that the bank is managed properly, the board must be certain that management has established a planning process and is planning continuously. Typically, at regular meetings board members of many banks are kept busy leafing through voluminous pages of materials and approving many housekeeping and other routine items presented to them by management. Special situations and significant problems are generally attacked with gusto, but planning often is left behind to be put on a future meeting agenda. Sometimes management may not want the board involved extensively in planning. Yet, in Chapter 3 it was emphasized that all managers in the bank must know the outline of the entire plan and the details of their own department's role in the plan in order to maximize their contribution to implementing the plan. The board must make certain that this happens.

Every manager in the bank should have helped create the plan, at least by proposing alternatives for inclusion, if not actually writing and drawing up parts of it. This is not an exercise in corporate or employee democracy; rather, it is an attempt to obtain the best ideas and thinking of the people who constitute the bank's most important resources. The board must make certain that the planning up process is constantly working. If fermentation starts to slow down, board members should throw in some ripe yeast by asking questions, such as whether alternatives were considered for any proposed point, why some ideas were rejected, and why the proposed course of action was accepted.

The most critical areas of any bank's international plan involve the selection of countries where business will be conducted and the types and volumes of business that will be carried out in each country. This subject is commonly referred to as determining country limits. In essence, a *country limit* is a total number expressed in currency units for all the assets, actual and contingent, that the bank has related to a particular nation. If a bank has no business outside the United States, theoretically it has only one country limit, which is for the United States and is expressed in U.S. dollars. The amount of the limit would be the same as total assets or the limit for total assets.

For a bank with international business, the countries where business is conducted must be identified by name, and a conscious decision must be made as to exactly how much business and what types of business by degree of risk should be obtained in each nation. This system of limits forms part of the bank's overall diversification effort and broad portfolio management strategy. To go a step further, a bank on the United States-Mexican border, for example, might decide to conduct part of its business in the United States and part in Mexico. For a $5 billion bank, the decision might be to limit its total of $250 million in Mexican exposure to assets with maturities of no more than five years. Of this $250 million, some sublimit might be set for five-year transactions, and the balance might be made available for credit extension of one year or less, thus ruling out long-term mortgage loans in Mexico, for example. Or the sublimit for term loans might be divided into categories for loans to the Mexican government or government institutions, loans to Mexican banks, and loans to privately owned Mexican businesses.

This brief discussion introduces the general topic of country limits, which is covered in detail in Chapter 12, in order to point out the board's involvement. The board's responsibility is to assure that an adequate system for establishing country limits exists and that limits for each country are reviewed periodically. Furthermore, not only must the board insist that care be exercised in selection of places where business will be conducted, but it also must make certain that countries with good business opportunities are not overlooked.

In addition to country limits, the board concerns itself with limits by various sectors of industry and business activity for international and domestic credit extension. Industrial sector limits also provide diversification, but cut across the portfolio on an entirely different grid in comparison to the country limits. Whereas it is hoped country limits will serve to minimize the impact on the bank of weakness in a particular national economy, industry limits should tend to prevent extensive damage from a worldwide downturn in a particular industry as a result of technological developments or economic conditions.

Again, a positive approach in this area of limits should be balanced against attempts to prevent or limit damage. Often board members have insights into industrial trends that offer a potential for maximizing the bank's opportunities on the basis of the skills of existing personnel or those who could be added and properly supervised within the bank's overall level of experience. Industrial limits will be discussed again in Chapter 12, but as with country limits, the board is responsible for seeing that a good system exists in this area, is functioning adequately, and is changed as required.

By the internal rules of most banks, total credit extensions to any one borrower or related group in excess of some amount must be brought to the board for approval and, of course, international credits would be caught in this net. Larger credits generally are passed up through the credit committee and the bank's management to the board or at least to an experienced and representative executive committee of the board, which will review the larger risks in some detailed fashion, one by one. It is in credit decisions that all of the experience, knowledge, and diversity of the members of the board of directors can be focused to greatest advantage for the bank. The directors can bring perspective from local and worldwide industrial, economic, political, and social trends to the activities of the bank's largest customers.

In addition, the board should be involved in consideration of any significant changes in the activities of the international division, such as adding or leaving lines of business, opening or closing overseas locations, and similar events. These matters generally would be part of the annual plan, except in unusual situations. However, more complete discussion may be necessary in a context outside of the plan, although not inconsistent with it.

For most banks, the planning aspects of the board's responsibilities should involve at least one extended review of the plan each year, with quarterly follow-ups. Country and industrial limits could be scheduled throughout the year, with a few at each meeting or every quarter, and credit extensions would be handled every month or more often, as necessary. Other special items would be presented as they arise.

CHAIRMAN, PRESIDENT, AND SENIOR MANAGEMENT

The most important contribution made by senior management to the direction of the international division occurs during the annual planning process and subsequent monitoring sessions, as described in Chapter 3. As the total annual plan, including the qualitative and quantitive goals, is assembled from all parts of the bank, numerous inconsistencies, conflicts, and differing priorities are bound to surface. It is management's responsibility to create a method to resolve these conflicts at the lowest level possible and, when all else fails, step in and make decisions on the unresolved matters or those that have worked their way up to the highest levels.

Ideally, the planning process involves upward movement from department or division units to group or area levels. Thus, assuming that the international division of a regional bank is part of a larger wholesale banking group, business development, customer and prospect calling programs, loan and other asset totals, and deposit and other liability totals would be harmonized within the group before group plans would be placed side by side with the other groups, such as retail banking, trusts, and investments.

In money center banks where retail operations around the world might form part of the international division, a more complex planning effort is required since the international effort forms part of its own group with, perhaps, commercial banking, investment banking, and retail banking operations worldwide. The same or greater difficulties would occur where retail banking might cover all retail operations worldwide, and commercial banking and other related functions are combined in a separate group with global responsibilities. In these more complex organizational structures, mostly at the money center banks, many more points of contact are needed at the lower levels to assure a smooth flowing together of the final pieces of the annual plan.

An example of such lack of planning and resolution of inconsistencies in one organization involved two separate physical locations in the same city in a country quite remote from the head office. Unknown to many, this condition resulted from the fact that the heads of the respective divisions were such intense rivals that personnel in the two divisions officially were not allowed to talk to each other. Fortunately for the profit centers of all involved, this situation is the exception rather than the rule. In most banks, representatives of different functions at least share the same buildings in foreign locations.

Planning together also can result in considerable savings in calling programs where extensive travel is involved. Whenever the same representative can adequately sell several services, this not only saves travel funds but wear and tear on corporate treasurers or other representatives of the customers, since more services can be discussed during each call, with experts brought in later after specific potential business has been uncovered.

Another area of high priority for senior management involves selecting, hiring, and appraising performance of international personnel. International bankers represent a considerable investment not only in salaries but in associated expenses, such as maintaining foreign offices and travel. Obtaining capable people from the steady stream of applicants, as will be mentioned in Chapter 7, requires input and leads from senior management, as well as some occasional selling of the organization to potential recruits by the top people.

This involvement is especially necessary because of the recent tendency for more and more top positions in the bank to be filled by people from the international division or by people with international experience from outside the bank. One of the greatest benefits to the commercial bank is the occasional recruiting of an experienced international monetary expert or banker, who has had years of experience not only with different countries, cultures, or credits but also working with various foreign problems or in managing various overseas operations. These foreign units in many instances are banks within a bank, in accordance with the concept described in Chapter 1. To bring in such a person to head wholesale banking activities, to serve as senior credit officer for the entire bank — or even as president or chairman — is not uncommon today.

On a management by exception basis, senior management must also become involved with the large problems, as well as the significant opportunities emanating from the bank's international activities. It is to be hoped that the opportunities, such as exceptionally large credits, acquisitions, or mergers, can be handled within the overall context of planning. Under these circumstances, senior management can work at its best to carry out long-range objectives in a noncrisis atmosphere. But occasionally, or perhaps too often in recent years when international banking has been under intense pressure as a result of the world's economic difficulties starting with the 1974–1976 recession, top management has been forced to operate under crisis conditions. Large credits that sour or foreign acquisitions that have gone awry demand top attention because so much is at stake.

When these problems arise or are detected, management can do much to help. Even before problems occur or are discovered, management can be checking constantly to assure that early warning systems are functioning adequately. Most future bad credits can be identified early and improved or restructured before disaster strikes. One of the best forms of detection is through a regular credit review process. Another way is through reading not just headlines but articles and journals that point out problems. It is relatively easy to review total credit extensions to particular countries or areas of the world on an ad hoc basis from time to time. Other problems often can be diagnosed and discussed if internal communications are open and free from recrimination.

Most decisions in international banking, as is true for most of commercial banking in general, are not made by one person alone. But although the committee system usually prevents or minimizes the number of bad decisions, it sometimes seems to also hold up early and decisive action to tackle the defining and solving of problem situations. At this point, alert top management, especially those members of the team with heavy credit experience, in the case of bad credits, can provide maximum aid in restructurings or workout situations.

Senior management can also contribute to the overall sound direction of the international division by maintaining lines of constant communication. Staff, credit, or other periodic meetings, which include international division representation, not only keep the division informed of overall developments within the bank, but permit an international contribution or feedback to the rest of the organization, so that others may be aware of worldwide trends and developments that could impact on other lines of the business.

CREDIT COMMITTEE

Probably the most basic consideration with regard to the credit committee from the international standpoint is where there should be a separate credit committee for international credits. To a large extent, the size of the banking organization dictates the answer to this question. In money center banks with substantial international divisions, for example, rules for extension of credit generally provide that each officer, by title, has a certain credit limit. Therefore, the larger the credit, the greater will be the number of lending officers required to sanction the bank's action. Since these large international divisions are well populated by lenders ranked by title and hence degree of lending authority, the approval mechanism tends to involve merely passing the credit file and related materials needed for a proper decision up the line to the requisite number of people. Seldom is it necessary to forage outside the international division for signatories on the approval document, except in cases of the largest credits, of course, when board of directors or executive committee authority would be required.

This process is referred to by some banks as a "round robin" method of obtaining credit approvals, or by others as a "walk around," since one lending officer, often a junior, as part of his credit training and to provide an opportunity to become more closely acquainted with other members of the bank, carries the credit file from officer to officer or at least keeps track of the credit file's whereabouts while also endeavoring to answer any questions about the credit under consideration. Under this system, there is nothing to prevent the calling of a meeting where all concerned with the credit sit together and discuss the matter for all to hear. This approach has great merit in new or nonroutine credit extensions. Nevertheless, in larger banks, most credit extensions are approved by means of the round-robin method and, accordingly, stay entirely within the international division.

In regional banks or banks with relatively small international departments in comparison with the size of the domestic lending departments, there is a tendency for the credit committee to be composed of a few senior domestic lending officers, as well as selected international lenders. Usually the international lending officers represent a minority on the committee and often a minority of one. Unless there has been careful development of staff from domestic units on the committee, the majority of the members are not experienced in international lending. Understandably, this situation sometimes creates difficulties for the development of a sound and profitable international loan portfolio.

A solution midway between the round-robin system and the meeting of one committee with a limited number of persons is to provide for two formal committees, one for domestic credits and the other for international credits. Usually in this situation there is some overlap in memberships on the two committees. The most senior domestic lenders or credit officers would be on both committees, but the international credit committee would have more international officers who are not members of the domestic committee, and the domestic committee could be weighted more heavily with domestic lenders. The one-committee approach has the advantage of obtaining broader perspective from the different domestic lenders and can also serve as a training technique for better educating domestic lenders with regard to international lending. However, in the two-committee approach, the international committee tends to be more effective, since its members by experience and training obviously are better equipped to handle international credit decisions.

Perhaps the smaller banks, generally those with the single- or even the dual-committee system, can obtain the best of all worlds by judiciously using both systems. The round-robin method of approval can be followed to the maximum extent possible for the more routine and less difficult credits in order to minimize the number of items for agenda at the regular meetings of all the members. This approach tends to put emphasis where emphasis should be placed, namely, on the newer and more complicated credits. At the same time, routine credit approvals can move more quickly, while allowing more opportunity for deeper consideration of the less routine credits.

Certainly the goal of the credit committee should be not equal time and effort for all credits but, rather, the highest-quality credit decisions possible. Nonroutine credits require more time for explanations, questions, and discussion. The round-robin system also eliminates some of the photocopying of credit materials, since the original set of approval materials should be attached to the credit file to maximize the benefits of this system. Routing materials with the credit file, of course, provides an easier opportunity for each approving officer to review the credit file, which can often give more understanding of the credit than summary materials that must be distributed as agenda items for a simultaneous meeting.

Accordingly, the credit committee with a regular meeting schedule tends to be found in regional banks and those with fewer lending officers, or officers with relatively low credit limits and banks with heavily centralized controls. The round-robin system tends to evolve in the larger, more decentralized banks with more lending officers and higher individual limits. However, there appear to be sound reasons even for single-committee banks to us the round robin on occasion, perhaps even as part of their evolution away from the single-committee approach. Any regularly scheduled meeting that can be eliminated or shortened but still accomplish quality work should be a net gain for any organization.

PRICING COMMITTEE

In many banks pricing decisions often tend to be difficult to separate from credit decisions. However, in some banks this is accomplished by providing no pricing information with credit committee materials. In these banks profitability is solely the responsibility of individual cost centers, and funding costs are made clear to all units of the bank, since some may be net providers and others net users of funds. In those banks where credit committees become involved with pricing, a pure credit decision may be relatively easy, and a pricing decision for a fee service where no credit risk is involved is obviously a cost accounting and marketing decision, not a credit decision. Yet, many banks tend to become bogged down in this area of credit and pricing, and much time supposedly devoted to credit decisions is really spent on pricing, often with less than satisfactory results.

Mixing credit and pricing is not wrong per se. If good credit experience and reasonable profits result, lending personnel must be making correct decisions in these two areas — and who should know better how to price a service than the lending officer who knows the credit? Economies in use of people result, since two different departments or areas of personnel do not have to know each relationship. Moreover, lenders obviously prefer to control pricing for their credit-using relationships because it gives them greater freedom. Others in the bank, however, may be responsible for demonstrating that each unit of the bank is operating at optimum profit or minimum loss and that there is a uniform schedule or method of pricing. In this atmosphere, international division credits and fee services often present some special problems. Before examining these problems, however, a few additional general observations seem in order.

Banks with confusion between the pricing and credit areas usually have weak or nonexistent cost accounting systems and, in addition, often have fewer or more highly centralized profit responsibility units. As final responsibility for profits after all costs moves out into more decentralized units, pricing decisions also tend to move to the decentralized locations. It is no secret that many banks are behind in the art of developing easy-to-apply systems for allocating cost of funds and various overhead items. Managers of manufacturing concerns use cost accounting techniques and output from their systems every day as the basis for sound pricing and purchasing decisions. Perhaps this area only seems complex or obscure to many bankers because money is the main raw material for the commercial banking business, and most bankers have not been involved with industrial cost accounting.

Since commercial banks usually operate under extremely competitive conditions in many different geographic markets with a wide variety of services, some of which are funds-intensive and others of which are people-intensive, line personnel responsible for sales must know the cost of their services as accurately as possible and have maximum flexibility with regard to setting prices. Therefore, overall restrictions and management controls in this area should be limited to assuring that services are sold profitably, that like services for similar customers are sold on a consistent basis, and that services of one part of the bank are not sold at prices that would undercut sales of other services of the bank.

One of the first problems faced by most international divisions under these circumstances relates to overdrafts and compensating balances. In many parts of the world, especially outside the United States, commercial banking operates on the overdraft system. Under the overdraft system, bankers periodically make credit decisions on the amount of lines of credit and then permit their customers to overdraw their demand deposit accounts to the authorized limits. Customers are charged interest for this form of borrowing, and interest rates are set on the basis of the cost of funds, the estimated usage of the line, the quality of the credit, and a margin for profit. Compensating balances do not enter into the picture, since they do not exist. Proponents of this system believe it to be quite efficient. Bankers think it is simple to administer, and customers think it is the ultimate in cash management, since funds deposited to the account immediately reduce borrowing costs.

Some argue that the U.S. system of not paying interest on demand deposits, insisting on compensating balances when loans or lines are granted, and then pushing to market cash management services is not only inconsistent and confusing but also tends to inflate bank balance sheets, because part of a bank's loan assets must be maintained by the bank's customers as deposit liabilities on the bank's balance sheet. Of course, these arguments are correct but do not take account of the history of U.S. bank regulation. Over the years the U.S. Congress has purportedly protected depositors from potential bank failures, which theoretically could be brought about by cutthroat competition in paying interest on deposits and by denying depositors earnings on their demand deposits. Apparently, bank failures stem from paying depositors interest, rather than from poor management or unsound loan decisions, according to the rationale behind this rule.

In addition, it is not only expensive but inconvenient for some customers to maintain substantial balances in currencies other than their own outside their home country if they have no need for such working balances in the currency. Moreover, such deposits may expose the customer to unnecessary and unreasonable foreign exchange risks. This may explain the absence of compensating balances to the domestic members of the credit committee of a U.S. bank, but often it leaves them far from comfortable. The vague feeling may linger that somehow international customers do not treat their bankers fairly because they do not keep substantial demand deposits, even if the borrowing rate to the overseas customer is increased in comparison with domestic loans with compensating balances. For some who are unfamiliar with international business, almost no risk premium suffices for foreign credits.

The next problem peculiar to international credit relationships concerns the provision of various fee-producing services, such as international funds transfers, collections, letters of credit, and foreign exchange. The international commercial banker generally works to establish credit relationships with selected customers, which will provide an opportunity to use these fee services, since they usually involve a much lower level of credit risk, if any at all, and provide attractive income. Domestic lenders on the credit committee may not see either the volume or variety of such income streams from their domestic loans and thus may disregard these activities in decisions on pricing international credits.

Moreover, the flow of international payments from some relationships may build deposit balances in other accounts that never are related or matched against credit usage. For example, assume that payments for outgoing collections for a manufacturing customer are routinely received through the same overseas correspondent banks. These correspondent banks may use little or no credit facilities; yet, they maintain with the international divisions dollar accounts that they instruct the division to charge when settling or paying for the collection items. A heavy volume of such items requires the correspondent to continuously transfer dollars to the international division account to maintain working balances. Other examples of this nature could be shown for foreign exhange and letter of credit activities or from payments related to other services of the bank.

Combinations of services and attendant income are really limited only by the imagination of the international banker, the quality of the international division's services, and the willingness of customers to use the bank's international services. Putting all of these activities into a compact pricing formula such as "10 percent plus 10 percent balances for a $1 million line" is not possible. More collection of data and analysis of the relationship are necessary to accomplish this. Such analysis of overall relationships, involving all income streams and all costs, is the only way to determine profitability, as opposed to pricing by formulas. Accordingly, in many cases, relationship analysis must be considered as an alternative to a pricing committee or at least as a supplement to the workings of such a committee.

The composition of the pricing committee, if one is deemed necessary, should include representation from all departments that sell services to the public. If this is impossible because of the large number of personnel involved, representatives of each division should at least be heard from when prices of their areas are presented for review. This assures that the committee members have some information from the personnel most knowledgeable about the service in question. Other representatives would include a member of the cost accounting or analysis department, which is involved with developing the cost information for the bank's services, and perhaps a person from the investment or treasury function of the bank.

Another alternative to the pricing committee is an expanded cost accounting or analysis department. By centralizing all listings of prices and methods for gathering information and allocating costs, this department has the ability to work with each department to review pricing schedules and policies, as often as needed, but preferably not less than once a year for every service. Any unresolved differences between the staff and line departments could be settled by an executive of a higher level than either of the two departments and thus another committee would be eliminated.

At most banks in the foreseeable future, the most important factors in connection with pricing of international services appear to be the quality and quantity of the cost and income information being used as input for final pricing decisions. Where credit extension also is involved, a broader approach requiring relationship analysis seems called for, and every reasonable effort should be made to avoid a dual responsibility system on a credit-by-credit or case-by-case basis. More important than a pricing committee is the proper establishment and smooth functioning of a modern cost accounting system. This system should be conducted continuously, preferably as a staff function or on a consulting basis, to assist each profit center to maximize its return but avoid glaring inconsistencies between the bank's different units that may be providing similar services to the same market.

INTERNATIONAL ADVISORY BOARD

In addition to the board of directors, senior management, and special committees, in many banks an international advisory board can provide useful direction for international activities. The creation and use of international advisory boards or groups with similar names is relatively new but has benefited both money center and regional banks, although the number of banks with international activities that use such groups is still relatively quite small. One of the largest banks to use such a board is the Chase Manhattan Bank. Members of its advisory board as of 1980 included, among others, Henry Kissinger, former U.S. Secretary of State. American Security Bank, with its close personnel ties and convenient access to international figures in the Washington, D.C. area, also has assembled a distinguished international board, which demonstrates how regional banks utilize the advisory group concept.

Members of international advisory boards, of course, are not per se members of a bank's board of directors. As indicated in the most common title for such groups, their role is merely advisory and hence no directors' liability is involved. Nonetheless, the role of the advisory board and its members can be as significant as the bank wishes it to be. The advisory board exists to serve the bank only to the extent that the directors and management decide. Therefore, its powers and duties in rendering its advice are limited only by its terms of reference.

Undoubtedly in some institutions, there may be some element of using the names of advisory group members to enhance the prestige of the bank and increase its international aura. However, to ascribe this as the only motive for any institution is to overlook the many tangible and intangible benefits that may be derived from such a group's association with a bank. At a minimum, as a source of contact for the bank's board, management, and officers, the advisory board serves to provide a stimulus for broadening the outlook of the members of the organization.

Beyond this function, the advisory board can answer specific inquiries on developments in international affairs that fall outside the regular disciplines of those persons concerned with credit decisions or economic matters. Questions on trends in foreign policy, military and strategic considerations, and technological changes from fishing methods to ocean mining, or almost any international event that might affect the bank, may be directed to the advisory board.

With preparation, such as common assigned readings, the advisory group might discuss with selected management representatives matters referred for exploration of possible alternative developments, probable developments, and suggested courses of action by the bank consistent with probable and possible developments. The advisory group could be asked for its opinions and recommendations, independent of anyone from within the bank. Going one step further, the board could be asked to list by order of importance the international events or trends, which, in its opinion, will have the greatest impact on the bank for a specified period of time in the future. In the planning process the international advisory board is an ideal unit to become involved with preparing the world outlook document, as well as parts of other planning materials.

The advisory group also might be consulted for background ideas and opinions in connection with opening or closing international offices, acquisitions, mergers, or divestitures, while, of course, leaving the business decisions and terms and conditions of such actions for consideration by the management and board of directors. Some banks refer the matter of country limits to the advisory board, either using the group as the country limit committee or using input from the advisory group as an ingredient in final decisions. On an individual basis, members of the group might be consulted for assistance on subjects falling under their special fields of expertise by discipline or geographic areas. In short, the uses of such groups are limited only by the ingenuity of and frequency of contact with representatives of the bank.

Contact with the group can be structured in the form of scheduled meetings with a business format to review or provide input for country limits, for example, or as more informal sessions, such as luncheon or dinner gatherings. To gain the most benefit from such groups it is important to spend some time during meetings or else have some other channel of communication to provide the advisory board members with a minimum level of basic information on the international activities of the bank. Furthermore, enough contact should exist between the group and various levels of management so that a free and frequent exchange of information and ideas can occur within the limits of the framework for time and remuneration provided in the arrangements between the bank and the advisory board members. Finally, some form of regular contact with both the international division and the board of directors should be provided.

As increasing numbers of banks become more heavily involved in international activities, it seems safe to assume that more banks will have international advisory boards in the future. Often for national banks in the United States, this is an excellent way to obtain the services of non-U.S. citizens. The existence of advisory boards tends to bring special expertise to bear on the bank's overseas business and helps to some degree in solving the problem of how to best use the limited time of the bank's board of directors. The advisory group might for some banks serve as a springboard for younger individuals to assume board of director membership after a trial period, during which management and board members can gain experience in working with the new outsider.

COUNTRY LIMIT COMMITTEE

In connection with the board of directors and the international advisory board, the function of approving country limits has been mentioned. In some banks country limits are set by the credit committee. Others may have a separate committee for this purpose. Regardless of the body that establishes country limits, the important factor is that some person or unit outside the international division is part of the process. Few banks now leave this responsibility solely to the international division.

By necessity the international division must initiate the country review process. Although a separate economics staff may prepare country studies, which will be discussed in Chapter 12, the international division formulates and implements plans for marketing, new business, and administration of existing business. Hence, it recommends the limits for each country where business is or will be conducted. In most banks, moreover, international staff, especially those who reside or travel abroad, are heavily involved in preparation of the country studies, as well as in proposing limits. International staff generally have the best contacts, experience, sources of information, and, in many cases, command of foreign languages necessary to develop material for the country studies or reports.

After country reports are prepared along with a recommendation for limits for doing business in each country, it is important that adequate study time be provided to members of the committee or other body responsible for approving limits. Preparation time or personal knowledge of each country, or, better yet, both, is necessary to conduct a thorough discussion with members of the international staff who carry on the bank's business in the nations in question. Discussion, involving questions and answers, is important in order to determine the level of the bank's experience, competence, and understanding of each country. Some banks and especially U.S. bank regulatory authorities have attempted to develop mechanical rating systems or percentage formulas, sometimes related to a certain amount of a bank's capital, to determine how much credit a bank should extend in each nation. However, none of these systems or formulas make much sense, because a balancing of all factors in differing degrees for each country is required for appropriate decision making. The most recent system in the United States, as an illustration, uses a percentage of capital limit to trigger notification to the board of directors through the examination report.

The total amount of credit to be extended in any country is basically a function of the bank's experience and understanding related to the country in question. Various banks throughout the world work across national boundaries on the basis of their specialized experience. Even in the largest, most experienced international banks, certain countries rank as the most important by volume of business and level of credit exposure. Accordingly, the role of the country limit committee is not to review the country studies and apply some mechanical formula, but to decide on the basis of all factors whether the business levels requested are prudent for the bank. In addition to considering the particular economic and political conditions in any country, the committee must satisfy itself that the experience level of the bank's officers and the type of business being conducted bear a reasonable relationship, on a country-by-country basis, to the risks and rewards involved.

Business conducted largely and funded entirely from offices within a country, short-term, trade-related transactions, or bank-to-bank business must be viewed differently, for example, than unsecured, cross-border term loans with long maturities. An analysis of the type of business and the history or bank's record must be coupled with current and future economic and political conditions and balanced with the experience of the bank's staff. For this reason, nothing can take the place of face-to-face discussion within the bank between knowledgeable individuals from inside and outside the international division. Therefore, the proper people to form a country limit committee must be brought together within the bank from wherever they are located outside the international division.

A regular meeting schedule must be set up to permit all countries to be reviewed, after adequate preparation and discussion, at least once a year or more often when special circumstances require it. In order that members may maintain proper perspective, the materials for each meeting of the country limit committee should include not only the country reports currently under review but a listing of all country limits and outstandings by general type of business, as well as a list of officers' titles and countries or geographic areas of responsibility. Special circumstances include not only negative or threatening developments within countries but positive developments and new business opportunities. Country limits must not be rigid but free to move up or down according to changed conditions. In addition to conducting the individual country reviews on a regular basis, it is the duty of country limit committees to assure that the review system continues to be flexible and sound and utilizes the best personnel resources and experience available to the bank.

7

International Division Personnel

Characteristics of International Personnel / Mercenary Theory of Employment / Position Descriptions and Performance Appraisals / Selecting International Personnel / Using Starting-Level Jobs / Internal Training and Development Techniques

P eople within the international division bring together planning and procedures in order to provide international services to bank customers. Although management outside the division establishes the planning process and defines the role of the division within the bank, international personnel develop the detailed plan. Their expertise comes to bear in the planning up. Moreover, they work together with other people from inside and outside the bank to achieve international goals by implementing and monitoring the plan.

Successful international division personnel usually have several common characteristics regardless of their experience or background. People with these characteristics may be selected for the international department from elsewhere within the bank, from recent school graduates, and from other banks and organizations. Particular care should be taken in selecting personnel for foreign assignments. Pay and benefits should be used as a means to provide equal pay for equal work regardless of location and not to induce people to serve abroad when they might not otherwise do so.

Great care also should be exercised not only in selecting each person in the international division but in first defining the jobs that each person will perform. Job descriptions should be written for each position on the basis of international planning goals and should be reviewed periodically as these goals change. Performance appraisals should be conducted at least annually on the basis of job descriptions in order to measure results objectively and provide a fair method for awarding salary increases and other benefits. Starting jobs should be designed and maintained so that new people can be rapidly absorbed within the division. These first positions have certain identifiable elements both for future clerks and potential officers.

After a new person has started in the international department, constant training and development are necessary to build upon the factors that correlate with success. Successful international bankers learn not only from formal training programs, specialized banking schools, and short courses but also from on-the-job experience. Formal programs outside the bank will be considered in Appendix C, and this chapter will deal with techniques that can be applied within the bank.

To maximize job experience, the size of each job must be considered carefully and job assignments rotated periodically. In addition, with proper preparation, certain routine activities such as regular staff meetings, prompt circulation of correspondence, and credit committee presentations can contribute to staff development.

CHARACTERISTICS OF INTERNATIONAL PERSONNEL

International personnel need a wider range of qualities and skills than are required for other parts of the commercial bank. Earlier chapters discussed the concept of a bank within a bank and the specialized nature of even the routine transfer of funds overseas and the accounting techniques required for foreign exchange, as well as the complexities of overseas lending. Accordingly, the international division utilizes the efforts of numerous highly trained clerks, as well as officers and specialized professionals, to carry out its functions.

Many people travel, some almost constantly, some reside abroad, at least for part of their careers, and others may never leave the United States or venture outside the city of their employer. Yet, all staff must be able to understand and relate to the international aspects of each function they perform. Account and lending personnel must be able to sell, and both operations supervisors and lending officers must be able to function effectively across different time zones, at great distances, and with different cultures and languages. The common denominator for all international division staff is a deep interest in international activities and an international perspective, or world view. Without such an approach to the work of the international division from every level, the employee will not only miss much of the excitement and satisfaction that comes from the unique and varied daily experiences within the division but may overlook important factors that can cause costly errors.

Accordingly, the first characteristic of all international staff should be an international perspective or at least the flexibility or willingness to develop such a perspective. If such a world view does not exist or a spark cannot be ignited quickly, it will probably be difficult for the employee in question to become an enthusiastic and effective member of the international team. As a part of this worldwide perspective, international personnel at all levels must have a genuine respect for different cultures, languages, customs, and business styles. This applies to the secretary or clerk who must be willing to check and insure the accuracy of a foreign language title or overseas address for an outgoing letter or payment order, as well as to officers and customer contact personnel.

A greater effort often is required to communicate in international work, whether it involves shouting over a poor telephone connection, mastering a foreign language, or making an extra effort to word a telex or letter as clearly as possible for a distant recipient. Compilation of mailing lists, updating of credit file index sheets, working through a letter of credit with foreign terminology, or translating and correctly analyzing a foreign financial statement can become a nightmare for those who do not thoroughly respect and sincerely appreciate other societies and the nuances and distinctions that each produces.

Attitude toward travel or residing abroad is a critical factor for the international banker whose job requires either or both. Increased salary and extended benefits cannot provide sufficient incentive to move or travel abroad. The desire to be overseas must exist for those stationed or traveling outside the home country, because that is the place of work. Greater salary and special benefits should be designed only to keep the overseas employee equal to others in the organization and to compensate for increased wear and tear or opportunities forgone, such as building increased equity in a family home. The mercenary theory of employment, which will be examined in the next section, usually does not work successfully for international banking, and when it does work, it seems to have only limited application to unusual situations.

A secretary or clerk with good job skills plus this world outlook should have no difficulty in becoming a successful member of the international staff. However, for the officers, professionals, and other specialized staff, analysis of qualities and skills required for international work is a bit more complex. All the qualities that produce a successful domestic lender, for example, should produce a good international lender, but the transformation is far from easily assured.

Odds for success are increased significantly in favor of the domestic lending officer who was born, was raised, or has lived abroad, knows a foreign language, or even travels overseas for vacations. Personnel department records can easily catalog most of these factors, and occasionally reference to the bank's personnel records can produce surprising results. For this reason, it is important to insure that forms for listing employee backgrounds, special interests, and skills have adequate provision for foreign language facility, travel experience, and similar information.

Obviously, a lender or thoroughly trained credit analyst who knows the bank's overall policies, business approach, and some of its domestic customers can make a significant contribution to the international effort with the right combination of the other characteristics and skills. Likewise, many domestic operations people have skills that are readily transferable to the international effort. Those concerned with operations related to domestic correspondent banking, in particular, seem to be excellent candidates for international work in many banks, since many of the domestic techniques are similar to those in dealing with foreign correspondents.

A willingness to understand and become knowledgeable about both operations and lending areas is another important quality needed in the international division. There is such an interlock between these areas in international work that every officer and most nonofficers must have sufficient knowledge to at least be able to communicate effectively from one side of the division to the other. Operations personnel must know when credit is being extended, for example, in a foreign exchange or letter of credit transaction in order to know if proper approvals exist. Lending personnel must understand, for example, acceptance transactions or funds movement to properly structure and document an acceptance facility or Euroloan agreement.

In order to maximize deposits and fee income from relationships involving extension of credit and all customer contacts, a detailed knowledge of the division's international services and operations capabilities must be acquired either during a formal training period or shortly after joining the division. Therefore, care must be taken by the division's managers during the hiring process to insure that all future lending officers have a spirit and willingness to master operations techniques and that all future operations personnel will learn the importance of credit extension.

Beyond a world outlook, including any language abilities, the willingness to travel or reside abroad, a basic domestic banking background acquired over the years or through a training or orientation program for the newly hired, and a willingness plus the ability to master operations matters as well as the techniques of credit extension, one other important skill stands out as necessary for the ultimate success of an international lending officer. That is the mastery of the application of the basics of international economics as used in country risk analysis.

All of the other abilities without a thorough understanding of international economics seem blunted, especially in the regional bank international division. Money center banks can afford to develop compartmentalized individual specialists in marketing, business development, merchant banking, correspondent banking, project finance, leasing, or other specialized lending areas, and even in country risk analysis, using those highly trained in economics or even political experts. But in the regional bank international division, multiple skills must be developed in each officer. The lending officer, although a "jack of all trades," must have good mastery of international economics, in addition to skills in handling operations matters, in marketing all of the bank's services available to international customers, and in structuring, documenting, and administering credits. This is essential, because often this officer is the only bank representative to live in or travel to the foreign countries under his jurisdiction. Hence, this officer's input for country analysis studies and guidance for increased or decreased credit exposure are significant.

MERCENARY THEORY OF EMPLOYMENT

The idea that people must be induced by increased pay or special benefits to work or travel abroad may be referred to as the *mercenary theory of employment*. This concept appears from time to time in both money center and regional banks, frequently in the United States, and sometimes has harmful, if not disastrous, consequences. Interestingly enough, the idea, when used, usually is developed or seized upon by noninternational division staff, sometimes even in personnel departments or senior management, especially those with limited or no international experience.

Since people applying the mercenary theory usually have not served abroad or, if they have served or traveled overseas, did so under unpleasant circumstances, they tend to view at least certain foreign assignments, if not all locations outside the home country, as unsatisfactory. Rather than attempt to seek out individuals and even whole families with special interests and a world outlook who would volunteer eagerly for foreign service, the proponents of this theory advocate increased incentive pay and benefits. With intensive recruiting efforts for limited assignments, willing staff sometimes are found and hastily relocated to serve out their terms with only brief, if any, orientation to the bank or country of their assignment. Sometimes only bachelors are selected. Permanent employment with the bank may or may not be possible after the end of the contracted term. Too often personnel recruited under such circumstances do not serve out their tours of duty or, if they do, they mark off each completed day on their calendar. In other cases, those who are unhappy with foreign living and working conditions develop various personal problems, cause poor morale among fellow workers, and turn in low-quality work performance.

For example, recent graduates with some business or accounting background might be hired as traveling auditors or foreign branch inspectors by banks with numerous international locations. Also, in other cases, younger bankers may be hired on a contract basis to serve as junior officers for a year or two in newly acquired or faltering operations with high turnover. In these situations, during their contract periods the junior officers are expected to train local staff as replacements and eliminate the need for future nonlocal nationals. Staff for such assignments sometimes are not citizens of the home-office country and are often called third country nationals.

If third country nationals or special hires are placed in a different pay category in between the pay levels for the local staff and personnel from the head-office nation, problems of attitude toward work and poor performance can develop over time. Accordingly, the better approach is an attempt to maintain equal pay for equal work regardless of nationality and to provide continuous employment on the basis of increasing responsibility over time, assuming employees can handle the responsibility. Thus, all workers will have the tendency to view themselves as permanent members of the bank team rather than contract labor and will contribute their efforts accordingly.

In some regional banks with limited foreign locations, the attitude may develop in the head office that those who serve outside the country are making a special sacrifice in their careers for the bank. This approach can lead to distortions in pay, benefits, and positions upon reassignment to the head office. Inequities then develop in the treatment of head-office staff. To avoid this problem, services of outside salary consultants may be used to compare pay and benefits with other banks and international firms if the bank does not have enough overseas staff to warrant development of in-house expertise in the personnel department.

Base salary, cost of living adjustments, hardship allowance, overseas premiums, tax equalizations, education allowances, and similar payments must be used to keep employees at all locations equal in living standard. Some posts are a hardship in the sense that certain services, goods, and activities common in the head-office country are not available. However, payments and benefits should be used to replace such items on the basis of the circumstances of each location in an attempt to maintain parity and not to exceed levels of head-office or other locations.

Moreover, care should be taken with regard to all special hiring situations and temporary foreign-based employees, so that the mercenary theory of employment does not take root anywhere within the organization. Although not always attainable, the goal for international banking should continue to be equal pay for equal work. Otherwise, morale problems develop, work performance suffers, and employees are either overeager or reluctant to change work assignments on the basis of factors unrelated to level of responsibility and career development. At one extreme, for example, situations often develop in which employees are reluctant to return to home country assignments.

Complicated formulas and detailed calculations along with numerous and repeated explanations may be necessary to administer the foreign compensation package of large international banking networks. However, the system must make sense and be uniform for all staff. Furthermore, those who have served abroad should be selected for future assignments on the basis of their on-the-job performance and actual work experience and not merely because they had the experience of working outside the head-office country.

On the other hand, the work experience in a foreign office often leads to increased responsibility on the job because of the need to act on more occasions without reference to head-office supervisors or staff. Also, the bank-within-a-bank concept broadens managers at the same time they are obtaining depth in various management skills. Therefore, officers may grow faster in a foreign post and be ready for greater responsibilities sooner than their peers who may have remained at home in a more controlled and supported atmosphere.

Finally, for the married employee, the attitude of spouse and other family members is critical. The mercenary theory often brings out of the head-office country willing workers but reluctant spouses and children. International banking in many locations in the world often involves a heavy social schedule. In some postings such activity is a way of life and a valuable source of new business, contacts, and information. In these situations the reluctant spouse or unhappy family usually detracts from or certainly adds nothing to the efforts of the most dedicated and able employee.

POSITION DESCRIPTIONS AND PERFORMANCE APPRAISALS

In preparing and updating position descriptions, reference must be made to the written objectives that result from the planning process. Budget numbers indicate the monetary amount of assets, liabilities, income, and expenses for which responsibility is assigned. Management objectives and project descriptions outline the areas in which managers are to achieve results. Job descriptions for new foreign branches or expanded functions in the head office usually can be based on similar existing positions. However, when organizational changes resulting from the planning process create new positions in terms of customers served and services offered, then entirely new and original position descriptions must be prepared.

In addition to the position, name or title, and location, most job descriptions also indicate the title to which the position reports, the amount of monetary responsibility involved, the number of people supervised, if appropriate, and a one- or two-line listing of from five to ten duties related to the job. Usually the duties are ranked in priority order and end with a catchall phrase for such other duties as are assigned, or with some similar statement. Detailed position descriptions are important in any organization because they are used to establish pay ranges and evaluate individual performance, as well as agree with the employee on the nature of the work expected.

Although most international banks have written job descriptions and some system of performance appraisal, usually in printed form, fewer than generally realized have developed a method to correlate in a satisfactory manner planning, job description, and performance appraisal. Assuming some type of annual planning system along the lines described in Chapter 4 is being used, it is not difficult to compare quantitative and qualitative goals with existing job descriptions and make revisions where necessary. With updated job descriptions in each personnel file, it then is even easier to relate performance appraisals to job descriptions.

When setting up position descriptions and salary ranges, it is useful that certain jobs have several levels for basically the same type of work. This is appropriate, for example, in areas in which skill often varies with experience, such as lending, developing or administering customer relationships, working with letters of credit, or dealing in foreign exchange in the operations area. The existence of different levels for similar work allows for continued promotion and salary increases, while necessary technical and management skills and experience are being developed.

It is characteristic of international commercial banking that relatively large numbers of well-paid and highly skilled people perform roughly the same type of work at many locations, with relatively frequent transfers of these people from one location to another. Moreover, when employees are transferred from one country to another, promotions and pay increases are more likely to be granted. Accordingly, as a rule, periodic reviews are required more often in international banking than in other businesses to assure that salaries, benefits, and pay grades stay in proper relationship for all positions in individual units within the international banking organization. Managers of each international unit should conduct such a review every two or three years at a minimum. If highest to lowest salaries are plotted in a giant triangular structure with lowest or starting-level salaries at the base of the triangle, it then is easy to compare similar salary payments and determine whether equal payment is being made for roughly equivalent work. If pay is not equal, the situation can be taken into account with other established criteria at the time of subsequent appraisals for the personnel involved.

SELECTING INTERNATIONAL PERSONNEL

Having identified the characteristics of successful international personnel, established written job descriptions, and instituted a system of objective performance appraisal, the next consideration is selecting and hiring candidates for international banking work. Obtaining international staff involves the establishment of a broad base of qualified job applicants. Except for the largest regionals or money center banks where unsolicited résumés roll in daily and routine recruitment takes place annually at numerous schools, colleges, and universities, the building of such a pool of applicants requires time and planning. Obviously, the first place to seek such applicants is within the bank itself.

Earlier in this chapter we mentioned the possibility of transferring to the international division domestic lenders or operations personnel with experience in the area of correspondent banking. In addition, the international division head, others in the division responsible for hiring, and the personnel department staff who serve the international division should be observing carefully the development of financial analysts, credit department staff, and accounting personnel within the area of the controller's function. Analysts working with international credits and controller's staff involved with international systems or foreign exchange calculations, for example, may be good candidates for future openings.

Even for the regional bank without an extensive or continuous campus interviewing program, updated materials can be sent routinely to a handful of selected area or specialized schools with strong international programs.

One of the most frequently asked questions about selecting international staff is whether foreign languages are necessary. Since the most widely used language in international banking is English, the answer to this question depends largely upon whether the person is fluent in English or not. In most places in Asia, Africa, and the Middle East where international banking is actively conducted, English is the most commonly used international language. In addition, most Europeans and many South Americans engaged in international transactions use English. However, in doing business in Brazil, Portuguese is more than helpful, and the same is largely true for Spanish in the rest of South America and Mexico, although English is used extensively in Central America. Accordingly, mastery of English is necessary in the long run for success anywhere in international banking, and other languages, if not required in some areas, are obviously helpful.

Unfortunately, pure language specialists seldom seem to have the proper mix of characteristics that correlate with success in international banking. As part of their world outlook and interest in travel, most successful international bankers have some degree of ability in a foreign language or even several languages. Most have such skill in connection with the other factors mentioned earlier. Foreign languages in addition to English are another tool for the international banker, but with language skills alone it is difficult to progress satisfactorily. Therefore, in selecting formal courses of study to prepare for international banking, a foreign language could be a major field of concentration, especially for non-English speakers. But foreign language study should not crowd out study of economics, accounting, finance, politics, and history, or courses that study different cultures or areas of the world in detail from various other aspects, as well as language.

In reviewing résumés, particular care should be taken to find those candidates who studied more than superficially and enjoyed accounting and corporate finance, as well as international economics. There is obviously a high correlation between success in credit analysis and lending and study of accounting and finance. Further, there seems to be an even higher correlation between studying accounting and successfully running the operations of an overseas branch or a domestic-based international division.

Most of the operations of international commercial banking revolve around prompt and accurate bookkeeping, based upon efficient accounting systems and well-designed reports. The ordinary debit and credit ticket or its equivalent in our computer age goes through numerous subsidiary ledgers en route to the general ledger. All of these records are produced daily and must be in proof with each other. For the major in languages or history, no matter how keen the interest in international affairs, the job in international banking with its ceaseless flow of accounting entries will soon become either bewildering or boring unless interest and ability can be developed through on-the-job training or additional courses in accounting. Every member of the international team needs to understand the bank's international accounting records in order to properly use and help improve the product of the system.

Selecting staff from other banks or institutions as opposed to hiring new graduates from schools, theoretically at least, should be much easier. The interest, skills, qualities, and background discussed here should be well evidenced by the descriptions of jobs held and work performed for previous employers. Of prime importance would be in-depth experience in several fields of operations or lending, or both, plus any time spent in management and in various locations in the world.

A common pattern for personnel from the money center banks with service records at several foreign locations is to return at some point to someplace they will call home. This could be a United States national returning to the international department of a hometown bank, but it might just as easily involve joining the U.S. operation of a non-U.S. bank or even settling permanently in a bank outside the United States. The point is that after moving around abroad for a number of years, there often is a desire to settle down in one place, either to educate young children or establish permanent roots. Candidates of this type are usually excellent for an international division since they bring all of their experience, contacts, and training from another institution.

Even in a bank that wishes to develop and promote entirely from within the organization, occasional exceptions must be made for the international division. This is especially true for the smaller bank since there is no way that a variety of offshore experiences can be duplicated by the smaller organization. Some of the best managed regional banks in the United States, for example, have brought in not only key international staff and international division heads but even presidents and chairmen with international experience. Far from stifling careers of others already in the organization, this often signals a renewed and increased commitment to conducting international banking activities and heralds a new era of expansion and greater personnel opportunity for everyone in the division.

The largest banks do not hesitate to leaven their mix with outsiders from time to time. Numerous former foreign service officers, ex-officials of the International Monetary Fund or World Bank, former U.S. Treasury Department members, and corporate financial executives all make significant contributions today to the international banking efforts of their banks. This is true not only in the United States but in money center banks of other nations also.

USING STARTING-LEVEL JOBS

Starting jobs are necessary in order to bring new people into the international division in a manner that facilitates training for increased responsibilities in the future and at the same time permits measuring their capacities to take on such future responsibilities. Potential officers are usually placed in starting positions after a brief period, sometimes called a training program, of touring various parts of the bank to observe and gain familiarity with various banking functions. This period or tour is discussed in the next section on training and development. In many international divisions and especially for operations and clerical personnel, the newly hired are placed in starting positions without any formal orientation.

Starting positions occasionally exist within developed organizations, and, of course, in a completely new operation, in a sense, all positions might be considered as starting jobs. However, more often for any section or division, entry-level positions must be created and, more importantly, maintained. If a person becomes rooted in a starting job, this defeats the whole purpose for the position, and it is then the duty of the supervisor to uproot the incumbent and bring in a new entrant before the arteries of the organization become permanently clogged.

Design or creation of starting jobs is a top priority for any manager or supervisor immediately upon assignment to a new responsibility. The number and level of starting positions to be designated is a factor of the size, turnover, and needs of the section or operation for which the manager is responsible, balanced against the supply of qualified personnel and the restraints of the manager's budget. Accordingly, starting jobs must be tailor-made for each operation, but several general guidelines and a few examples can be helpful in approaching this task.

Although starting jobs will be filled only with qualified hires or transfers to the international department, the object of having a period of both orientation and measurement is not to test whether the new people can fulfill the entry-level position. There should be no question of the person's ability to succeed in this first job. Instead, the orientation and measurement period is used to determine how quickly the new person can learn, adapt, and expand capabilities that may be applicable in the next position after the entry-level position. At the same time, management has the opportunity to double-check its initial decision to take the person into the department and the supervisor also has time to become better acquainted with the new person, discover special skills, strengths, and abilities, and consider the next position.

On this basis, the starting job is in no sense a created "make work" position. The job must be vital and challenging, and at the same time allow for easy measurement of results and introduction to as many aspects of the work of the department as possible. Therefore, the entry-level job must be carefully supervised. The larger the division or international banking operation, the more possibilities exist for entry-level positions. However, even in the relatively small international department, several key starting jobs exist or can be created and maintained without much effort.

On the operations side of the division, sections dealing with reports, controls, systems, and procedures often provide good starting positions for future operations section heads of foreign exchange, paying and receiving, collections, or letters of credit. Preparation of the various reports needed by management, carrying out control or audit functions, revision or writing existing or new procedures, and design of new or modified accounting systems are all excellent ways to gain breadth and depth in the operations area while permitting frequent contact with existing section heads, auditors, systems and other specialists within other departments of the bank, and even some of the more senior people in the international department. In smaller international divisions, especially where these duties may be combined into one unit, this area also might provide an excellent starting-level position for future lending or account officers.

On the credit or lending side of the division, the traditional starting jobs are well known and easily defined. In the larger international banks, new graduates and first-time employees often arrive after some brief, format orientation period as platform assistants. In this position, they immediately assist seasoned account and lending officers, who become their mentors and teach by the case-study method as the juniors carry out investigations, prepare routine letters and memoranda, and generally try to do anything the senior permits and assigns. Under this arrangement the officer signs or at least checks every piece of work at some point in the process or at the end of the task until the junior earns his or her own authority to sign on behalf of the bank.

In smaller banks a greater volume and variety of credits can be observed and worked with by a credit analyst. Spreading statements and reviewing or assisting in preparation of materials to be presented to the department's or bank's credit committee is an excellent introduction to the lending function and brings contact and discussion with the lending and account administration personnel, who in the near future may need their own assistants.

In large international banks where numerous openings arise for service in foreign locations, the entry-level positions for platform assistants must be kept free of career assistants in order to permit orientation and development of the steady stream of candidates for foreign duty. More will be said about this situation under training and development; however, obviously here again is one of the key points where clogging of the arteries must be avoided. The motto here must be "foreign assignment, up or out."

A less traditional entry route for the future foreign officer or lending account officers, particularly in smaller international banks, is through the operations side of the division. The systems and procedures section already has been mentioned, but even the paying and receiving officer's job, for example, should be considered for new employees who have completed a tour of the credit function. Operations functions provide background and perspective, as well as specific opportunities to assist customers, especially correspondent banks. This is a significant part of the work of many account officers and shows how to serve customers' needs with noncredit as well as credit services of the bank. For those bound for foreign posts, early management experience in the operations sections can be provided before dealing with similar functions in what is often a completely different culture.

INTERNAL TRAINING AND DEVELOPMENT TECHNIQUES

At the risk of oversimplification, training will be viewed for the purposes of this section as an input from management, including explanations, discussions, courses, lectures, and assigned readings. Development will be considered as the result of a person's understanding and fulfilling the requirements of an assigned job. Although admittedly arbitrary, these definitions may help us better understand the means by which the growth of international banking skills and mastery of techniques peculiar to this craft can be encouraged. These definitions are arbitrary because they obviously overlap and one can be emphasized to offset an absence of the other.

For example, training to a large extent depends upon the size of the particular operation and amount of the overall international budget. However, even in the smaller operation, carefully planned job rotation can speed development in the absence of an extensive or even any formal training program. More importantly, time is probably the most serious restraint on training in any organization. Therefore, every organization must make time for training, and for the new or inexperienced international division or for one that is expanding rapidly or must supply a steady stream of personnel to man foreign posts, time for training must be given a high priority. Responsibility for training usually cannot be turned over to outsiders or even assigned to a designated training officer with successful results. Training is a responsibility of management and involves all managers and, to some extent, all staff. Accordingly, management must set the priorities for training and relate training with development, which again involves management through arrangement of a logical plan of job rotation.

At the present state of the art in international banking, clerical personnel and operations officers probably tend to grow more through job rotation than formal training programs, whereas lending or account officers receive more formal training. But even the lending or account officers rely more on job rotation than on formal training to learn their jobs.

For larger organizations with a steady flow of large numbers of international trainees, in-house training programs can be made quite extensive and run continuously. A mixture of formal classroom work and job rotation and observation can be operated with a minimum of instruction personnel and without placing too heavy a burden on the personnel whose jobs are being observed. Although proper scheduling, visits, and observation of different functions can be used in any size bank, the goal of such scheduling should be to prevent too many trainees from overwhelming any particular section or area by arriving at inconvenient times from the standpoint of vacation schedules, audits, or work difficulties. One person should be placed in charge of handling introductions, clearing ahead with the departments or sections being visited, and making last-minute adjustments to the schedule when necessary to route trainees to another department better able to receive them at the time. Once a list of areas and functions to be observed has been drawn up, this can be used again or modified over time.

For university graduates with no previous banking experience who are destined to become account and lending officers or foreign branch managers, a typical training program might extend from four to six weeks or more and encompass some or all of the main areas of domestic and international banking operations. Included would be a tour through a domestic branch, from tellers through the proof, bookkeeping, and check processing functions. Daily audit routines would be observed, and time actually serving as a teller or platform assistant to help answer all types of routine and nonroutine inquires is usually well spent. Following the checks from the branch to the bank's centralized check processing facility is a next logical step, if time permits, and then visits may be made to the signature control and demand deposit processing areas, and then on into the specialized international sections for collections, letters of credit, money transfer, and foreign exchange. The loan department should be visited to learn how loans and credit extensions of all kinds are booked, how interest accruals and billings are handled, and how loan documentation is collected, checked, accounted for, and maintained in safekeeping.

Next on the itinerary would be the credit department for a study in credit investigation methods and spread and analysis of foreign financial statements. If financial projections for term loans and project lending are prepared or checked in a specialized section, this area also is an excellent place to do actual work for some time. Obviously, more departments and sections could be added to this list, but these suggestions at least cover the basic points. Permanent assignment to an operations department or lending administration area would then follow completion of this tour through the bank.

With or without the in-house or outside training programs, the most important stimulus to growth of international officers still

comes from on-the-job experience. Maximum development, therefore, comes from a carefully thought-out progression of different
job assignments over the years, or job rotation, for short. Every
organization regardless of size can provide the opportunity for job
rotation if managers are willing to plan a logical schedule of job
assignments for each member of the staff and further are willing to
persist in carrying out the changes necessary to meet the schedule.

Unfortunately, after a while in some organizations there is a
temptation to leave people where they are until some outside event
changes the order. This, of course, is reactive rather than active
management. Inevitably, even the reactive organizations change,
but the difference then is a scramble to merely fill jobs rather than
have the flexibility to make changes to create opportunities for
individual growth. Every opening in an organization can present an
opportunity for someone's development or it can be viewed only as a
slot to be filled and forgotten.

The manager or managers responsible for setting up the job
rotation schedules must establish them and keep to them. The
advantage to writing down the schedules is better discipline for the
manager. The disadvantage is premature disclosure with adverse
effects in the event that the needs of the organization change before
the next job assignment can be arranged. Although job rotation is
not change for the sake of change, various alternatives almost always
seem to exist for logical moves and allow for balancing the needs of
the organization with the growth of the individuals involved.

Accordingly, on balance, it seems better that each manager have
his rotation plans for key personnel constantly in mind but reveal
these changes only at the time they take place. If questioned by
subordinates, it is better to reveal only general patterns and alternatives, as career paths can be made only in the context of the needs of
the organization. For persons being assigned to foreign locations or
to particularly complicated jobs, it may be necessary, however, for
the manager to provide longer lead times in notifying of such
changes and to help more in preparing the person involved.

Job rotation also involves a willingness to share knowledge, expertise, skills, and experience with others by example, explanation,
discussions, or formal presentations. This involves the supervisors in
taking time from routine work during working hours or outside

working hours, if necessary. Occasionally it involves creating training materials where none exist or at least obtaining such materials where they do exist and then using them. Finally, it involves people with the proper attitudes to teach and to share and have patience with others. Often this means going over the same materials, job descriptions, or explanations with a succession of jobholders.

For example, a senior credit department supervisor might work with a constant parade of new recruits. Some routine can be passed on by the incumbent to the newcomer, and Chapter 11 discusses how procedures manual sections can help ease the burdens of training. However, to insure high standards, it is necessary for supervisors to go over, and sometimes over and over, the ground rules also. Accordingly, the ability to teach effectively is a key attribute of successful supervisors in the environment envisioned here and is the critical element for carrying out training and development after programs and job rotation schedules have been arranged.

Even with frequent job rotation or as an alternative to an otherwise planned rotation program, establishing and changing the size of a job must be considered from time to time. To permit optimum development, a job should always be a bit larger than the jobholder can fulfill at the exact moment. Occasionally, outstanding performers will sense the next moves and seize the right opportunities without prompting, but more often even the eager and talented need a nudge now and then to keep them moving within the framework of the organization's priorities. This usually reflects no weakness on the part of the employee, but stems almost entirely from a lack of perspective that only the person's supervisor can have, based upon a network of contacts and feedback from the next higher level in the organization.

In international lending, job size is often easy to adjust by adding or substituting relationships in different countries. But new functions can also be added, such as more involvement in country analysis, the taking on of new projects, or assumption of responsibility for specialized lending techniques, such as Export-Import Bank programs in the United States, for example. The size of operations and administrative jobs can also be changed, of course, as there almost always are tasks to be done that could fit in with one area as well as another. In dividing up these extra tasks or other duties, the primary consideration then can be job sizing, with numerous changes to make the coat slightly larger than the person wearing it.

One of the most useful training techniques is the section or division staff meeting. Although some may argue that the function of a staff meeting is communication, this objective is not inconsistent with training and education. To maximize the training function of staff meetings, as broad a group as possible should participate on a consistent basis. The trade-off occurs in balancing the number of participants; giving time to each to speak for a few minutes; allowing for questions, discussion, and announcements; and keeping the total meeting within the range of about one hour, as a rule of thumb.

Such a formula rules out meetings with more than fifteen to twenty attendees, or in the alternative having only selected persons speak and report while others merely listen. If the manager in charge of the staff meeting minimizes his or her own initial remarks and leads quickly into comments by others and then channels and shapes any questions and discussion to the goals defined in the management plan, the meeting can become a learning experience for all. The results of the staff meeting should be written and circulated to the next higher level of management, for there can often be a training as well as a communications function to be performed at this level also.

Another excellent training device is the weekly collection and circulation to all officers of the smaller division or section of all routine correspondence and memoranda prepared by each officer in the unit. Although this practice again could fall under the heading of communication, assuming that the first copies of such correspondence have been filed in the appropriate credit or other files, the main purpose again is training. Each person can see the similarities or differences between his or her work and that of others and keep in mind such examples for future use. In effect, each item in the correspondence file serves as a mini-case study.

Finally, nothing can take the place of reading. Many materials of excellent quality, covering most aspects of international banking, are now available. For further study, representative basic reference materials are listed with brief descriptions in Appendix G.

8

Support Function Personnel

Domestic Branch Offices and Services Manuals / Domestic Banking Units and Matrix Management / Credit Department Functions / Economics Department Activities / Loan Administration Department / Investment Department Coordination

Although international division personnel often tend to operate their unit with the characteristics of a bank within a bank, this does not mean the international division functions autonomously. In fact, international personnel are supported in carrying out their duties by personnel from several key divisions and parts of the commercial banking organization. At the same time, some of the units that may provide support functions, in turn, are dependent upon efficient international operations and cooperation to serve their customers. Therefore, strong links must be forged between international division staff and personnel of these various other areas in order to assure maximum success of the other areas and the international division. The supporting areas and the international division function as the spokes of a wheel. Without strong, firmly connected spokes, the total effort of the bank to serve its customers effectively will collapse. International wholesale or

157

commercial banking business, for example, is generated through the domestic branches and banking departments, which deal with the bank's local customers. Such business includes but is not limited to loans, letters of credit, collections, funds transfers, and foreign exchange.

The credit department of the bank, among other duties, maintains credit files, analyzes customer financial statements, and exchanges credit information with other institutions. The economics department supplies valuable information on local and world economic and industrial conditions and especially assists the international division in its planning process and in preparing country studies.

The loan department provides vital support functions in record keeping and related areas. The investment department can help develop international relationships, especially among correspondent banks, and also provides services that complement those provided by the international division. The international and investment departments at most banks especially must cooperate closely in connection with the commercial bank's conduct of bankers' acceptances business.

Almost every department and division in the commercial bank deals with the international division to some extent, including, for example, the personnel and public relations departments and even the trust division, which might use international services in the course of collecting foreign assets of a decedent's estate. However, these other departments are considered outside the scope of our present study. The work of the internal auditors, accounting or controller's department, and house counsel in connection with the international division is included in Chapter 9.

DOMESTIC BRANCH OFFICES AND SERVICES MANUALS

The contribution of domestic branch offices to the volume of international activity of any commercial bank is dependent upon several factors. Some commercial banks, of course, have few, if any, branches. Reasons range from the almost exclusively wholesale nature of their business to banking laws such as those found in the United States, where state legislatures can forbid even national banks operating within the states to have more than one office. Many large banks, especially in nations such as the Western European countries, Japan, and Brazil, where the entire economy is heavily dependent upon exporting and importing, conduct as much, if not more, of certain types of international transactions from their extensive branch networks than from their head-office international divisions.

In these countries, international payments and receipts, collections, letters of credit, and foreign exchange are handled by personnel located in branch offices convenient to importing and exporting customers, even in remote geographic locations of such nations. In many banks, however, not every branch office or agency is equipped to provide all international services. For example, one regional or city office might cover an area or smaller city and handle more complex transactions, including financing of trade transactions. But in Western Europe in particular, almost every branch of any bank at least can handle international payments and deal in foreign exchange or foreign currencies.

In many other countries and especially the United States, the effectiveness of domestic branch systems in building profits from international transactions is related more to the training provided to the personnel in these offices. Large European banks commonly have three routes for their personnel trained in international business. In addition to working in the head-office international division or foreign branches, there is the opportunity to be stationed in those domestic offices that provide international services in large volumes. Secondary school as well as university graduates generally undergo a period of formal, specialized, or on-the-job training, either in the head office or at bank-operated training schools.

Many banks in the United States and other countries could greatly increase their share of international business by training domestic office personnel in international transactions. International services then can be provided at greater convenience to their customers, who need not send employees or messengers to usually congested downtown or center city locations to conduct routine international business. Branch offices near harbors or airports are the most likely candidates to supply international services, because more customers will be near these transportation centers.

To expedite the providing of international service in domestic bank offices, a services manual, as well as a procedures manual, is indispensable. A services manual also is useful for the personnel of the domestic commercial banking departments, whose customers may use international services. Whereas a separate international procedures manual or special procedures that are included within the domestic branch procedures manual concentrate on the various accounts and controls to be used in carrying out international transactions, a services manual deals with obtaining clear instructions for executing international transactions and the mechanics of complying with these instructions. At a minimum the international services manual should contain brief, but accurate, descriptions of the various international services, with information on which sections and persons to contact in the regional or headquarters international operation. For those services that branch offices can initiate, sample application or instruction forms and directions to enable the customer to complete the forms should be included in the services manual as well.

By way of example, applications for international funds transfers should permit the customer to choose between telex or cable transfers, airmail payment orders, and purchase of drafts. The distinctions between these three forms of payment and the charges for each should be clear to the customer. The description section of the services manual should enable branch personnel to give good explanations and answer most routine questions. The funds transfer application should contain contractual wording of the rights and duties of both the bank and the customer and should have a space for the customer's signature. In a similar manner, application forms should exist for issuing letters of credit and accepting documents for collection. Also, the routine for entering into foreign exchange contracts and the steps for buying and selling foreign bank notes should be included in the services manual.

All the contractual language on such forms should be cleared by the legal department of the bank or by outside counsel, and the forms should be reviewed from time to time for changes, especially in the event of any problems. In no event should any bank personnel ever attempt to carry out transactions without signed written instructions from the customer. Action in the absence of signed in-

structions is a clear invitation to liability on the part of the bank in the
event the transaction is not executed to the customer's satisfaction.

Without a written record of the customer's request and words to
define the role of bank and customer, the bank has no recourse in
the event of problems. When bank personnel complete application
forms, even greater problems can arise. Although assistance might
be given appropriately in the form of suggested answers to questions
related to completing the various forms, if a customer cannot complete a funds transfer or letter of credit application, either the wrong
employee of the customer has been assigned this task or the bank
probably should not be dealing with the customer in question.

Although the domestic office originally receives instruction forms
and initiates routine transactions, specialized international personnel in the head office or regional international operations unit
usually will be responsible for carrying out or completing the transactions. This allows foreign accounts to be controlled in concentrated locations where only certain personnel are authorized to
create entries and, at the same time, permits review of the application form or transaction by specialized personnel.

In the event of any questions by either branch office or international unit personnel, communication before attempting to execute
the transaction is better than trying to patch together an unclear
transaction after the instructions have been transmitted to another
part of the globe. In international banking, as in any other endeavor,
it pays in the long run to get things done correctly the first time
around. On a routine telex funds transfer, for example, the cost of
one exchange of telex inquiries after transmission often can more
than double the cost of the original transaction, to mention nothing
of the delay involved.

Over and above handling of routine international transactions,
domestic branch personnel can play a leading role in identifying and
developing new international business for the bank. A branch customer usually will inquire first of his local banker about exporting or
importing or sending funds abroad. The alert domestic office
banker likewise should ask his customer about initial receipts or
transfers of funds abroad. Such activity or request for credit information on foreign names is often the earliest indication to anyone in

the entire bank that a previously totally domestic client has decided to look outside his own country for new business opportunities.

Nor should the domestic banker wait until the customer inquires about doing business internationally. On calls to both office and plant, the local banker should repeatedly ask whether the customer has considered, depending upon the nature of the customer's business, buying, selling, licensing, or investing internationally. Expressions of interest should be brought to the attention of head-office account and international personnel for study and assistance with preparation for follow-up calls. Finally, specific international opportunities obtained through the international division should be made known to local-office customers.

To encourage international business development, experienced international personnel should visit from time to time at least with domestic office managers, if not individual customers, and discuss important customers. If time and personnel levels permit, occasional joint calls should be made by domestic office international division officers to encourage local customers to consider overseas business opportunities. When local customers start conducting international business, a regular pattern of joint calling may be necessary to advise and assist the customer not only in keeping apace but in staying ahead of growing needs for international services.

DOMESTIC BANKING UNITS AND MATRIX MANAGEMENT

Domestic banking departments, unlike domestic branch offices, usually are not equipped to handle the execution of international transactions. Such transactions almost always will be handled from the inception by the head-office international division, since domestic banking departments seldom contain any operations personnel. However, the domestic commercial account officers spend more time on calling customers, selling services, and meeting with their customers, since they are not burdened with the daily routine of running a branch or similar operation. Accordingly, domestic head-office account personnel, especially since they usually deal with the larger firms, can make a significant contribution to assisting their customers in the conduct of international activities. In this regard the same international services manual used in the domestic branch offices may be of great use.

Many domestic officers in certain banks spend most of their time serving their customers' international needs. As seen at the end of Chapter 3, a modern marketing strategy to reach and serve multinational corporations involves close coordination between domestic and international banking staff. Furthermore, a series of organizational changes may be necessary so that most banks may accomplish delivery of international services to such customers. Ultimately, at many of the larger international banks, domestic and international functions will be merged into a unit with worldwide responsibility, if this has not been done already. Even in the regional banks, especially within the United States, such consolidation is taking place. Often the surviving amalgamated unit in these smaller banks is called the multinational division, which embodies the former traditional international department, foreign offices, and international operations along with domestic corporate banking staff.

The greatest challenges under these circumstances revolve around training personnel and determining departmental jurisdiction, issues which are covered in greater detail in other chapters of this book. These two main issues are not only problems but solutions. Complete cross-training of lending and account officers to provide both domestic corporate banking and international services improves the delivery of international services to the multinational corporation. Similarly, strict enforcement of the basic concept of departmental jurisdiction permits specialization, economies of scale, and more convenient service for customers.

However, pending the utopia of complete cross-training of all personnel and the smooth implementation of rules of departmental jurisdiction, two other solutions may have application for many banks. One concept, the relationship profitability analysis, comes from the field of cost accounting and seems particularly applicable to smaller or regional banks. The other idea, matrix management, derives from a popular current technique of business administration and has been successfully used by several commercial banks, especially some of the largest and most international money center institutions.

Relationship analysis consists of complete accounting for all income streams and expenses for each major customer and assists the effort of assessing accurately and rewarding fairly both domestic and international personnel, who are working on the same account relationships. Although such an approach may appear to involve some element of double counting, this should be acceptable since there is also quite obviously a duality of effort. Moreover, there can be no quarrel with a result that encourages greater effort on the most profitable relationships and has increased overall profits. Furthermore, although relationship profitability analysis might involve some additional expense, the process is subject at some point to automation, which can at least contain, if not actually decrease, total expense. In any event, there seems to be no wiser use of scarce resources than to establish an independent unit to centralize all data and fairly determine which relationships are of greatest value to the bank and how much profit results from the efforts of several units of the organization.

Matrix management, although not inconsistent with relationship analysis, is more than an outgrowth of such analysis. Nor can there be any doubt that matrix management also is expensive. The profit center accounting apparatus must be greatly expanded, totally integrated, and carefully overlapped. Basically, *matrix management,* from the standpoint of commercial banking, involves the establishment of numerous profit centers, which view the same customers and transactions from several different perspectives, often as many as three or four.

For example, individual customers may be served by various bank units that have geographic responsibility. Such units might include domestic, international, or multinational departments or divisions, and each unit would strive to maximize profits by its geographic classification. Of interest to the international division would be profits from the head office; from each foreign office, branch, or subsidiary; and from regional groupings. At the same time, every customer within the bank might be assigned to an industrial grouping that has worldwide relationship responsibility.

Examples of industry or business groupings include petroleum and energy, metals and mining, aerospace and electronics, government organizations, and financial institutions. Each of these market segment groups likewise is striving to maximize profits. A further grouping of profit center units might be organized by product or service. Cash management, merchant banking, and letters of credit and collection units fall into this third line. Finally, the treasury and foreign exchange responsibility might work at the fourth level to maximize return by obtaining the lowest cost sources of funding for loans and money market activities.

The matrix management system is not free from conflict and is not meant to be. In fact, means must exist to resolve conflicts, by working across some axis of the matrix. Thus, serving the Bethlehem Steel account relationship might involve the officers of a California bank responsible for calling on relationships in eastern Pennsylvania or the northeastern United States, the personnel responsible for the mining and metals industry, and merchant banking staff raising funds by means of a syndicated loan to expand an iron ore mine in western Africa.

Theoretically, in this example, although officers from all of these units might at one time or another visit the customer, it is more likely that officers of one unit would maintain primary, continuous contact by a routine calling program. The officers of the other units would visit the customer on a less frequent basis, or only when needed, or would work through the primary account officer to assist with preparation for visits and sale of specific services.

Clearly, matrix management may not be the solution for every bank's organizational problems. However, it is currently being used in whole or in part by more and more banks of all sizes and nationalities. The concept in some form certainly has some validity in the area of implementing bank marketing strategies for multinational corporations. It appears likely to remain a part of the commercial banking scene for some time and a permanent aspect of the organizational structure of many major money center banks and some regionals.

CREDIT DEPARTMENT FUNCTIONS

Historically, the credit department, until recent times, has been in most banks a staff department, charged with well-defined functions of a routine nature. Within the last few years, however, the role of this department has changed dramatically, especially in those banks that have experienced a high percentage of problem loans. Although most banks had or continue to have a separate international credit unit within the international division for all or certain functions, some banks today have put all credit department functions into a unit completely outside the international division and reporting up a separate chain of command. In some cases this arrangement is designed deliberately to serve as a check-and-balance mechanism with regard to the international division. In other cases the main purpose is to increase efficiency by specialization of functions.

With inadequately trained staff, such an arrangement can stifle the international division and impede delivery of international services involving extension of credit to bank customers. If the credit department takes over total responsibility for credit decisions, as opposed to preparing analyses and recommendations, then the international division becomes only a marketing arm of the bank. International officers, in effect, make no credit decisions but only initial recommendations. The role of the two departments becomes completely reversed, and the international division attempts to sell short, marketing credit services over which it has no authority. The ultimate result of this turn of events is quite likely a distorted and decreased international division, which loses creditability with its customers until finally little or no international business is done effectively.

One of the easiest and often most overlooked functions of any credit department is to maintain the credit files for each borrowing customer. This function involves not only storage but also release of files to authorized personnel only against signed check-out slips. Sometimes financial statements, especially annual reports, also are maintained in a separate filing series by the credit department. Further, the credit department is responsible for properly filing materials, marked for filing, in the correct files. Credit and statement files are the most important daily working tool for the lending officer and also are used by credit investigators for answering inquiries, by auditors, and by loan review personnel. Accordingly, misplaced files and sloppy and inaccurate filing can slow the work of the bank significantly. With an improperly functioning filing operation, secretaries, as well as officers, spend a great deal of their time searching for credit files or material that should be located in a particular file or section of a file. Because of the importance of proper filing, this subject will be considered in further detail in Chapter 13 on office management.

Beyond maintaining credit and statement files, credit department personnel usually are responsible for spreading or transferring information from customer financial statements to bank forms, which tend to present balance sheets, income statements, other financial information, and key ratios in a uniform format. This facilitates evaluations and comparisons of financial statements for the same customers over different time periods, between various customers, and between a customer's financial condition and industry standards or averages.

In the international area, where different languages, different accounting systems, and different auditing standards are involved, this task of spreading financial statements can be far from routine. Different items can be included in the same balance sheet caption in two different systems, for example, or items that are hard to translate and define can be complete mysteries, defying imagination as to where they should be included in the bank's standard format. To help the credit analyst, most major accounting firms with international offices, many foreign banks, and, increasingly, the Robert Morris Associates publish or provide guides to foreign accounting systems and translations for financial statement terminology.

Greater standardization is gradually occurring with time, especially as the major international accounting firms and their standards, as applied by their foreign accounting correspondents, are increasingly used around the world. This is one area of standardization that all international bankers should encourage. It is hoped that all nations will follow uniform accounting standards as soon as possible but retain their own cuisine forever. Obviously, multinational corporations and other organizations with worldwide activities are instrumental in hastening this development, since it is necessary for one accounting firm to work with the multinationals in all countries where they have activity.

The next traditional function of the credit department is to conduct credit investigations of potential or actual customers. All new depositors, as well as new borrowers, should be investigated with other banks and other organizations before delivering checkbooks or extending credit. At least annually, even the most satisfactory borrowing account should be reviewed with other institutions. Credit department investigators use different forms, checklists, standards, and terminology around the world, but usually two investigators within the same system clearly understand each other. Also, usually more will be stated in clear language in person or over the telephone than in writing.

Bank credit investigations, or at least the written results of such investigations, often tend to be less thorough than various special services such as Dun and Bradstreet, but few, if any, of these special services are of uniform high quality around the world. Accordingly, the most that usually can be expected from the credit investigation process is warning of any major problems or clues warranting further research. Usually such further investigation should be undertaken with the assistance of international lending officers, who can often learn more from their counterparts in other banks.

Bank credit investigators tend to work well with credit personnel in other banks but often overlook their counterparts in companies, which may be suppliers or extend credit in other capacities. Contractors, which perform services for major corporations, for example, are usually investigated thoroughly by their corporate customers. The corporate customers want to assure themselves that the contractors have the capacity to complete major contracts, which might be vital to the continuous functioning of one of the corporation's plants or other units.

Much of the bank-to-bank investigation process concentrates on whether each bank is increasing, decreasing, or holding level the amount of credit being extended to a particular customer. This approach is useful in avoiding "the musical chairs" scenario, in which all other banks pull away from a borrower, leaving the last borrower locked into a deteriorating credit. When completing the report of an investigation, the name, address, and telephone number of the person contacted should be recorded along with the date of the contact.

The reciprocal of the credit investigation function is answering credit inquiries from customers and other banks performing credit investigations with the subject of the inquiry. The answer to an inquiry depends upon the combination of any investigatory work performed by the bank plus any direct experience of the bank with regard to deposits or lending.

Written answers to credit inquiries should be provided only on nonliability paper or accompanied by the statement typed at the end of the answer to the effect that all information is provided without warranty or liability regarding accuracy and is intended only for the confidential use of the inquirer. Further, although it is not a legal requirement, it is useful to keep a running record in every credit file of the inquiries answered, with a date and the inquirer's name and address. Then, if the credit standing of the subject of an inquiry deteriorates, the bank is able to contact its customers and suggest that they may wish to update their files with regard to the subject of an inquiry of a previous date, since such information can change over time.

ECONOMICS DEPARTMENT ACTIVITIES

The role of the economics department has been referred to in Chapter 3 in connection with the bankwide planning process. There, the economist's role in preparing documents relating to the general world outlook, country studies, money market development, and industry studies was considered. However, the functions of this department are sufficiently important to the international division to warrant separate discussion, focusing on the economics department alone.

In this modern age no economist can ignore significant developments in any part of the world when analyzing the bank's home economy. Although the economist's duties may concentrate on analysis of economic changes in a particular nation or region surrounding the bank's headquarters, the impact of international events must be considered in regard to other nations and the head-office country of the bank. Moreover, economic developments cannot be considered in any nation without due regard to political factors. Accordingly, the bank economist or economics department collectively analyzes considerably more than purely economic matters.

Political changes, foreign policy, and strategic, military, and social developments, at least in the world's major nations, must be assessed constantly. Regional groupings, whether common markets in Europe or Latin America or commodity producer alliances for oil or sugar, as well as international bodies, especially but not limited to the International Monetary Fund, must be monitored for actions that could directly affect the bank's home country, foreign markets, and the world monetary system. Changes in any of these areas could have important consequences for many bank customers. Furthermore, industrial trends for such changing industries as steel, shipbuilding, petroleum, chemicals, and textiles, and increasingly with time other industries as well, tend to be global or at least have global ramifications.

For those reasons, today's bank economists need to have an extremely broad viewpoint, as well as specialized analytical skills. The bank's economists thus make ideal intellectual sparring partners for international division lending officers. Such exchanges may point out future opportunities and danger spots for lending or other international banking services or areas that justify future investigation and information gathering.

The bank's economists should be in constant communication with other economists from around the world and may even travel abroad from time to time to visit other economists and especially central bankers. Such travels may be undertaken alone or in conjunction with international account officers, usually those who deal with central banks, regional and international development banks, and monetary agencies.

Even in those banks whose members of the economics department do not travel regularly, constant communication can enable the international officers who do travel to bring back information to assist the economists. From piecing together the experiences and observations of international officers and the viewpoint and analysis of the economists, a better total picture than either group could develop alone often emerges to the benefit of all parties concerned. Constant interaction is particularly useful with regard to industry studies, which are usually prepared under the direction of the economics department.

Beyond worldwide industry studies or analyses, the economics department in most banks directs and organizes the preparation of country studies of the various nations around the world where the bank does business or is considering future business. Again in this area, continual interplay between traveling or overseas-based international officers is necessary to maximize the collection of accurate and timely information.

Most banks have established requirements for regular reporting by their overseas units, so that a steady flow of current economic and related information flows back to the headquarters economics department. In the event of questions or need for further details, overseas officers often have immediate access to senior financial or central bank officials in the countries where they are located. In this way, trends and developments can be spotted quickly and communicated promptly for information and, if necessary, decision making.

In essence, the economics department in most banks ideally performs as the head-office intelligence agency, directing, collecting, analyzing, and distributing information from an industrial, national, and worldwide economic perspective. Many of the ideas, methods, and systems of overt national intelligence gathering could be adapted to the bank's economics department. The foreign-based and traveling international officers serve as the arms of this effort, as well as being the beneficiaries of the end results of the economics department's work.

LOAN ADMINISTRATION DEPARTMENT

The loan administration department is one of the most vital supporting departments of the international operation. This is because this department controls the original records of the bank for what usually is the greatest volume of international assets. This department also is responsible for calculating and accruing interest and fees on these assets, among other functions. Similar statements can be made about the loan department with regard to almost every domestic lending unit of the bank. However, special attention is needed in many, especially smaller, banks, because of the tendency to make an exception in the case of international loans and not have these functions handled by a separate department. This same issue occasionally arises in the overseas branches and other lending offices of even the largest banks.

Because of differences in handling interest calculations based upon LIBOR instead of the prime rate in the United States or the usual base rate in other countries, for example, or because of complexities related to handling syndicated loans and loan participations, or for various other reasons, loan department functions are sometimes left within the control of the international division. Usually, of course, in domestic lending departments, the loan department exists completely separate from and outside the chain of command of any lending officer, even at the highest level.

This separation of function is necessary not only to obtain economies of scale from work specialization but also for the sound control purpose of minimizing opportunities for defalcation. For international lenders, who usually have heavy travel schedules, as well as other duties related to country analysis, in addition to normal workloads for handling credit extension and account relationships, the concept of specialization makes even more sense than for domestic lenders.

International lending officers should not be burdened with interest calculations, accruals, and billings, from the standpoint of an equitable workload alone. Furthermore, the control basis for separation of function is also equally, if not more, applicable in the international area, since disbursements of international loan proceeds often are accomplished through funds transfer services that may be under the control of the international division, especially in smaller banks or separate offices of larger banks. The potential for harm under these circumstances is obvious, since the same unit extending credit might have the operations capability to transmit loan proceeds.

A bank's loan administration department should function to serve all lending units of the bank. Access to the work areas of the loan department should be limited strictly, with admittance of employees outside the unit only on an exceptional basis. For convenience, the loan administration department usually is located near vaults for storage of original loan documents and has convenient access to computer terminals used to calculate interest and fee accruals and prepare billings. Frequent and thorough audits and numerous daily and weekly internal control routines are needed to keep vital asset records in good order in this department.

No loan asset should be booked or entered upon the bank's official records and no authorization to disburse the corresponding loan proceeds should be given until the loan administration department has received and reviewed for completeness a loan booking memorandum and all loan documentation and has verified that credit approvals for granting the loan are in order. The loan booking memorandum should contain all loan details, including amount, interest rate, fees, payment dates, and similar information needed to administer the loan during its life, without reference to lending officers.

All original documents, including any promissory notes or other instruments of indebtedness, loan agreements, guarantees, security documents, and legal opinions, should be in the bank's standard format as previously approved by bank counsel, or in a form approved by counsel on an exceptional basis. In checking for credit approvals, officers who initial or sign for approval should have sufficient authority to approve the loan or authorize disbursement, as established by the bank's rules for extension of credit.

In most banks, loan department personnel are not expected to read each document for content but only review for existence and form. Many banks use loan document checklists during the course of the credit approval process or provide that in complex loans a memorandum by counsel stating that documentation is in order will suffice for the loan department's purposes. The main idea of this process, of course, is to assure that loan proceeds are not disbursed before all necessary documents are collected and approved by lending officers and counsel when necessary.

Because of the detailed nature of its work, the loan department commonly is divided into sections or organized so that all work is reviewed by at least two people. Instructions on the loan booking memorandum should be particularly clear about interest rates, which can be fixed, tied or related to, or floating over LIBO, U.S. prime, or other base rates, and about commitment and other special fees. In setting up diaries or ticklers and other special instructions for internal loan department files, most banks rely on standardized checklists, which build upon information provided in the booking memorandum. Setup of all such records should be carefully checked independently within the department, especially since most loan record keeping is handled now by computers, and information incorrectly entered often requires great effort to change. Detailed information on withholding and other taxes is also collected and housed in the loan administration department.

Another function of the loan administration department is to preserve exact records of LIBO, prime, and other base rates and the exact method by which these rates were established. These records are needed not only to verify interest rate settings, but also may be used in legal actions where defenses may be raised by borrowers in future litigation initiated by the bank to collect sums owed to it.

On the basis of information generated from the records and controls, billings or invoices for interest, fees, and repayments are prepared by the loan administration department. As in setting up information, all billings should be independently checked within the department. In many countries with exchange control regulations, billings must be airmailed or even telexed well in advance of due dates to allow borrowers to make timely application to central banks or other monetary authorities so that payments will be made in time. To expedite the work of these government agencies and avoid confusion and inquiries, all billings should be in a clear format that is consistent from billing to billing.

When the bank is authorized to charge borrowers' accounts on their books to collect interest, fees, and repayments, the loan administration department should be certain that entries are passed. In the event of questions or problems in obtaining payments, lending officers should be advised promptly so they may take appropriate action. In this regard the most important daily document produced by the loan department for any lending unit within the bank, including the international division, is the *daily past due report.*

It is imperative that the past due report be prepared promptly each day, so that an immediate search for incoming funds can be initiated. Often, correspondent banks, especially in major centers such as New York, inadvertently delay payments as a result of high volumes, weak systems, and poorly trained personnel. Delayed receipt of interest or loan payments then involves assessing responsibility for delay and collecting interest on interest, if possible. As a matter of good form, all late payments should be the responsibility of the borrower, who owes and should pay late interest or even interest on interest, which involves adjustments to loan department records or future billings. However, in practice, much of the lending bank's time is often spent with correspondents in expediting the resolution of late payments.

Finally, the loan department also is the custodian of all original loan documents, which must be kept in the bank's vaults when not in use. All documents should be lodged with and removed from the loan department against signed receipts. Multiple forms for this purpose are common and quite helpful. If lending officers believe that frequent reference to loan documents will be necessary, they should obtain duplicate documents or make photocopies for appropriate credit files before lodging original documents for storage in safekeeping with the loan department. Finally, according to some loan agreements, it is necessary for the bank to note loan repayments on the reverse side of promissory notes, and the making of such notations is an additional duty of the loan department.

INVESTMENT DEPARTMENT COORDINATION

The international and investment departments of commercial banks generally become involved with each other in two main ways. In its role of maintaining liquidity or holding a reservoir of funds for use by the lending areas of the commercial bank, the investment department may place bank funds in instruments or institutions that are considered as foreign risks. This, of course, amounts to extension of credit through the investment department to international division customers. Also, in providing its usual customer services, the investment department identifies and executes investment transactions on behalf of international customers. In some banks a third area of interaction occurs in connection with handling bankers' acceptances.

As to the liquidity function, investment department personnel always must be certain that credit approvals in good order exist for dealing with any name. As to foreign names, including branches of foreign banks located in the country of the investing bank, credit approvals must be processed by the international division. That division may initiate the approval process as part of a twofold strategy of developing a relationship with the foreign institution and providing an outlet for bank funds. Or the investment department through its contacts in the money market might determine that it would be advantageous to conduct business with a foreign name. Then, approval should be requested from the international division so it can determine whether the proposed institution is creditworthy and suitable for establishing a relationship.

When the international division decides that a foreign bank is acceptable for money market activity, it is generally best to obtain approvals for all types of routine money market lines. These include placement of Eurodollars or other Eurocurrencies, depending upon the bank's home country currency and foreign exchange policies, sale of federal funds if locations in the United States are involved, purchase of certificates of deposits, and purchase of bankers' acceptances. Although the degree of risk varies slightly between each of these different forms of investment, if a bank meets the credit standards for any of these instruments, it usually meets the standards for all. Also, this variety is necessary in order to provide the investment department with sufficient flexibility, for, although these different forms of investments have separate markets, emphasis changes from time to time from one investment to another as a result of rate differentials.

Eurodollars and other Eurocurrencies, both placements and deposits accepted, may be handled by the international division, the investment department, or other specialized units, depending upon the organization of the bank involved. In any case, all activity must be coordinated at least daily by the investment committee or at some other central point where the liquidity position of the bank is monitored. This committee or other responsible unit decides what amounts, rates, and maturities meet the bank's current requirements. The international division should be represented on the committee or have input to the responsible unit to give international views on rates and markets. In smaller banks, the Eurocurrency function is often combined with the foreign exchange dealers, since both functions and their controls follow virtually identical work patterns involving the making of contracts by telephone or telex, the sending of confirmations, and the arranging for deliveries of funds.

Federal funds, or fed funds, of course, are a feature of the United States bank-to-bank money market. But U.S. branches of foreign banks usually participate in this market and both U.S. and foreign banks find fed fund activity a logical part of the correspondent relationships. Money market activities, including fed funds when the parties are in the U.S. market, are an ideal way to initiate a relationship between two banks. The transactions should be mutually beneficial and are easy to handle.

On this basis reciprocity is involved. Each bank needs approved facilities for the other, and both parties should strive to be able to quote a two-way rate at all times. This means that banks that tend to be net placers of funds on balance or net takers on balance should take or place some amounts on as consistent a basis as possible. Otherwise, the general position will become known in the market, and the bank over time will not receive the most competitive rates. For international names, it is the duty of the international division to assure that reciprocal lines are in place.

In serving the bank's international customers, the investment department makes available its full range of investment opportunities. These include those already mentioned plus the usual range of domestic instruments, such as certificates of deposit and commercial paper, for example. Bankers' acceptances are often attractive to individual corporate, institutional, and even personal accounts. Before the advent of the negotiable certificate of deposit, bankers' acceptances were one of the most common short-term investments and are still favored by many investors since they generally are supported by underlying trade transactions and thus are considered to be self-liquidating.

Bankers' acceptances raise several unique questions involving coordination between the international and investment functions. Bankers' acceptances usually are created by the international division in the course of carrying out international trade financing transactions. From Chapter 2 it will be recalledthat bankers' acceptances may be held as supporting instruments for funds disbursed by the bank, or they may be sold to parties who, in effect, fund the transaction financed by the bank but rely on the credit of the bank. Moreover, the international division or unit receives a commission for creating the acceptance, which involves a credit risk, since, if the bank customer cannot repay, the bank must grant a loan upon the maturity of the acceptance.

At this point the issue is raised as to which unit within the bank should decide on whether to hold the acceptance in portfolio (and, in effect, fund the transaction) or sell the instrument (and, if so, at what rate). The better view is that the international unit that created the acceptance should decide whether to fund or sell the instrument. However, in those banks that separate funding from lending areas or funds usage, the investment department may hold and fund acceptances, as well as decide when and at what rate to sell them. This could create friction if the investment department is not selling acceptances at the same pace the international division is creating them, assuming some overall internal limit has been reached for the amount of acceptances that can be funded at any one time.

Reasons for slow sales could range from an inadequate sales effort on the part of the investment department to an increase in market rates after the creation of acceptances. Obviously, if money rates decline below the level carried on acceptances in portfolio, these instruments would represent attractive investments and perhaps could be sold with a further margin or profit being retained by the investment department.

The main reason that investment departments in some banks handle sales of bankers' acceptances is to prevent unwanted competition in the same markets between other instruments of the bank, such as commercial paper and certificates of deposit, and hence prevent increased cost to the bank. However, in the United States, bankers' acceptances are bought and sold in a specialized market through dealers in New York City. Thus, regional banks have two separate markets, one for purchases by local area customers, and another for purchases by New York City dealers. Both markets require intensive cultivation for most regional banks, and frequent communication and careful coordination are required to maximize international commissions and minimize the overall cost of funds to the bank.

9

Control Function Personnel

Auditors and Lawyers / Internal Audit and Legal Controls / Working with Auditors / The Audit Report and Follow-Up / Bank Controller Function / House Counsel and Outside Counsel / Selecting Foreign Counsel

T he functions of various types of auditors, accountants, and lawyers have been grouped together in this chapter, which explains how these specialists help control the international function. Auditors usually come into international division units on a periodic basis to assure that certain rules and standards are being adhered to. They also can be sent in or called for anytime in the event of unusual problems. Lawyers, on the other hand, usually must be consulted or involved in the division's activities on request. However, there is no reason that house counsel also should not conduct division reviews regularly without permission of the division. But in most banks today this is not done.

Simple but frequent checks, reviews, and questioning of routine actions performed independently by people within the international division or departments working closely with it often can identify or prevent problems before they become serious. However, more

179

thorough periodic reviews performed by completely independent outsiders are necessary to supplement such internal steps and to satisfy specific requirements. Few organizations in the United States, for example, are audited more frequently or in more detail by government regulators than banks.

Working with outside auditors and bank examiners requires a special approach so as to minimize disruption to work flows and misinterpretation of auditing reports. In many situations much work remains to be done after the final audit report. This work must be fitted in with the regular work flow. Simultaneously various other new objectives that result from the planning process must be accomplished. The bank's controller or accounting department often becomes involved in monitoring the clean-up process resulting from the audit and is especially important with regard to tax matters and reporting to stockholders and regulatory authorities.

In many commercial banks, especially regional banks, house counsel either does not exist or does not have a well-defined role in relation to the international division. Introduction of relatively simple procedures and new work habits often can handle legal matters adequately and minimize the time required on the part of lawyers, either internal or outside. Furthermore, total or excessive reliance on outside counsel in most parts of the world today tends to be not only extremely expensive but often inconvenient to the bank and its customers. Successful banks, by carefully defining the functions of inside and outside counsel, fully utilize the services of all lawyers in the most efficient and cost-effective manner. In this regard, selecting counsel in foreign countries and working with them are often challenging tasks that require special considerations.

AUDITORS AND LAWYERS

Internal auditors are full-time bank employees who belong to a separate audit department. To be completely free of influence or control by anyone inside the bank, the head of the audit department should report directly to the board of directors or a committee of the board. In some banks the internal audit staff still tends to concentrate heavily on the prevention of defalcation and fraud. However, most banks have long ago moved forward from the old-fashioned approach that consisted basically of counting cash and balancing accounts. Most internal audit programs now involve checking actual work methods against written procedures and recommending changes in work routines and revisions in procedures where necessary. Thus, most auditors now work to assure not only compliance with laws, rules, and regulations, and generally accepted accounting principles, all established from outside the bank, but also with rules and standards established internally.

Most controversy in the area of internal auditing at this time concerns the role of the auditor in reviewing the quality of assets, especially loans and other extensions of credit. In smaller banks it is often difficult to find or train internal auditors for handling international extensions of credit. Some banks have completely separated the review of credits from other audit functions on the grounds that the audit staff is not qualified to perform the specialized credit review function. Other banks compromise by providing some role for audit personnel in the credit review process, such as membership or representation on the committee that oversees this activity.

Still other banks, including many with extensive overseas branch networks, have relied successfully for years upon traveling internal examiners who are trained in reviewing credit extension and auditing other functions. To be absolutely certain of maintaining complete independence from any influence within the bank, there can be no doubt that the internal audit staff should have the the qualified personnel and leadership necessary to properly review all credit extensions, as well as other functions.

Independent public accountants are required now for U.S. banks whose equity shares are publicly traded. The origin of this requirement is the U.S. Securities and Exchange Act, which established the Securities and Exchange Commission, whose duty is to protect the investing public by assuring full disclosure of pertinent information about an organization with public ownership. More banks in Latin America are beginning to use outside public accountants, but European and Asian banks seem to be behind in this regard.

Because public accounting firms check for compliance with generally accepted accounting principles as well as consistency in preparation of financial statements, their approach to the international division, as compared to that of the internal auditors, tends to place more emphasis on broad accounting concepts rather than mechanical nuts and bolts. However, this is not to say that such broad concepts do not have their more practical aspects, including, for example, recognition of income in proper periods or the question of adequacy of loan loss reserves.

By illustration, on the question of allocating income to proper periods, it would seem preferable to amortize over the life of the loans what are called front-end fees for taking participations in syndicated loans, as opposed to management fees for extra work required by the lead banks in preparing or marketing the loans. Yet, many banks at this time do not amortize such fees, but instead take all such amounts immediately into income during the year of receipt of the fee. The same issue arises regarding fees paid by exporters to banks to subsidize low or fixed interest rates on export financing transactions, especially those to communist nations, which prohibit paying interest rates above certain levels.

In connection with the adequacy of loan loss reserves, the public accountants by necessity must become involved deeply in the review of loan asset quality. One aspect of this question, which remains unresolved, is the relationship between the adequacy of loan loss reserves and the bank's total capital. In essence, the final test of the adequacy of a bank's loan loss reserve is its capital.

U.S. national bank examiners, like internal auditors and public accountants, tend to become involved in every aspect of international activity, but they place special emphasis on overall management approaches, systems, procedures, and controls. In the United States, national bank examiners may be employed by the Office of the Comptroller of the Currency, the Federal Deposit Insurance Corporation, or the Federal Reserve System. Although the U.S. Comptroller of the Currency once followed the more traditional concepts of counting cash and balancing accounts, during the last several years the shift to broader management principles has been rapid. This has been a result of a deliberate plan to completely overhaul the examination process.

In this regard the U.S. national bank examiner has come to play a role more akin to a management consultant by suggesting, urging, and pushing laggard banks into line with what is regarded as normal banking industry standards, while at the same time adopting many of the best approaches of successful banks as new standards. The Federal Reserve, as if to complement this effort, has tended to concentrate more of its efforts on gathering not only information, of a raw statistical variety, such as loans outstanding to individual countries, but also on how different banks approach various specialized international activities, such as analyzing countries and establishing country limits.

At the same time that Federal Reserve and Comptroller of Currency personnel have performed their functions of gathering information, enforcing industry standards, and examining banks during the last several years, both agencies plus the Federal Deposit Insurance Corporation have been busy proposing new rules and regulations for the control of international banking in the United States. More of this rule making will continue in the future as the result of ongoing projects aimed at limiting the amount of loans by U.S. banks to foreign nations when economic and political risks are believed to be excessive. An example of this effort is the recent expansion of the scope of 12 *United States Code* 84 to combine certain loans to foreign governments and government agencies from the same country for the purpose of applying the limitation of 10 percent of a bank's capital accounts for total loans to any one borrower.

Because of the close relationship between auditing, examination, regulation, new legislation, and rule making, inside or house counsel must be in close and continuous contact with the international division. Emphasis should be placed upon review of examination reports and understanding of new activities being undertaken. In a money center or large regional bank, one or more full-time attorneys may devote substantially all of their time to the bank's international work. In smaller banks only part of the in-house lawyer's time may be available for this purpose. Because of the specialized nature of international banking legal matters, the smaller bank may find it advantageous to engage the services of an outside legal expert in international banking. Such an expert not only may render advice in connection with new or pending legislation but also may be helpful in introductions to overseas counsel.

In the United States, special demands are being made upon banking legal experts because of recent new laws and legislative proposals. Reform of outmoded U.S. commercial banking laws is being given impetus by various forces, including the large numbers of foreign banks that are making acquisitions and starting new operatons in the United States. Until the International Banking Act of 1978, foreign banks in the United States could conduct business in more locations and under less stringent conditions than prevailed for U.S. banks. Many U.S. banks are attempting to use this situation as a means to reform U.S. laws to permit commercial banks to compete with foreign banks and even other U.S. nonbanking institutions by obtaining the same freedom from restrictions enjoyed by these other institutions. This involves fundamental changes in the rules, such as commercial banks crossing state lines to establish branches and determing whether commercial banks in effect should continue to be taxed in the form of lost earnings on noninterest-earning reserves that must be deposited with the Federal Reserve banks.

All of this effort requires close reading and interpretation of new and proposed laws by those in the commercial bank involved with the legal, accounting, and international functions. Many banks believe it is of vital interest to testify before congressional committees and to work with various regulatory agencies and bankers' associations in order to influence the content of new laws and regulations under these laws. The only alternative may be to stand by and permit U.S. commercial banks to operate under one set of rules while other financial competitors spread across the nation and continue to operate under other, more lenient rules or no rules in some areas.

Foreign banks operating in the United States must work closely with their legal division under these circumstances, and increasingly lawyers and legally trained persons are moving into top management and policy-making positions within U.S. banks in recognition of this situation. Outside the United States, banking regulation is increasing in many nations as laws are changed to impose special restrictions and local ownership requirements on foreign banks. Under these circumstances international banks must make greater use of foreign counsel in order to comply with new laws.

Foreign counsel are members of the bar in the countries where they reside and hence are experts in the laws of their countries. In addition, most foreign lawyers who work with international clients are well versed in comparative law. This means that such lawyers will be able to work easily with the bank's domestic counsel to explain new laws and regulations, as well as to structure agreements and carry out assignments, including litigation when necessary. They may explain the nature of their work and their countries' laws with analogies or comparisons to legal steps and laws of the bank's home country.

INTERNAL AUDIT AND LEGAL CONTROLS

Internal departmental audit controls consist of those routine checks that can be performed by personnel in the international division or closely related departments to prevent or minimize errors or problems. It is important that such checking be carried out frequently, usually on a daily, weekly, or at least monthly basis, and that it not require much time. This refers to relatively simple tasks that require minutes or an hour or two at most, as opposed to days. Furthermore, such routine internal auditing should be performed by persons completely unrelated to the original job, including preparation of entries to the books, of course, Finally, some form of written evidence should exist to show when the check or audit was completed and who performed it. A printed checklist with names of routine chores and spaces for dates and initial is quite adequate for most international divisions or overseas branches.

Any internal departmental audit routine must be tailor-made to the unit involved, but a few common ground rules for establishing such routines can be easily set forth. For example, in designing such routines, reference should be made to the division's chart of accounts and procedures manual, subjects that will be covered in Chapter 11 in detail. Next, past audit reports may point out particular problem areas on which future emphasis should be placed. Last, common sense should be applied to select and concentrate on areas where passage of time will make a trail of activity difficult to reconstruct, because of heavy volume or inconvenient filing methods, or will make checking too late to be of any reasonable use.

Examples in these last areas would include a daily review of numbered form sequences for drafts and payment orders; daily checking to assure that all debit and credit tickets have been initialed by a maker, checker, and authorized signer, or the equivalent for computer entries; and prompt follow-up for confirmations of foreign exchange or Eurodollar transactions. Obviously, a missing draft or payment order must be traced immediately. Insufficient initials on tickets or other irregular entry of information into the bank's books could indicate improper preparation involving in- adequate descriptive detail, wrong accounts, or even more serious problems. Also, by some strange rule, missing confirmations almost always seem to be for transactions in which there is some misunder- standing as to detailed terms.

Much of the daily, weekly, and monthly internal audit routine involves assuring that all accounts and subsidiary ledgers are in balance with each other and the general ledger. The sooner that imbalances are discovered, the easier it will be to locate mispostings and pass correcting entries, since fewer days' work will have to be reviewed. It is important to keep clean records of when accounts were balanced and what correcting entries were passed. Unfortu- nately, it seems to be one of the oldest rules of accounting that a higher percentage of errors occur when attempting to correct er- roneous entries than in processing routine entries. Further, it should be recalled that few businesses other than banking attempt to create a daily balance sheet or have so many subsidiary ledgers regrouping the same basic information in so many different ways. International banking only increases the number of records and steps to be checked and balanced with the many records in foreign currencies and other detail that are required.

With such a volume of accounts, including the many bank ac- counts maintained by each bank engaged in international activity, frequent and independent reconcilement of accounts is a constant task. To monitor the task of reconcilement, a separate report or reconcilement register is necessary. The purpose of this register is to indicate the date of the last reconcilement for each account and what employees performed the work. This record should be examined no less frequently than every few weeks or once a month to assure that the people doing reconcilements are not falling behind in their work. Even though bank account reconciliations may be performed by people completely outside the international operations, it is nec- essary that someone in the international division spot check the register. In an overseas branch a senior officer should review this record. Often, bank statements and supporting data are slow to arrive and must be requested urgently by telex to keep records current and to continue investigations needed to complete reconcilements.

A good example of control from outside the international division by a closely related department occurs in the process of booking a head-office loan. Here, the loan administration department has the occasion to compare the details on the loan booking memorandum with the document used originally to obtain credit committee approval of the transaction. Further, the loan booking memorandum is an important instrument, because it must contain sufficient information to properly administer the loan during its life without future reference to the lending officer. As discussed in Chapter 8, this administrative work includes properly accruing interest and other fees, and preparing and issuing invoices for all fees, interest, and repayments.

The loan administration department is also a point where legal department controls cross the path of the international division. In disbursing loan proceeds, the lending officer must turn in not only a booking memorandum with the details of the loan in summary form for entering information in the bank's primary records but also the loan agreement, promissory note, and other related original documents which must be placed in the bank's vaults for safekeeping. At this stage all documents must conform to the bank's documentation standards, which have been approved previously by the bank's counsel, or they must be approved on an exception basis by counsel, if they do not conform.

Other control points involving the bank's legal department require vigilance on the part of international division personnel, who must properly notify counsel of unusual circumstances for otherwise routine transactions. Letters of credit, acceptance transactions, and collection items, among others, often raise important legal questions that should be addressed before attempting to complete the transaction. Many problems in these areas are easy to spot, because they result during the course of attempting to modify or add to one of the bank's standard forms, such as special additional wording on applications to the bank for issuing a letter of credit. Standby letters of credit are especially troublesome in this regard, and quite large sums of money are often involved. Every such instance should be brought to the attention of an experienced officer, who may then decide whether or not it is necessary to refer to counsel.

In the United States, the so-called anti-boycott laws have been particularly difficult for many banks in connection with handling letter of credit transactions. These laws are found in two places, the Internal Revenue Code and the Commerce Act, and apparently are not consistent with each other. Some smaller banks have thrown up their hands in disgust and refused to handle letters of credit that might require review rather than spend the money for the legal talent needed to advise on coping with these laws. Unfortunately, when U.S. exports are involved, this seems counterproductive to the effort of reversing balance of payments deficits. As more and more legislation of this kind affecting the international division is passed, involvement with the bank's legal department or outside counsel is bound to increase, perhaps at an even faster rate than during the last few years. Therefore, it is important to have good lines of communication between the international unit and international legal advisors.

One bank has solved this problem quite handily by assigning on a full-time basis to the head-office international division one lawyer, who makes personal rounds to visit each officer weekly. Far from turning up more work for himself in the long run, this lawyer "nips many problems in the bud" and in reality practices preventive "legal medicine" instead of dealing with basket cases, for which drastic "legal surgery" may be too late. Moreover, with time the officers of the bank become quite adept in identifying and defining potential legal issues with this routine. Most quickly learn to know which matters should and which should not be referred to counsel and when they should be referred. This lawyer has trained the international officers to do part of his work for him at considerable savings in time, work, and money to all parties, including the bank's customers who are the ultimate beneficiaries of this farsighted approach.

WORKING WITH AUDITORS

Before starting any audit, whether by internal bank auditors, public accountants, or government bank examiners, the auditors should introduce themselves to the division or unit head. If the auditors are not known personally by the banker in charge of the operation being audited, and since auditors often do arrive unannounced, suitable identification should be required or confirmation obtained. In a head office there are usually fewer problems of this kind, but in remote foreign locations, great care should be exercised in identifying unknown auditors. It could prove to be more than embarrassing to provide unlimited access to bank records to impostors, whose purposes for obtaining bank information undoubtedly would be contrary to the interests of the bank and to its customers as well.

Beyond serving as a checkpoint for proper identification, the introductory meeting is useful to make arrangements concerning working space, schedules, and clerical support to type confirmation requests or perform other tasks under the control of the auditors. At this or another meeting before commencement of the audit, it also is necessary to define the scope of the audit. Some bankers and auditors have approached the audit process as if it were an adversary proceeding. According to this mentality, the auditors try to score as many points as possible as measured by the length and number of items in the final audit report, whereas the bankers being audited try to eliminate every possible item by promises of instantaneous corrections or vehement denials.

A far more sensible attitude toward the audit process is to consider the auditos as management consultants with unlimited investigatory powers. On this basis the bankers being audited should provide, if the auditors are interested, a brief summary of the conditions of the operation, including both strong and weak points. Good managers know their problems and good auditors will find them anyway, so it seems better to clear the air immediately and save everyone's time.

Serious operating deficiencies and past due loans, as well as other problem areas, should be discussed along with the timetable and steps for correction. Based upon such disclosures, a preliminary outline of the audit scope can be drawn up, subject to modification on the basis of further information that may come to light during the audit. Usually at this stage, the auditors request certain basic information that is necessary to aid in the completion of their work. Also, background information on officers and key clerical personnel and a list of names and titles of all staff along with job descriptions should be provided.

Chapter 11 will discuss the central liability ledger in greater detail, but information from this record or its equivalent, as of the date of the commencement of the audit, is a basic requirement for every major audit. With such information, the auditors have at their fingertips summary details of all credit exposure to each customer, arranged by customer, along with amounts of all deposits with the bank. The auditors also should be supplied a copy of the division's or branch's current final plan document and copies of monthly management reports issued since the date of the last audit. Further, the auditors should be given the manager's audit file, which contains past audit reports, replies, and any evidence of actions taken to correct past situations that were the subject of previous audit comments.

During these early meetings, key officers and staff members who will be working with the auditors should be introduced to the auditors. All of the parties involved in the audit should try to assure that all questions and work assignments are funneled through these key persons so that others in the division will be able to continue with regular duties to the maximum extent possible. Occasionally, during the course of an audit, auditors will ask questions that fall outside the area of responsibility or competence of the person being questioned. Then, in an effort to be helpful, incorrect answers or misinformation may be given in response. To minimize the possibility of such occurrences, at the start of each audit all staff should be cautioned to refer questions they cannot answer to supervisors. Reference by the auditors to the job descriptions provided at the beginning of the audit also can be helpful in this regard.

From time to time as logical work units are completed during the audit, short meetings should be held with the auditors to review batches of preliminary or draft comments. If the auditors have received wrong information or been inadvertently misled in their investigations, this is the time to set matters straight. Also, during such sessions, further drafting of the comments agreed upon can be undertaken with a view toward the means and timing for corrective actions. In short, there should be neither surprises to management nor inaccuracies of narrative in the final audit reply.

THE AUDIT REPORT AND FOLLOW-UP

Assuming that the auditors have received promptly the basic information and clerical support needed for their work, that replies to their questions have been accurate, and that all draft comments for the audit report have been reviewed with management, the production of the final audit report should be welcomed by both management and the auditors. Obviously, the auditors consider each completed audit as a major work unit in their normal routine. Management should consider the final report in comparison with previous reports as a measure of its performance and as a list of objectives to be accomplished during the period of the next plan. These objectives would include not only corrective actions but improvements to enhance future operations of the department.

Upon receipt of the final report, a formal reply should be submitted by the head of the division or unit that was audited. Replies to each comment should be brief, stating agreement with the comment and indicating the action to be taken for correction or implementation of the agreed upon improvements. If management does not agree with a comment, the reply is the place to enter management's views into the record, but this should occur only rarely.

At the same time the formal reply is prepared and dispatched, every matter or closely related matter requiring corrective action and implementation or improvements should be written in separate memorandums addressed to appropriate officers. Responsibility for each corrective action or improvement should be given to designated persons and time limits for written evidence of progress should be established. Within these time limits, further reports should be submitted to the division, branch, or unit manager for use in determining whether further steps should be taken or whether the situation may be considered as settled.

Corrective action and improvements usually fall into one of three broad categories involving (1) change in work habits, (2) change in existing written procedures and work, and (3) major change, including preparation of new procedures. When a satisfactory written procedure exists but has not been followed, the person in charge of corrective action should explain the procedure to all parties required to follow it, prepare memorandums stating that reinstruction has been given, and obtain signed copies of such memorandums from each person involved. Copies of all these materials should then be placed in the main file of audit-related materials.

If there is a change in a written procedure, more time is usually required for corrective action and subsequent reinstruction. Copies of related memorandums and the revised procedure should be reviewed by the division head and added to the audit file as well as the procedures manual. It may be necessary for major changes and new procedures to be included in the division plan and handled on a project basis. Monitoring then could occur through the mechanism of the monthly management report, as well as through specific follow-up on the total audit report.

The next event in the audit cycle occurs when a higher level of management reviews the final report and reply of the division or unit that has been audited. Managers who have run a division or other unit and have been through the auditing process usually have learned by experience how to read an audit report. But for those who have not had this or equivalent experience, evaluating the audit report may present problems.

A thick report with long and detailed comments, supplemented by a thorough reply, may lead to the rapid conclusion that serious problems exist. But this is not always the case. Nor does a relatively short report always mean that a clean bill of health has been given. Only one or a few large nonperforming loans could seriously weaken the department and the entire bank. Or records could be in such poor condition that the usual auditing steps could not be completed. Therefore, the only way to properly evaluate the audit report and reply is to deal with the substance and not the form.

Comparisons must be made with previous reports and replies. Considerations must be given to trends over time periods. If the same old problems persist with new problems being added, obviously there has been deterioration, and questions must be asked or action taken. But if old problems have been eliminated and new, more sophisticated improvements are being suggested, this may indicate a positive trend and even substantial progress in implementing new procedures and systems.

Good auditors use responsible judgment in not loading the audit report with more than management can accomplish before the time of the next audit. This does not mean that problem areas are glossed over. Problems are defined, but recommendations are limited to what can be completed reasonably before the next audit. Naturally, this means that the same problems might be mentioned in future reports for action on other aspects, unless management races ahead of projected schedules for correction. Moreover, good auditors should be constantly raising standards and learning new techniques from their own study and experience in auditing other operations. Accordingly, even the best managed division can be improved over time, and the audit process is a convenient and proper method to identify, discuss, agree upon, and carry out such improvements.

BANK CONTROLLER FUNCTION

The accounting or controller's section of the commercial bank often becomes involved in the aftermath of the auditing process. The bank controller is responsible for maintaining the general books and records of the bank and for preparing various financial statements and reports. These reports and especially the bank's financial statements, which must conform with generally accepted accounting principles and be prepared on a basis consistent with previous statements in order to be certified without qualification by the bank's outside auditors, are submitted to shareholders, regulatory authorities, other banks, customers, and, of course, management. Managers at various levels within the bank also require further detailed information and reports from bank records to do their jobs properly.

Accordingly, any changes in procedures that affect the reporting process involve the controller. In addition, in some banks the controller's division is responsible for subsidiary records and perhaps also the preparation and distribution of new or revised written procedures and the development of new accounting systems. Even in those banks that control some subsidiary ledgers and records and handle procedure writing within line units, the controller usually reviews all new or changed procedures. In many countries, the international division also works closely with the controller on tax matters, since taxes involve another form of government reporting.

Therefore, as a general rule, no financial information or reports other than the bank's annual report or quarterly report to shareholders should be given to persons or authorities outside the bank without permission or review by the controller. In foreign branches or other units, where it is not feasible to have preliminary review by the head-office controller, copies of all reports submitted to host country authorities should be sent simultaneously to the head office, and only forms and systems approved in advance by the controller should be used for this purpose.

Taxes involve another area in which specialized personnel, usually reporting to the controller, can assist international managers. Foreign taxes that are withheld or paid by the bank on interest or other earnings may be used as a credit or deduction in some nations to reduce tax liability in the home- or head-office country. To obtain all tax benefits and be able to quote interest rates accurately and competitively, tax experts must follow changes in the tax laws of the head-office country and nations from which the international bank receives earnings.

Furthermore, the definition of what constitutes doing business in a foreign nation usually poses important tax questions for foreign banks. Accounting or legal experts available through the bank's tax section or legal department must be relied upon to make certain that the bank complies with local laws in each country in which it makes loans or conducts other banking activity.

HOUSE COUNSEL AND OUTSIDE COUNSEL

Earlier in this chapter when defining house counsel and outside counsel and discussing internal controls we briefly touched upon some of the functions of these legal experts. Now we are ready to examine these important jobs in a more comprehensive manner. First and foremost, of course, house counsel should be certain that international division personnel, as is true for all others in the bank, are aware of laws and regulations that apply to the conduct of international banking and are complying with them. If house counsel cannot develop sufficient expertise immediately in all of the legal aspects of international banking or stay up to date with changes, help should be enlisted in the form of special or outside counsel to cover international matters.

Just as every bank always should have strong correspondent banking relationships on a continuing basis in each city or country where it conducts business, house counsel should have frequent contact with at least one of the major law firms that specializes in international banking matters. Such a relationship often provides another early warning system for new developments and possible problems, as well as opportunities for the bank. Firms that specialize in legal work relating to international banking generally cover such fields as banking regulations at home and abroad and the legal aspects of international transactions, such as letters of credit, acceptances, funds transfers, and foreign exchange, as well as deposits and loan transactions. Usually these firms have extensive experience directly and through their correspondents in creditors' rights, loan restructurings, and efforts to collect problem loans, including litigation.

In addition, more law firms today are specializing in dealings with particular institutions, such as the Export-Import Bank of the United States or the World Bank Group, including the International Finance Corporation, which has developed a highly successful and a rather unique approach to handling the legal aspects of project financing in developing countries. Further, it is often through specialized international firms that introductions to qualified foreign counsel can be arranged as the bank undertakes business in countries where it has not previously done business.

House counsel also should review and approve all standard forms and documents used within the international division. In foreign offices, these forms and documents will require review by foreign local counsel, and often modifications will be necessary in order to comply with local laws. The house counsel of the larger banks with extensive foreign offices have, in the course of this task, a great opportunity to encourage the development of standardized forms for funds transfers, collections, letters of credit, foreign exchange contracts, and, naturally, loan documentation.

Loan documentation, especially for Eurodollar loans, should start from a basic standard draft document, although tailoring is required for each particular loan. In working with term loan documentation, time can be saved for international division lending officers, house counsel, and outside counsel, if certain standard procedures are followed. After completing the credit approval process, the lending officer responsible for making the term loan should draw up a checklist of requirements for inclusion in the loan documentation, including the loan agreement, any guarantees or other security instruments, and legal opinions.

Items on the checklist then should be divided into negotiable and non-negotiable categories. The lending officer should next consult the bank's standard loan agreement and meet with house counsel to have clauses prepared or modified to cover all the requirements on the checklist. After completion of a revised draft loan agreement, house counsel should send a copy to foreign counsel in the borrower's country for review and comments by local counsel there. This process should be followed regardless of the law chosen to govern the agreements, since even if the law of the bank's country applies, a judgment may have to be enforced locally. Only after agreement on the terms of the loan documents by the lending officer, house counsel, and foreign counsel should negotiations with the borrower and his lawyer be initiated.

Depending upon the complexity of the loan documentation, the amount of the loan, the presence of counsel for the borrower, and the experience of the lending officer, house counsel or foreign counsel or both may be needed in negotiating the loan documentation. House counsel and foreign counsel obviously should be involved when loans are declared in default, accelerated, or enforced. All collection efforts and especially litigation will involve extensive coordination and communication between lending officers, house counsel, and foreign counsel. Special care must be taken when the bank has syndicated portions of the loan to other institutions. In these cases the lead bank generally has a fiduciary duty to the participants, and under the laws of most countries many aspects of the rights and duties of the parties involved in syndicated loans have yet to be clearly defined in detail as the result of laws or court cases.

Before lodging executed agreements for safekeeping under the control of the bank's loan department, house counsel should sign off on a memorandum stating that nonstandard documents have been reviewed and are in satisfactory form and substance for the bank's purposes. At this time the loan department also should review the bank's comprehensive checklist for loan documentation and be satisfied that every necessary document has been submitted on the bank's standard forms, or that this requirement has been waived or modifications have been approved by house counsel. If these procedures are followed, much soul searching and agony will be prevented in the event it is ever necessary to use the loan documentation in litigation to collect any amounts owed to the bank.

Before leaving the subject of bank counsel, it must be stressed again that in most situations no amount of work after the fact can repair the damage that can be done by hastily prepared or unreviewed documents in any area of international banking. Time invested in preventing problems and reviewing transactions beforehand is well spent, since matters are seldom, if ever, resolved in the bank's favor after a transaction involving bank obligations has been entered into or loan proceeds have been disbursed. The bank law department that practices preventive medicine is far happier and less crisis-ridden than house counsel who must constantly handle emergency cases, many of which then require expensive referral to outside counsel.

SELECTING FOREIGN COUNSEL

Use of foreign counsel is so frequent and so critical to success in international commercial banking that several special factors should be taken into account when selecting foreign counsel. From the standpoint of timing, foreign counsel should be chosen, whenever possible, before the bank undertakes any business in a country. House counsel, outside counsel, special international counsel, other foreign counsel in neighboring countries, public accounting firms, bank customers, and correspondent banks in the bank's home country and in the foreign country are all good sources of names and introductions to potential foreign counsel. Law directories and similar reference books can provide factual background on these firms and often list existing clients. However, there is no substitute for visits and personal meetings.

After collecting a reasonable list of names and arranging introductions, house counsel or an international division lending officer, or, if possible, both should visit foreign lawyers in person. International calling officers with responsibility for calling on customers in foreign countries constantly should be meeting new foreign lawyers during trips to call on potential customers. House counsel, likewise, should be meeting foreign counsel during travels or at legal seminars and other meetings, some of which might be held in the head-office country.

In meeting with potential foreign counsel it is important to establish early in any conversation whether or not any conflicts of interest exist. This usually can be accomplished by having each party run through its list of clients that do business internationally. For a bank it is important to listen for the names of potential, as well as actual, customers when a potential foreign lawyer describes the scope of his firm's activity. In larger and more internationally established nations, a segment of the bar often specializes in serving foreign clients.

In smaller countries or nations with limited experience in dealing internationally, it might be necessary to work variously over a period of time with several law firms, since only a few firms in smaller legal communities can afford to specialize in dealing with foreign clients. At the same time, these firms might represent potential or actual local customers who engage in international business. Also, since most law firms tend to be relatively small in many countries and therefore subject to substantial changes in their abilities on the basis of only a few changes in key personalities, it is prudent for the international banker and house counsel to be in frequent contact with several members of the local bar in each country where the bank does business.

Foreign counsel should be able to speak and write effectively the language of the bank's head office. Although specialized calling officers of the bank may be able to converse in local languages with foreign counsel, house counsel and others in the bank's head office may not be language experts. Thus, language ability is important to save translation expense and time, especially on complicated legal matters and cases involving litigation.

Firms with several or many members are usually more suitable than sole practitioners, since travel, time, and distance factors often make it difficult to coordinate busy schedules, and partners or associates can take over and meet with the traveling banker in the absence of others in the firm. Larger foreign law firms tend to have more specialists in the fields with relevance to international business, such as taxation, for example. Further, it generally is preferable to select firms with litigation specialists, all other factors being equal. Although international bankers do not set out to become involved in lawsuits or make problem loans, if difficulties develop, litigation may be necessary. At that point it is expensive and time consuming to obtain another firm and bring its personnel current on a transaction that may have been initiated by another firm.

Between personal visits and work on actual transactions much can be done to keep foreign counsel informed of the bank's activities. Annual and quarterly reports, other bank publications, news releases, and even copies of appropriate internal correspondence should be mailed periodically to foreign counsel. The better any lawyer understands his client, the more likely he will be able to work effectively for a client and protect the bank's interest. It is particularly important to maintain communication when the lawyer and client are many miles apart in different nations and often different cultures.

Finally, in order to avoid any misunderstandings, it is useful for house counsel to establish with foreign counsel, at the time the latter are engaged, the details regarding such matters as fee levels, billing and payment arrangements, and routine reporting requirements for legal work performed. Moreover, all billings and reports should be reviewed by house counsel for consistency and good order. This is particularly useful if, as is customary, the international lending officer has the most frequent day-to-day contact with foreign counsel.

Such a practice enables the officer to work on a day-to-day basis with the lawyer without reference to the question of fees, which can be handled lawyer to lawyer. In establishing the basis for fees with foreign counsel, it is important to allow sufficient time and explanation to cover this point in detail. In some legal systems, lawyers work mainly on certain types of cases on a contingent fee basis, whereas in other systems, billing by the hours of work performed is more common. For the sake of good order, such details should be confirmed in writing before foreign lawyers start to work.

10

Correspondent Bank Personnel

Need for International Correspondents / Characteristics of Correspondent Relationships / Criteria for Selecting Correspondents / History of Typical Relationships / Administering Correspondent Relations / Personnel of Specialized Institutions

U p to now all personnel discussed in this unit, with the exception of outside auditors, bank examiners, and outside counsel referred to in Chapter 9, have been employed within the bank. Even in those outside functions there are counterpart or reciprocal staff at most banks, such as internal auditors and house counsel. The board of directors, other persons on committees mentioned in connection with the direction function in Chapter 6, support function personnel discussed in Chapter 8, and the international division staff discussed in Chapter 7 are all part of the same commercial bank organization, although board or advisory committee members may not be full-time bank employees. Now we turn to consider correspondent bank personnel who are employed by other banks.

This chapter first examines the need for developing correspondents, the general characteristics of correspondent relationships, the criteria used for choosing correspondents, and the usual steps in the historical development of a typical correspondent relationship. Next, the organizational setting for personnel administering correspondent activities is considered. Finally, although they are not correspondents in the exact sense of the term, the role of personnel in certain specialized banking and banking-related institutions is discussed.

These specialized organizations often are instrumental in successfully delivering a complete package of international financing services. Among these specialized institutions are the Export-Import Bank of the United States, the Overseas Private Investment Corporation, and the Foreign Credit Insurance Association in the United States, and the International Finance Corporation of the World Bank Group. Most developed nations and even some developing countries have analogous entities or programs.

Therefore, the theme that unites the topics of this chapter is working together with personnel of other banks or international financial institutions to accomplish the primary objectives of the international commercial banking function. The key to working together in most situations is reciprocity. If business is referred back for business received, the relationship will grow and prosper.

As we have seen in several other areas of this study, although there may be many characteristics common to the domestic function being considered, several unique or distinguishing features characterize the international aspect of the function. This is also true of correspondent banking. But above all, reciprocity dominates this area, since it is the key to a continued relationship and long-range profitability. Volume, as well as quality of transactions, is critical, since it is costly to maintain a network of foreign correspondents.

NEED FOR INTERNATIONAL CORRESPONDENTS

Although a totally domestic bank can grow quite large in its local area without becoming significantly involved with more than a few domestic correspondents, this is not the case when the bank moves out internationally. Any bank doing international business needs numerous foreign correspondents if it is to succeed. At the same time, relationships with other banks in the headquarters country also increase as a result of becoming involved in the Eurocurrency market. Hence, the development of correspondent relationships is one of the earliest and most important tasks of any bank starting to do business internationally. Foreign currency accounts must be established to handle payments and all types of transactions involving payments. As the international bank grows, more correspondents are needed, although emphasis can change as the larger banks establish hundreds or perhaps thousands of foreign offices. Put simply, international banks need other banks, and international banks conduct a great deal of business with other banks.

Probably to a higher degree than in almost any other profession or business, international bankers work together. In a real sense, the international banks of the world form an interlocking network. An unusual occurrence or problem in any part of the grid has, in most cases, an almost instantaneous effect throughout the network. Hence, international bankers are mutually interdependent, often view world developments in the same light, communicate and exchange information with each other frequently, and spend a great deal of time together. The 1979–1981 freeze on Iranian assets by the United States is only one illustration of this phenomenon; almost every banking transaction anywhere in the world between Iran and the United States, from payment orders to term loans, was disrupted by the freeze.

All banks, regardless of size and number of international locations, need international correspondents in order to provide the usual range of international banking services, because delivery of many international services is not complete until someone in another part of the world has been reached or has initiated the transactions involved. Funds transfers, foreign exchange contracts, and collections are a few examples. Even major money center banks with extensive foreign branches, subsidiaries, and affiliates need many correspondents to reach remote corners of the globe. No bank as yet has its own offices in every country, and many nations are so large that even multiple offices in many key cities are not adequate to serve customers' needs in these areas.

In carrying out activities around the world, correspondents conduct several different functions, often simultaneously. Accordingly, correspondent banks and their personnel may be classified as partners, customers, suppliers, or competitors, or sometimes combinations of these functions. The dominant role of each function at any time or for each individual transaction depends upon the stage of historical development of the banks involved, the level of the correspondent relationship between the two banks, and the non-bank customer, if any, in any particular transaction involving the two banks.

For regional or smaller banks with few or no overseas offices, the bank's correspondent banks overseas are key partners in delivery of banking services to and receipt of business from outside the home country. For large banks with locations worldwide, correspondents more often tend to fall into the customer category, although correspondents also are used to deliver services to remote locations or places outside money centers where the home country bank has no direct overseas representation.

If both a bank and its correspondent have the same customer, an element of competition is injected into the picture, although both banks may cooperate to deliver different services or parts of the same service to the customer at home and overseas. Larger banks and those with more developed services and skills in some particular area obviously are those banks most likely to be suppliers of specialized services and techniques for international banking. But any bank, regardless of size or stage of development, can become a supplier by virtue of developing unique services or skills and marketing them effectively.

CHARACTERISTICS OF CORRESPONDENT RELATIONSHIPS

A basic characteristic of correspondent banking is established by the law or set of rules that governs the relationship. Usually, correspondents serve as agents to carry out routine banking activities for each other. Such agent activities, for example, include delivering the proceeds of payment orders and telex payments, cashing or buying drafts, handling incoming and outgoing collections, and confirming, advising, and negotiating letters of credit. In carrying out these and other activities, employees of correspondents must take care to follow instructions exactly, not exceed their authority, and not make unauthorized statements on behalf of the other bank.

Whether involved in exchanging credit, country, or other information, acting as agents, buying services as bank customers, or selling services as suppliers, all correspondent relationships are characterized by one common element, namely, working together in accordance with instructions or previously agreed upon ground rules. These rules may originate in customs and practices that have developed over time to govern almost all correspondent relationships in general, or they may result from special communications between particular banks involving repeated personal visits or calling, discussions, and exchanges of letters, telexes, and other information, including specific written agreements.

With the heaviest volume of transactions being conducted between different locations of the same bank, it is true that correspondents of the larger banking organizations in these same locations may receive a smaller percentage of total business than local banks. However, business between correspondents and the larger banks with dozens or hundreds of foreign offices often grows absolutely after opening of branches, as more transactions are generated between the two countries and the local banks in each location are used to complete delivery of services to the cities outside the main international financial centers of each nation.

Business shifts and the balance between correspondents can be dramatic, however, when a large bank opens its first branch or office in a country and directs all of its other foreign branches and offices to direct business for that country to the new branch. These new units then often can become profitable overnight as other offices of the bank open accounts and direct foreign exchange transactions, payment orders, collections, and letters of credit to the new location, as well as introduce customers and refer lending or other opportunities involving the extension of credit.

On the other hand, whereas larger banks may be opening new branches to build up or round out their foreign network of offices, other banks are starting up or expanding their international activities. These banks need new correspondents and more attention to handle their heavier business volumes, and many banks prefer to devote more effort and a higher standard of care to those correspondent banks that are not likely to become their local competitors in the near future. In addition, many banks of quite large size from different countries for various reasons have not chosen to create extensive foreign branch networks. Their business volumes can be huge and highly profitable for those banks fortunate enough to be their correspondents.

Furthermore, there is a certain logic to this natural process of growth in correspondent banking relationships. In entering a country to do business for the first time, it is common for a bank to obtain basic information about the country, business methods, and local banking practices from another banker, in addition to specific credit information about potential customers, Also, in extending credit for the first time, in most countries the banking industry should be the easiest industry for the inexperienced international lender to understand. Moreover, the new international banker may have previously either met or been introduced to local bankers at gatherings of international bankers or other occasions.

Usually, and especially in developing countries that utilize foreign sources of capital, a correspondent banker will work harder and provide more collateral business to the banks that extend lines of credit in useful amounts. Particularly in smaller countries, some bankers may have more foreign bankers calling on them than they could ever possibly hope to work with economically. Accordingly, obtaining a profitable share of business by developing an effective correspondent banking relationship in such circumstances involves extending a useful amount of credit, building new business to be directed to the correspondent, providing good service, and making frequent calls to maintain and expand close personal ties.

Because of the necessity for correspondents to carry out international services and the time and effort needed to develop and maintain these relationships, correspondent relationships should never be entered into casually or terminated abruptly. Knowledge of each other's operations, based upon exchange of information and personnel, should be at such a level to justify normal credit extension over a long period of time, although most credit extension between banks is on a short-term and transaction-oriented basis. In extreme cases quick action may be necessary to avoid or minimize losses. Although such instances are rare, banking, as each generation of new bankers must relearn, is an industry in which entities are subject to failure and exit from the market in most countries. However, most correspondent relationships involving credit extension are modified over time according to profitability conditions rather than lack of creditworthiness.

In measuring the degree of profitability, it is necessary, however, to take into account income and expenses related to all forms of business between the two institutions. To disregard volumes and sizes of payments, collections, letters of credit, acceptances, foreign exchange contracts, special time deposits, and money market transactions, such as Eurodollars accepted and placed, federal funds bought or sold, and the fees and other benefits from these activities, and measure only advances or funds usage against average balances is not only shortsighted but inaccurate. Business referrals, introductions, and other activities that may be difficult to quantify are other factors needed to complete the periodic profitability review of any correspondent relationship.

In some banking systems outside the United States, standby lines or funding facilities to provide dollars to banks lending in dollars are required by local banking authorities to cover the contingency of capital controls or a breakdown in the Eurodollar market. Obviously, the total of such commitments for all banks must be kept to some controlled limit, since if conditions warranted funding under any facility, all such facilities could be used simultaneously. These standby lines or funding commitments are usually granted on a basis of from one to three years. For U.S. banks, the provision of such facilities to their correspondents for a commitment fee can be an additional source of income and a useful way to maintain a closer correspondent relationship.

Although not always true, many developing nations have established a pattern of assuming some sort of responsibility for troubled local banks in order to preserve the credit standing of the nation and its institutions in the international market. Orderly liquidation with government supervision, as opposed to abrupt collapse, is at least the minimum position even for countries that tend to let banking entities enter and leave the market freely. Although government support is meant to protect depositors as well as the nations's reputation, and accordingly should not be used to allow either lower banking standards or less care in selecting correspondents, such support under certain circumstances can be documented in many countries. Hence, it is a factor to be given some weight when considering extension of credit to banks in such countries.

In any event, bankers usually are the first to become aware of or suspect problems with other banks. The style and client mix of overaggressive or improperly controlled banks can be important warning signals to experienced bankers. Even close observation of the conduct of routine day-to-day international transactions can give valuable indications about the quality of a bank's procedures or management methods. For these reasons, foreign exchange traders, other money market personnel, and operations officers of the international division are important sources for judging a correspondent's conduct. They should be consulted periodically and pass information about observation of unusual situations or significant variations in business patterns and styles to their supervisors and officers responsible for extension of credit. Officers of a bank have at least a moral duty, most bankers believe, to inform managers of their correspondents of suspected irregularities, especially in the foreign exchange area where abuses sometimes can be detected more readily by fellow foreign exchange dealers in other banks than by persons within the same bank.

In summary, international correspondents are indispensable. Also, with persistence in development and consistency in performance, correspondent banking relationships can be not only mutually profitable but also relatively free of major problems. If serious problems cannot be corrected or eliminated with reasonable effort, obviously, selection of a new correspondent is warranted. But most well-thought-out correspondent relationships over the test of time grow to the benefit of both bankers and their other customers.

CRITERIA FOR SELECTING CORRESPONDENTS

Selection of correspondents is based upon the internal policies of the banks involved, especially regarding extension of credit, the volume of activities between any two banks on the basis of historical, economic, and political factors, trade patterns, and the personalities of the individuals and institutions involved in conducting the particular relationship in question. As in any relationship involving extension of credit or potential extension of credit, the basic working tool of the banker is a properly maintained credit file. Although it is necessary to regularly obtain, spread, and analyze financial statements of foreign correspondents, it also is helpful to have on hand current annual reports for leading banks in each country where the bank does business or plans to do business, even though they are not correspondents.

Brief review of these banks' annual reports by lending and account officers before filing often yields valuable insight into the activities of the correspondent's competitors and thus facilitates comparison and better understanding of the correspondent. New banking developments are often mentioned in these annual reports along with extensive coverage of general, economic, and related political changes in the bank's market areas. Also, and sometimes more importantly, having current financial statements at hand, ready to be spread and analyzed in detail when needed, frequently enables a bank to take prompt advantage of a new business opportunity involving extension of credit to a new banking relationship, such as a confirmation of a letter of credit issued in favor of an important customer. For these reasons, international bankers are assiduous collectors and readers of annual reports of foreign banks.

Most banks of any size internationally mail out 1,000 or more annual reports each year, and the larger banks mail out many thousands of copies. As in other areas of correspondent relationships, reciprocity applies, and receipt of an annual report should prompt a return mailing of the recipient's annual report if this had not been done already. Follow-up lists should be used in the event that annual reports of correspondents are not received promptly, so that requests can be made for any missing financial statements in order to process on a timely basis regular annual reviews of credit facilities being extended. Annual statements should be sent to key personnel who will oversee the line renewal process in the correspondent banks.

The next level of activity in the selection process, beyond exchange of annual reports between two banks, usually is the initiation of a regular calling program. Most banks with established calling programs try at a minimum to visit each other at least once a year. If a correspondent relationship exists between two institutions and the volume of business warrants, more frequent visits may occur. During such visits the correspondent's competitors in the same city may be visited briefly for the same reasons that the banks read the annual reports of their correspondent's competitors. Moreover, the question of one bank serving many competing banks in the same city arises frequently and must be settled acccording to the policies of each institution involved.

Usually, stronger links can be forged between two banks if one bank is not also working with the other's competitors. Most bankers are quite open with each other, and the alliances between different institutions are well known to all parties. Yet, circumstances frequently arise, especially in countries with only a few banking entities, where choices for correspondents are quite limited. In particular, in the communist or socialist nations of Eastern Europe and elsewhere, one bank, usually designated as the foreign trade bank, frequently is the only choice and hence is literally everyone's correspondent.

When business is directed between banks by the bank's customers at either end of a transaction, occasions arise for using different correspondents in the same location. Therefore, the rule is that multiple relationships in the same country or city may develop as long as the parties are aware of the circumstances, business volumes warrant it, and the relationship is mutually profitable. All banks should handle all business on a confidential basis, and business between banks is no exception. However, situations arise every day when a choice for directing selected business between more than one similarly situated correspondent must be made. Then all of the previously mentioned factors come into play along with the factor of reciprocity, which will be discussed shortly in greater detail.

After the exchange of annual reports and the start of personal visits, the strategy for developing a network of international correspondents is simple to define but almost always difficult to implement. The goal is to find compatible and reliable working partners or, in short, a "good fit" in every city or area of the world where the bank does business. Implementation of this strategy takes a great deal of study, collection of materials, travel, and time. Obviously, links should be established first with nations where the greatest volumes of the bank's activity are being directed.

For regional or smaller banks, at first it may be expedient to conduct all overseas banking activity through a larger domestic correspondent. However, as business volume increases, it soon becomes apparent that it will be more convenient to have a direct relationship in one or more key cities overseas. At the time it is decided to establish direct relationships instead of continuing indefinitely to work through a more established domestic correspondent, some thought must be given to the qualities sought in new correspondents.

Large overseas correspondents, especially in countries with nationwide banking, may be more convenient to work with for payment order and money transfer services, as well as collections and letters of credit. These larger banks usually have huge branch networks, reaching every area of their nations, and uniform and efficient internal systems. The smaller bank, on the other hand, may not represent a proportionately important share of business to the large correspondent, even when an account with important balances in the eyes of the smaller bank is maintained with the larger correspondent.

Nor is there likely to be a reverse flow of business and introductions from the larger correspondent to the smaller bank, especially if the larger correspondent already has long-standing relationships with larger institutions in the smaller bank's nation. Therefore, closer relationships usually can be established with correspondents of more equal size and stage of development. If the small bank picks a smaller or more regional correspondent for a particular nation, that correspondent can use its own domestic correspondents to carry out transactions to the far corners of that country.

Yet, all banks have some successful relationships with banks much smaller or larger than theirs. Much of the success in building correspondent bank relationships results from the chemistry between the people in the two banking organizations. If the relationship works and is profitable, these are the results that count. Sometimes it may be expedient to start an initial account relationship in a country with the most friendly and eager of several large, well-known, and creditworthy banks. With time and more travel, if the initial fit does not seem proper and other institutions seem more suitable, a second relationship can be started with others. In countries where there is significant activity, two or three correspondents may be needed.

Moreover, in certain nations without nationwide banking, it may be necessary to select correspondents in each of several important cities in the nation. Should the needs and volume of activity for a particular customer justify it, accounts can be established for handling a specific flow of repetitive transactions, whether they be payments, collections, or letters of credit. Therefore, it is reasonable for most banks to exchange signatures and authentication documents with several banks in each country to obtain good direct communications and adequate geographic coverage.

HISTORY OF TYPICAL RELATIONSHIPS

After some study of the banks and banking system of the country in question, a collection of annual reports to start files on different banks, and visits or other opportunities to meet several bankers from the location under study, the first step of a typical correspondent relationship is to exchange signature lists and establish authentication arrangements. Exchange of books or microfiche lists containing the sample signatures of persons authorized to sign instructions to carry out international transactions permits signatures on instruction documents to be examined and compared with the samples to verify the authenticity of instructions. Drafts, payment orders, letters of credit, ordinary letters giving instructions, and other instruments all must be signed by persons whose sample signatures are in possession of the correspondent bank receiving the instructions.

Authentication arrangements consists of the mutual exchange of code materials to permit telex, cable, or voice messages to be confirmed by use of codes. Thus, these authenticating codes take the place of signatures in situations where signatures cannot be used. Because of the potential for misuse if in the wrong hands, signature lists and code materials are kept under tight security, removed by authorized personnel only when needed, and put back under security immediately after use.

After the establishment of authenticating arrangements and exchange of control documents, the two banks involved now have a secure means for communication. Actual transactions can be conducted by means of reimbursement through accounts with other banks. When sufficient transaction volume builds, a direct account may be opened by one of the banks with the other. Volume can be monitored easily by the international division or through the bank units that receive and reconcile bank statements. If two accounts, one with each bank by the other, exist, the relationship has developed to a level of reciprocal accounts. By now, of course, not only transaction messages but annual reports and information on economic, political, and banking developments are flowing between the banks. Credit information on customers or potential customers in each bank's market area is being exchanged, and regular visits between bank officers and perhaps senior management are occurring.

Before or after development of account relationships, but after exchange of control documentation, banks may work together in areas involving the extension of credit. Handling payment orders and confirming letters of credit may involve credit extension. Either such transactions must be approved by lending officers, item by item, or a regular facility or line must be established for the usual international transactions. The existence of a line permits authorized personnel to conduct transactions that meet the conditions of the line. If the banks decide to enter into foreign exchange contracts with each other, both banks will need to set up foreign exchange lines. Should the banks decide to invest excess Eurodollars or other Eurocurrencies with each other, placement limits or lines for such activity must be approved in accordance with each bank's procedures for authorization of credit, also.

Beyond these usual lines for international transactions such as foreign exchange and Eurodollars or Eurocurrencies, other, more specialized links involving extension of credit may be established. For example, foreign banks operating branches in the United States may deal in federal funds, in which case fed funds lines might be set up, since this is another market where reciprocity is customarily involved. Banks also buy each other's bankers' acceptances from time to time for investment of excess short-term funds, necessitating another line for this type of credit extension, and a non-U.S. bank may wish to have a facility to draw drafts on its U.S. correspondent, which accepts such instruments and thus creates bankers' acceptances, another type of credit extension. Since all these different types of transactions involve either different degrees of risk or different departments or both, at each bank extending credit, separately worded lines are needed for each activity. Obviously, economies of scale are achieved in processing such line approvals together. This process is described more fully in Chapter 12 with the topic of annual reviews. Samples of credit extension to banks are shown in Appendix E.

Credit extension need not end at this stage, however. Beyond the usual short-term money market, trade, and foreign exchange activities, it is not unusual for banks, especially from nations that are net importers of capital funds or short of foreign exchange, to borrow term funds from their correspondents. Long-term placements to deposits are found, as are direct term loans either with or without mention of the borrowing bank's customers. If the borrowing bank names its customers reborrowing from it, the term loan or facility is often referred to as a repass loan or repass line. Repayment by the customer is not a condition for repayment to the correspondent of such loans, of course, but the identification of the ultimate customer provides better understanding of the specific purpose for borrowing the funds. This process may lead to new customers for the lending bank, provided the borrowing bank is agreeable.

Often, customers of a bank may be considering trade or investment activities in a correspondent's country. Introductions of such customers not only provide new business opportunities for the correspondent, but maximize the chances for the introducing bank to maintain a greater degree of influence with the customer going outside of the home country. Both banks under these circumstances usually work together closely to provide a specific level of service to the mutual customer. This involves exchange of credit information, transfer of funds, and facilitation of guarantees, if necessary, among other matters. Examples of this types of activity are the waves of U.S. investment into Europe during the late 1950s and 1960s and the reverse wave of Western Europe, Japanese, and other foreign investment into the United States, which started to increase dramatically during the 1970s.

The German correspondent of a U.S. bank may have a great interest, for example, in having its customer's new U.S. company bank with the German bank's U.S. correspondent rather than do business with the U.S. branch of a competing German bank when the German correspondent has no nearby U.S. operation. With the proliferation of foreign-owned banking operations in the United States, this example in fact is becoming quite typical not only with European but also Asian, South American, and other banks.

ADMINISTERING CORRESPONDENT RELATIONS

The organizational pattern for handling foreign correspondent banking relationships has been changed rapidly in recent years and parallels to some extent the evolution in organizing to serve the needs of specialized industry or customer groups, including domestic correspondent banks. Historically, in most banks foreign correspondents fell within the province of the geographic areas of international divisions. Within geographic areas, the country desks handled correspondent, government, corporate, and some personal banking customers on the basis of the domicile of the customer. For example, whether they were individuals or institutions, all of a bank's customers located in France dealt with the French desk of the European unit, and so on, country by country.

With increasing specialization in serving government, corporate, and even personal customer needs in many banks, some banks began to consider organizing specialized units of separate correspondent banking officers. The postwar growth of the foreign exchange and Eurodollar markets, with attendant need for numerous bank lines and more voluminous credit workloads, further prodded the decision makers in this direction. Accordingly, during the early 1960s several of the largest international banks established separate correspondent banking units, usually starting with their European banking business. Because of the large number of money center plus regional banks in the United States as a result of U.S. banking laws, many foreign banks have developed special units to handle U.S. or North American banking relationship, since some group Canadian and U.S. business together.

Almost any bank that has a sufficient number of foreign correspondents, including even smaller regionals that do not organize by specialized industries, can gain some immediate economies of scale by organizing some of their international correspondent banking for separate staff to handle. Specialized knowledge of banking laws, accounting practices, the common skiiis for analyzing bank financial statements, and bank management fit together conveniently with record keeping for reciprocal business and the voluminous credit processing for virtually identical types of credit extension and services involved.

Although there may be some trade-off as a result of partially duplicated travel schedules by officers responsible for geographic areas, even this can be minimized if the correspondent banking unit staff members stay mainly at home to receive foreign bankers and make only a few well-planned trips each year to major money centers, such as London and Tokyo. As an alternative, with close coordination and proper preparation, geographic area officers in some banks can handle much, if not all, of the foreign calling for the specialized correspondent unit. With adjustments in reciprocal business flows and account balances by one central unit and constant personal attention, it may be possible to optimize the profitability of all relationships and, hence, increase total profitability. As part of this process, it is imperative that the correspondent bank unit have a good system of collecting and preparing reliable summaries of all data measuring activity with each correspondent.

This data should include activity under all lines such as current outstandings, average outstandings, high and low points, number of individual transactions, and the average size of each transaction. Since different lines are usually administered by different units of the bank, the collection task can be quite formidable unless data processing systems and standard procedures are used. However, only with such information, including, of course, account balances, incoming and outgoing collection statistics, and other similar data from outside the credit line data base, can an accurate and complete profitability analysis be prepared. Without a thorough profitability analysis built up from the various components of each relationship, it is dificult, if not impossible, to know what business flows to change so as to improve profitability. Also, without such an analysis, it is difficult to convince a correspondent to increase business, change patterns, or bear higher charges.

In adjusting business flows to maximize profitability, it is essential to have adequate coordination between the officers in charge of the correspondent banking function and the officers responsible for operations activities, such as money market transactions, collections, letters of credit, and funds transfers. On the basis of statistics for incoming business from all banks in a particular country, many banks periodically redirect their outgoing business for each country. Thus, to an extent not inconsistent with specific customer instructions, geographic proximity, and operating constraints, the bank that sends the greatest volume of business for a month or calendar quarter will be scheduled to receive the greatest share of outgoing business for a like period.

To simplify operating instructions and stagger workloads for accounting and subsequent account reconcilement work, some banks direct all undesignated transactions for a day or week to the same bank in one city. Correspondent banking staff must make certain that planned changes in patterns are communicated, fit into such schedules in each operating section, and are followed by staff, who in the heat of battle may overlook such modifications. During visits between correspondent bankers, the business volumes are discussed and compared in the context of reciprocity, profitability, credit extension, and any other special situations relevant to the relationship.

Also, during visits and by means of written materials, correspondent banking personnel constantly exchange ideas about new opportunities for profit, on the basis of new services, customers, or geographic areas, and about potential dangerous activities and new world trouble spots. This aspect of correspondent relationship is intangible in the sense of being hard to quantify in terms of profit or expense. However, there can be no doubt in the mind of any experienced international banker that this is an invaluable benefit. Many a banker has been saved by timely warnings or put on the early trail of excellent business leads by foreign correspondent bankers.

PERSONNEL OF SPECIALIZED INSTITUTIONS

This chapter is the most appropriate place in our study to mention the personnel of various specialized organizations, whose services complement the activities of the international commercial bank even though they are not part of the correspondent network. It is important to remember that although these institutions may seek the goodwill and close cooperation of the commercial banker, in most cases they are not directly dependent upon the commercial bank for their profitability. Since many are government-owned agencies, maximizing profits or earning any profit may not be a priority or even a goal of these entities, which were created and exist to serve other constituencies.

Understanding this situation is the key to working with the personnel of these other organizations, which are often slow to respond to both opportunities and potential danger, especially in areas involving extension of credit. In most transactions involving such institutions, another constituent almost always ranks higher than the commercial bank, which is often perceived by these institutions as overly concerned with earning a profit and too exacting with regard to credit standards and market practices.

Export finance institutions of many nations, including the Export-Import Bank of the United States (Eximbank), sometimes fall within this category. Creation of exports is the overriding justification for these government-owned agencies, and Eximbank, for example, must devote a considerable portion of its limited personnel resources to fight periodically for its survival at the hands of the U.S. Congress. Eximbank's rates are low and terms are long. Country relationships rank high as a priority on the basis of perceived long-run, U.S. strategic and foreign policy interests, and delays in repayment or default cause nowhere near the problems or pressures that emanate from the U.S. commercial bank regulatory process, for example.

Neither is new business as urgent, nor ultimate loan documentation at some of these institutions as detailed as most commercial bankers would like. With low interest rates, there are usually more customers than resources, and lending is based more upon credit allocation than upon long-term business development considerations. Commercial bankers are under pressure to conclude transactions, develop customer relationships, and produce income streams. These relationships for the commercial banker involve close administration of loans from the standpoint of defaults, covenants, and applying pressures to constantly protect the commercial bank. Eximbank, on the other hand, sometimes is more content to conclude a transaction and, barring negative long-term trends in a nation, let nature take its course. This does not mean that Eximbank's loan loss record is bad; far from it. In fact, it is the envy of almost any international commercial banker.

However, Eximbank personnel are not impelled to be closely involved in their customer relationships. Dangers and weak credits are often first spotted by commercial bankers, initiative for corrective action usually must be taken by commercial bankers, and Eximbank participates and approves proposed measures on a timetable and with an attitude consistent with its priority of working to cause new exports to flow. Eximbank involvement in any transaction usually lags as soon as the exports flow. Commercial bankers, on the other hand, work continuously to build account balances, seek to finance new transactions for the customer, whether or not they involve exports from a particular country, and generally increase their involvement with the customer over time. Eximbank by the nature of its activities does not become interested to any great extent again until another export transaction looms on the horizon.

However, U.S. and, increasingly, foreign bankers must work with Eximbank (or its counterparts in other nations) in certain cases or lose business, because many nations through similar government agencies compete for the same export business. If the commercial bank does not stand by its customer and work effectively with the export agency to develop and complete a competitive total package, another bank may disrupt the relationship with its customer. Under these circumstances, large exporters often work more eagerly and directly with export agencies than commercial bankers. Furthermore, the large multinational corporations usually have more sophisticated project finance experts than the smaller exporters. The smaller exporters in turn tend to work through their commercial bankers, since they often cannot afford the time and effort to deal with Eximbank directly.

Overseas Private Investment Corporation (OPIC) and similar development institutions work on still a different set of criteria. OPIC, for example, is an outgrowth of the U.S. foreign aid effort and its activities are closely related to U.S. foreign policy goals, although over the last decade or so it has evolved into a more autonomous organization than it was originally. Accordingly, OPIC is primarily interested in encouraging U.S. direct investment in selected overseas nations. It accomplishes this objective by providing direct loans, guarantees, and insurance coverage for such events as war, nationalization, and inconvertibility to projects with equity investment by U.S. nationals.

OPIC is relatively small by international standards and has political appointees at the highest levels. Over the years its policies and personnel have been subject to somewhat rapid change, and it must battle periodically for charter renewal with the U.S. Congress as Eximbank must do. Under these circumstances, the main problem encountered by commercial bankers in dealing with OPIC is unpredictability. If projects concide with particular OPIC and U.S. foreign policy goals at the moment, joint efforts can be quite successful. However, because of the need to spread its risk, coupled with its relatively small size, a continuous pattern of operation in the same country is difficult to develop. Accordingly, long-term corroboration is not easy, although some U.S. companies have financed a series of similar activities in different countries, with successful results.

The International Finance Corporation of the World Bank Group (IFC) exists to encourage the development process in less developed countries by working with private, as opposed to government, investors from all World Bank member nations. Typically, IFC projects fit in with World Bank priorities and long-range development plans. Thus, IFC is almost always on the cutting edge of developing private activities in the emerging industries in less developed countries. Planning from all aspects, including technical, marketing, and financial, is thorough and careful, and legal documentation probably ranks as the best of its kind in the world.

Few IFC projects have failed, and IFC staff are highly qualified and represent nationals from every area of the globe. Yet, IFC is more team oriented and effective than most commercial banks in the field of project finance for the countries where it works. Unfortunately, not enough commercial bankers have worked with IFC over the years, although many multinational corporations have worked with IFC personnel, some repeatedly on various new projects. With recent expansion of IFC's capital base without a concomitant increase in staff, IFC is seeking to work more closely with commercial bankers. A large challenge for IFC staff will be to maintain quality in project execution and not dilute their necessarily high standards as their activities expand over the coming years. Most commercial bankers have yet to discover IFC and could gain not only important new customers but valuable knowledge and experience in the field of project finance by working with IFC.

Because of program and policy changes and a constant parade of new projects throughout the world, it is necessary for commercial bankers to maintain close contact with the export banks and foreign investment agencies of their own and other nations, as well as the World Bank Group, especially the IFC, and regional development banks, such as the Inter-American Development Bank. A continuous calling program and reading of the annual reports, news releases, and other publications of these entities are required to be informed adequately to assist customers and consider participating in significant new projects involving international financing and commercial banking services. Nor should possible money market and deposit relationships be overlooked in dealing with these institutions. Most need deposit accounts at commercial banks to collect and disburse funds and conduct foreign exchange transactions, and short-term investment of excess cash is often directed toward commercial banks that have supported their programs, assuming rates and other terms meet market conditions.

PART III

Procedures

11

Operations-Related Procedures

Procedures, Systems, Reports, and Controls / Administrative Functions / Chart of Accounts and Procedures Manual / Central Liability Ledger / Foreign Currency Accounting and Limits / Funding International Loans

E arlier chapters of this book have studied the organizational structure, services, planning, and personnel involved in international commercial banking. From planning, people receive the direction for creating, selling, and supplying various international services. Procedures, related materials, and work methods, as discussed in this chapter, are the tools created under management direction for use in delivering services and maintaining control of international functions.

Procedures and related work methods in the broadest sense include individual procedures and collections of procedures, which usually are referred to as procedures manuals, as well as systems, reports, and controls. Charts of accounts are included in procedures manuals, and systems include accounting systems, which produce reports. However, the concept of operations-related procedures involves more than bookkeeping or accounting.

In fact, the management of the administrative functions involved in these operations-related activities usually determines the success or failure of the commercial bank's entire international effort. Lending or account officers concentrate their efforts on working with existing customers and developing new business, whereas individual operations sections deliver various individual services, such as foreign exchange or letters of credit. Yet, all of this effort must be harnessed together, coordinated, directed, and controlled for the international division to succeed.

This chapter defines the distinctions between procedures, systems, reports, and controls, deals with how these tools are created and used and how responsibilities are organized in this area, and explores in detail several important international banking tools, namely, the central liability record and the foreign exchange accounting system. In addition, controlling foreign exchange exposure and funding international loans are discussed.

Chapter 12 then deals with credit-related procedures, which also could be administered by the same unit of the division that is responsible for operations-related procedures functions. Although this may be the case in a few banks with new or limited international business, credit-related procedures usually are administered separately within the lending or geographic part of most international divisions. Chapter 13 completes the procedures unit of this book with a survey of office management, which involves general techniques and routines applicable throughout the commercial bank international division.

PROCEDURES, SYSTEMS, REPORTS, AND CONTROLS

Procedures in the widest sense of this term as used in this chapter cover not only individual procedures and procedures manuals but also systems, reports, and controls. On the other hand, in the narrow sense international division procedures are written instructions or descriptions for carrying out routine international functions. These functions would include using the various international division accounts, processing series of individual customer-related transactions such as collections, international funds transfers, and foreign exchange, handling bookkeeping and other record keeping, and preparing reports.

Procedures should be written, approved by bank management, indexed, and collected in a loose-leaf book to facilitate future changes. Collections of written procedures are called procedures manuals, which are described in further detail in a later section of this chapter.

Systems in this study refer to written procedures and related accounting or other records that are used to accomplish bookkeeping or other record-keeping functions. For example, the central liability ledger is a system involving application of a written procedure to enter certain information on the bank's accounting records so as to monitor total credit extensions in accordance with certain classifications. As another example, a bank's credit approval system consists in following written procedures to prepare and collect certain documents, which are sent to designated officers for making credit decisions.

Reports are written documents circulated on a scheduled basis to provide information to persons directly involved, indirectly involved, or totally uninvolved in the origination of such information. Reports help the people who receive them to better manage or control the activity reported upon or else to utilize the information reported in their own activities, such as business development. In international banking, as in any other organized activity, if reports are not used and therefore are not needed, they should be discontinued. Directions for the format, preparation, and distribution of reports usually are included in the procedures manual. Information from accounting systems or other records is used to prepare reports. Reports may be prepared manually by taking selected information from the bank's records or by word processing machines, mechanical bookkeeping machines, or computers, which print out reports on paper or microfiche.

Controls consist of regular reports, steps, or checks on a periodic or surprise basis that determine whether procedures are being followed and systems properly used. Controls usually are written as procedures or parts of procedures and are evidenced by reports or other records to indicate that the steps or checks have been performed. Chapter 9 discussed controls, ranging from daily or less frequent audits or checks performed within international division units to broader checks and balances involving other parts of the bank and specialized internal and outside personnel. Account reconcilement obviously plays an important role in this entire area of controls.

The creation and use of procedures manuals, systems, reports, and controls require special personnel and careful management attention, because procedures and systems change from time to time to keep pace with the changing requirements of the international division. Some reports, such as those included in the monthly management report, which was discussed in Chapter 4, relate to the budget and planning process. Furthermore, controls must be described in the procedures manual and changed when procedures and systems are modified on the basis of feedback from both the auditing and planning processes.

The operations sections, lending or account units and administrative parts of the international division, all deal with procedures, systems, reports, and controls. Because some organizations use an accounting and procedures manual that is mainly applicable to foreign branches or other separate operations or to the delivery of and accounting for nonloan services, sometimes the idea develops that only foreign branch or operations personnel should be concerned with procedures and systems. This attitude is dangerous. All international personnel, including lending and account staff, must understand thoroughly and use properly all applicable procedures, systems, reports, and controls.

ADMINISTRATIVE FUNCTIONS

Having distinguished between procedures, systems, reports, and controls and agreed that creation and use of these tools are indispensable for a successful international division, it is now necessary to determine which parts of the commercial bank or international division units should be responsible for the functions relating to these tools. In theory at least, it should be possible in some banks to have a separate section of the bank outside the international division write procedures. A section to prepare methods and procedures might exist in the controller's or accounting department of the bank, for example. Systems could be designed by accounting or computer experts, and the bank's internal auditors could tell the international unit what reports and controls are necessary.

This arrangement would leave all international personnel free of procedures-related duties to concentrate their efforts on sales and delivery of specific services from letters of credit to loans. Unfortunately, this theory does not hold up in practice in most banks. Many banks do not have specialized and experienced international personnel in their methods and procedures units, even if they have such units. Other banks have no units of this type. The accounting staff of some banks may be concerned mainly with the bank's general ledger and reports to outside agencies and regulators. Especially in regional banks, the bank's controller may be satisfied to leave detailed, subsidiary record keeping for foreign currency accounts to the international division. Computer programmers must be given detailed explanations and work closely with internationally experienced personnel. Under these circumstances, some international division staff must be involved with procedures and systems design and modifications to some extent at almost all times.

In addition, procedures, systems, reports, and controls must be related to the planning process and monitoring the plan by means of monthly management reports. The preparation of the plan, including the budget, and the monthly reports can be almost a full-time task for several persons even in a relatively small international unit. Furthermore, feedback from the audit process involves implementation of corrective action and new methods that are closely related to procedures, systems, reports, and controls.

For these reasons, in most banks it is expedient to establish within the international division a separate section or several sections staffed with qualified personnel to handle preparation and implementation of procedures, systems design, and work on computer programming or with computer programmers. This section or one of the several sections in the larger international division unit also can be responsible for planning, budgeting, monitoring the plan, supervising preparation and distribution of reports, and application of various controls.

Staff in these same sections also might be assigned responsibility for various housekeeping functions related to premises for foreign offices, capital appropriation requests, equipment, furniture and fixtures, and stationery, supplies, and similar items. These activities comprise the administration function, which was described in Chapter 1, and parallel the geographic or lending and account administration function and the operations component of the international division. This general administration function concept includes almost everything other than directly dealing with customers, running the operations sections that provide funds transfer, collections, letters of credit, and similar services, and carrying out strictly daily routines, such as bookkeeping and communications.

Depending upon the size of the international operation, these administrative duties may be concentrated in one relatively small section or diffused among different specialized staff units that may parallel each other to some extent on the organization chart. In the smaller organization, internal control functions, as discussed in Chapter 9, can be easily combined with the procedures and systems function, since the personnel in this section are usually completely independent from other parts of the international department. Other duties for this section might include revaluation of foreign currency accounts to obtain monthly profits or losses for foreign exchange, and similar functions, where independence from the rest of the division or unit is required.

Almost every bank takes great care in selecting account officers and foreign office managers. Most also have learned from experience the importance of quality operations personnel to handle the business generated by the account officers. But only the most successful institutions have extended their efforts to the administrative functions, which are vital to the entire international organization. The administrative area that is responsible for operations-related procedures and controls is indeed the key ingredient for the successful international unit. Unfortunately for the long-range success of many banks, it is often the most neglected area. Its absence or disregard can become readily apparent within a few years, at most. Frequent operating errors, necessitating extra time for investigations, correcting entries, refunds, and apologies, as well as lengthy and detailed audit and examination reports with serious substantive comments, often indicate absence of procedures, systems, reports, and controls.

Also, in the smaller international organization, where most of the procedures and control functions can be tightly grouped, the first-level position in this area of the international unit can be an ideal training ground for other positions in the division or unit. Seasoned officers in this area with proper credit and operations experience often make ideal candidates for managing foreign offices. In larger banks, the same results can be achieved by rotating selected officers or future officers through the administrative area, and experienced personnel with foreign duty usually can make immediate contributions of significance to the organization upon return to the head office by placement in the administrative area.

CHART OF ACCOUNTS AND PROCEDURES MANUAL

Perhaps the easiest way to understand the function and importance of the procedures manual is to try to visualize an international commercial banking unit without one. Few international operations can operate successfully in the long run without written procedures. Often, low staff turnover, steady repeat business, and a dominant market position can mask the absence of written procedures. But when change occurs, developments can be overwhelming.

Without a procedures manual, all directions and instructions are given verbally. As in the age before written history, work methods are passed from person to person. Key people with seniority and good memories become the walking encyclopedias of expertise in their areas. When the auditors arrive periodically, they, too, perform their work against this verbal backdrop or their own accumulated knowledge of how they believe the department or section should run.

But should staff turnover increase, large losses occur, repeated errors of a similar nature be noticed, or even rapid expansion with a change in key staff take place, the operation may flounder, and more questions about work methods will be asked from outside the division than can be answered readily by the staff available.

One of the best ways to obtain information and determine priorities for preparing procedures is by examining accounts to which clerical errors or differences are charged. All amounts required to correct errors should be charged to one account or related subaccounts. One of the first procedures to be written should require that error-correcting entries be processed only after certain authorized staff have reviewed and approved the circumstances of each error. Written explanations of the origin of all errors should be documented in brief memorandums. As a monthly internal audit, a designated employee, usually in the procedures or control section of the division, should review all entries to the errors account and make certain that approvals are in order and that explanatory memorandums exist for each entry. Then the memorandums should be examined for patterns, which could indicate the need for new procedures. Often human errors or matters calling for reinstruction of staff cannot be remedied by writing or revising procedures. However, in many cases, clear patterns emerge or point to particular types of transactions or even sections of the division that need attention from the standpoint of procedures.

Other internal memorandums, as well as audit reports and management replies to audit reports, should be accumulated to become the basis for new or revised procedures. Even copies of routine correspondence may contain the raw material of future procedures. All of these documents should be collected and sorted by topics. From these items, a rough index or outline can be constructed. A typical index of general subjects for an international division procedures manual is shown in Appendix D.

There is no standard requirement for the contents of an international procedures manual, but most manuals contain the chart of accounts, account descriptions, and the basic routine for the standard international operations, such as funds transfers, foreign exchange, collections, and letters of credit.

The backbone of the procedures manual is the chart of accounts, which is a collection of account descriptions. Every international operation has or can easily prepare a listing of the general ledger accounts that it uses when passing daily entries. Often in this age of computers, an index of account titles must exist with identifying account numbers. Using this or some other listing as a starting point, each account should be defined in writing. This definition should include the use of the account, reference to related accounts, how to use the account by making entries in the account, how to relieve the account, and which persons are authorized and not authorized to use the account. If repeated errors of a similar nature have been experienced, the description could include negative instructions with regard to such transactions and refer to the titles and numbers of the proper accounts. When such a chart of accounts is made available to personnel preparing debit and credit tickets or entries, errors obviously should be reduced and reversing entries minimized.

To supplement the chart of accounts and the collection of correspondence and memorandums and fill in the bare spots of the rough outline for the growing procedures manual, notes from personnel interviews may be used. Key staff, including those walking encyclopedias, and especially experienced clerks who know their jobs well, can explain their work. Others then can write these descriptions for review and comment, if the officers and clerks themselves cannot produce first-draft, written descriptions.

One person or group should be given responsibility for collecting and arranging the chart of accounts and draft procedures. If the bank has a procedures section, all materials should be referred to it for clearance with other departments involved and for final shaping into a standard format. If no such section or department exists, these steps should be performed by the assigned international personnel, and, with time and indexing, a partial procedures manual should emerge. As new procedures are added and existing procedures revised, this manual should serve as a reference work, an auditing standard, and a training tool.

For most banks, the manual or at least parts of it can be used as a training source for general programs or as instruction material for specific job orientation. If used for training purposes, only relevant parts of the manual should be distributed under careful supervision. Control functions for use in auditing should be separated from routine descriptions, and portions should be distributed only to those persons who need to know this information to perform their jobs.

All copies and sections of the manual should be controlled to avoid its contents being misused or falling into unauthorized hands. Usually, a system of numbered copies and signed receipts for each manual is advisable. A master list of manual holders is also helpful for distributing revisions of various parts of the manual. Obviously, such a control mechanism should apply also to holders of portions of the manual, as there is no reason that every person needs an entire copy. In fact, newer style procedures manuals increasingly are designed to facilitate distribution of only parts of the manual. Since a well-used manual changes frequently, a loose-leaf format is obviously desirable.

CENTRAL LIABILITY LEDGER

The central liability ledger, sometimes called the customer liability record, is subsidiary to the general ledger that is used to record all customers' liabilities owed to the bank, or, stated in reverse, all credit extensions made by the bank to its customers. Customers, as used here, include, of course, other banks as well as business entities and governments. Accordingly, information in this record usually is arranged in alphabetical order by customer name. The purpose of the central liability ledger is to provide at all times a complete and up-to-date picture of credit extension, including commitments to extend credit of every type to every customer or customer group. Therefore, if customers are related or different names form part of the same group, appropriate cross references should be made in this record.

The entire process of collecting information, processing it into the central liability ledger, and producing summary reports of outstandings is referred to here as the central liability system. In order to be accurate and useful, this information system is updated every business day, and the central liability legder is proved daily, weekly, or monthly to appropriate general ledger accounts, such as loans, foreign exchange, letters of credit, acceptances, and Eurodollars placed, to mention only a few. A detailed procedure is required to provide instructions on how entries are to be processed and which employees are responsible for the daily proving of each account. In banks with sophisticated computer programs, the creation of the central liability record is quite simple, since all entries contain the names of customers and appropriate accounts. The computer program that handles the general ledger accounting then can rearrange the same information by customer name order, with detail for the type and amount of each transaction.

The central liability ledger is not a peculiar feature of international banking, since many commercial banks maintain such records, regardless of the domiciles of their customers. However, because of the numerous categories of credit extension, including commitments, that can arise from conducting international banking business, the need for a centralized liability record becomes critical at a much earlier stage in international, as opposed to domestic, banking. For this reason, in some banks the concept of this record has originated in the international area of the bank and then spread subsequently to the domestic units of the bank.

For each customer name in the ledger, breakdowns are developed for the various categories of credit risk. The customer names might appear in the left-hand margin of the record, and the headings for the risk classifications are listed from left to right across the top of the ledger. Actual amounts of credit outstanding and commitments under each risk category then would appear beside each customer name and stretch across the face of the record. For example, risk categories for nonbank customers might include term loans, short-term loans or advances, temporary overdrafts, acceptances created, letters of credit opened, and outstanding foreign exchange contracts.

For bank customers, most of these same categories would apply, including term loans, short-term loans, advances, overdrafts, acceptances, and foreign exchange contracts. But, in addition, for banks there would be categories for confirming letters of credit, for deposits in due-from accounts, and for Eurodeposit placements. For banks in the United States, there also would be facilities for federal funds transactions and purchase of certificates of deposit. By way of further example, for banks dealing with Japanese long-term credit banks, there also could be facilities for purchase of long-term debentures.

A continuous, up-to-date record of total credit exposure is necessary so that the officers authorizing credit extension may stay within various limits at all times. Those usually consist of specific limits approved by the credit committee for each type of credit facility, aggregate legal lending limits in accordance with various banking laws, such as the U.S. limit on loans to any one customer or customer groups of not more than 10 percent of total bank capital, and prudent maximum lending limits, which sometimes are referred to as house limits by some banks. However, it must be emphasized that not all categories of credit extension are additive for all purposes in the strict legal or regulatory sense, since various facilities involve different degrees of risk. Deposit placements and foreign exchange contracts usually are outside the limit for loans and have separate limits under most regulatory systems.

A five-year term loan, for example, involves a much greater risk than an obligation arising from a future foreign exchange contract that will mature in one month. Yet, the central liability ledger provides a string of numbers beside each customer's name for all categories in the record. To some persons, it may be tempting to add all of these numbers in one grand total rather than by similar or related degrees of risk. However, such a total gives a distorted or exaggerated picture of risk, even assuming a business failure involving bankruptcy. Nevertheless, it is absolutely necessary to have all of this information together in one place.

Foreign exchange contracts that might go unfulfilled in such an event could be satisfied by others in the market, perhaps at a different rate, not a cost equivalent to the original contract amount. For this reason, although foreign exchange contracts may be included in the central liability ledger, they are usually totaled outside total customer limits for loans and other credit extensions in a separate category. Some banks include in total outstandings relatively small percentages of the total future foreign exchange contracts, representing the estimated cost to cover in the market in the event of the customer's failure. However, use of some arbitrary percentage may mislead officers or others less experienced with international activity and may mask total volumes of foreign exchange, which should be reasonable for each customer in relation to foreign sales, purchases, licensing, or other activities. Accordingly, the best view is to include gross foreign exchange contracts in the central liability record rather than exclude such information or take some arbitrary percentage. However, users of the information must know that to some extent they are adding "apples and oranges," and not equivalent degrees of risk.

The total picture of actual outstandings and firm commitments to lend, which is provided by the central liability ledger, is especially useful when reviewing customer relationships in connection with receipt of financial statements and when considering new or additional extensions of credit or terms and conditions, including requirements for security. This total picture, along with historical usage of various credit facilities, deposit averages, and fees from services, also is vital for making decisions on pricing. In essence, information from the central liability records ranks beside financial statements and customer profitability analyses as a tool for lending officers and credit analysts in understanding their customers. In addition, internal loan review personnel, internal auditors, outside auditors, and bank examining authorities all need the information provided by the central liability ledger to accurately assess the activity of any bank or unit and prepare requests for confirmations of actual outstandings, as discussed in Chapter 9.

The total picture from the customer liability ledger is the key to understanding the application of bank policies, gauging the experience of lending officers with relationship to their accounts, and generally considering all the factors that enter into diversification or portfolio management. Moreover, without the central liability record, the frequent task of preparing requests for audit confirmations becomes a long and laborious task, since the alternative to taking this information from the centralized record is to collect this information from each subsidiary ledger, account by account, in order to build up a complete record for each name or to mail out individual confirmation requests for each account to each customer.

Since firm commitments are indispensable to a complete picture of a customer's relationship, it is necessary to provide a feature for reducing or increasing commitments when actual outstandings change or a facility is used. Because of the variations that can exist for different types of commitments, special directions or instructions regarding commitments must be maintained with the central liability ledger record or built into any computer program. Because of the close relationship between loans and commitments, it is sometimes suggested that the central liability ledger be combined with the loan department records, especially when the records are computerized. Although this is possible both in theory and practice, such a combining does not always produce the efficiencies and economies of scale anticipated.

Basicallly, the loan department, as explained in Chapter 8, is concerned with proper accrual of interest and fees, preparation of billings, proper application of payments, and control of documentation related to loans. The central liability system, on the other hand, is a basic information source and tool for decision making. Speed, accuracy, and breadth of information about all of a particular customer's activity from various locations of the bank are required. More than loan and loan commitment accounts are involved. Accrued interest for any loan accounts can be obtained from the loan department and interfaced with the liability ledger, but it is the total picture from throughout the bank that is most important.

With these two different approaches, especially for a bank or unit that does not have either a good loan accounting system or a central liability system, it may be preferable to have each department concentrate on its own system first. If proper consultation takes place during the early phases, future conflicts can be minimized, both systems can be up and running more quickly, and combining, if believed necessary, can occur at a later date. This is certainly the best course, if unproven computer programs in either or both areas are being used. In some larger banks, separate central liability departments have been created to deal exclusively with collecting, processing, and reporting on customer outstandings for different users within the bank.

In establishing a new central liability ledger in any operation, as is true for many other accounting applications, it usually is advisable to use hand-posted or mechanical bookkeeping or machine systems until staff in all departments are familiar with the procedures, even if ultimate use of the computer is contemplated. With proper functioning of the hand-posted or machine system, a second or third step can be taken with the security of possessing a system that already works. When the computer system starts, the old system can be run parallel until the new system proves out.

In overseas locations without access to reliable computer technology, color-coded cards can be used to advantage. Each category of risk can be identified by different colored card stock. Liabilities for each customer can be grouped in a well-ordered rainbow of cards, with customers arranged alphabetically. Posting can take place, for example, from tickets or summary documents that have passed from the originating section or department to the general bookeeping function and, where necessary, the foreign currency control ledger. All of one category or risk can be posted easily, after arranging the tickets or information in account order (alphabetically, according to customer name), by moving from one card of the same color to another. Monthly or more frequent proofs to the general ledger accounts can be made by adding the balances of each color series.

Even when going to the computer, movement by stages is recommended. Hard-copy printouts should be used at first to provide a medium for making handwritten and initialed corrections that can be reviewed by a supervisor for a pattern of errors. Daily proof work is thus facilitated, and sources of errors can be traced and eliminated. Perhaps the ultimate in this record is microfiche. By this point, errors should be rare, and formal correcting entries will be used when necessary to keep the customer liability record in balance, both with general ledger and with section or departmental accounts.

Before leaving the subject of the customer liability ledger, it should be noted that in many international operations, this record easily can be used to calculate country outstandings. This is accomplished by arranging customers alphabetically under country headings and providing for appropriate subtotals. If countries are grouped by regions or areas, the subtotals can build up to totals for tailor-made country units or blocks, which could correspond to administrative units or even individual lending officers. Should any unused balance of a country limit be treated as a commitment on the country total line, a warning system for reaching country limits can be created. The significance of this feature will become clear when we deal with the subject of country limits further in Chapter 12.

FOREIGN CURRENCY ACCOUNTING AND LIMITS

Whereas the central liability system is used to maintain a day-to-day record of all credit extensions by customer, country, world area, and type of risk, the foreign currency control ledger or the foreign currency accounting system is necessary to ascertain exposure at least daily, if not more frequently, for most international banks, by each currency in which the bank conducts its business. One end product of the foreign currency accounting system is the net foreign currency position report, which informs appropriate management within the international division and in other bank units of the total levels of foreign exchange exposure or positions by each currency.

Net positions are either long (called overbought) or short (oversold) and tell management how much of each foreign currency as of the date of each report it would be necessary to buy or sell if the bank were to liquidate all its foreign currency assets and liabilities and bring all its accounts back into the home currency of the bank. The net position is not to be confused with profit or loss, although the foreign currency accounting system also is used to periodically produce the amount of foreign exchange profits or losses. Net positions gauge the levels of risk or exposure by currencies. Estimated percentage changes in currency values can be applied readily to net positions. This information helps international managers decide, in conjunction with demand and supply information about particular currencies and the bank's future requirements, whether to buy or sell foreign currency to decrease its risk, maximize profits, or minimize losses.

If a bank has a net long position in a foreign currency, this means that after meeting all liabilities in that currency, the bank would have assets left over in the currency that it would be necessary to sell to eliminate all its activity in the currency. A net short position means that a bank would be required to enter the market to buy a foreign currency in order to terminate its activity in that currency. Should a bank or bank unit with a net long position in a particular currency have a limited need for the currency in the future or feel that the currency may decline in value relative to the home or local currency of the bank or unit, some asset in the currency should be sold or some liability increased. Selling or decreasing the balance of a due-from account or funds deposited with another bank, on the one hand, or increasing a due-to account or funds deposited with the bank, on the other, would accomplish the desired result. When a bank is evenly matched in a currency, its net position in the currency is said to be square or completely hedged.

To learn how profits or losses result from foreign exchange transactions, it is necessary to understand that all accounts that are used to record transactions involving foreign currency are maintained in two currencies, the foreign currency and the local (or home) currency of the bank. For example, when a foreign currency check is cashed or purchased, an exchange rate that produces an equivalent in local currency is used, and both the foreign currency and local currency amounts will be debited to the bank's records for its due-from account in the particular currency. This debit produces a new balance in the due-from account, both in the foreign and the local currency.

When a draft drawn on the same due-from account is sold to a customer who wishes to purchase foreign exchange to pay an obligation, foreign currency and local currency equivalents are again entered into the account. This time, credits to the due-from account produce a new balance in each currency on the ledger record. Assuming the bank buys foreign currency at one rate of exchange and sells it at another rate more favorable to it, the amounts in the balance columns of the due-from account after a series of transactions soon have no relationship to either the buying or selling rates. In fact, after huge volumes of transactions, the relationship can become completely distorted; the foreign currency column can be positive whereas the due-from account is negative, or vice versa.

Periodically, therefore, it is necessary to revalue each foreign currency account or apply to the foreign currency balance in the account an appropriate rate on the basis of the latest rate quotation. If there is a profit in the account, it will be necessary to pass an entry only in local currency to debit the account for the excess amount of local currency over the actual local currency amount required to equal the foreign currency equivalent at the current rate. The offsetting credit for the entry is foreign exchange profit. If a local currency credit is required to bring the balance of the local currency to the current rate equivalent of the foreign currency, then, of course, a loss results.

Repeating this process account by account for each foreign currency, usually at month end, produces a total net loss or net profit in foreign exchange for the period. All the foreign currency account balances now have a current or realistic equivalent in local currency, until new entries for regular transactions are passed through the accounts or the exchange rate changes again.

The foreign currency ledger, or foreign currency control ledger, as it is sometimes called, is therefore merely a collection of all of the bank's accounts that are maintained in two currencies, foreign and local. Entries to the general ledger are processed each day in local currency only, but all entries involving both a foreign currency and a local currency are also recorded each day in the separate subsidiary foreign currency records, with their local currency equivalents. Each day, at least, personnel in charge of the foreign currency ledgers summarize all account information by currencies and prepare the net position amounts for each currency to be reported to management. Periodically, usually at the end of each month, the foreign currency accounts are revalued to recognize all profits and losses. Personnel that are separate from those entering information or handling the foreign currency control ledger bookkeeping should conduct the revaluation process under appropriate supervision for the sake of good control, and all unusual results or problems should be promptly investigated.

Because fluctuations in the relative values between various foreign currencies and the local or home currency can create foreign exchange losses, as well as profits, international banks usually set limits on the net position in each foreign currency. These limits are reviewed periodically and changed as necessary. Separate limits should be set for net overbought and net oversold positions in each currency, depending upon the outlook for each currency.

Although theoretically it is possible to be totally hedged or square at any one time in any or all currencies, in practice this is not possible. Too many transactions of various sizes are being run continuously through the due-from accounts of most international banks on any one day to make it economical to hedge every transaction. Foreign loans or foreign time deposits can be and usually are hedged by matching liabilities or assets or by entering into foreign exchange contracts to fix profit at the inception of each loan or deposit in a foreign currency. However, because of the activity in the foreign currency due-from accounts, most international banks, especially smaller banks or units, tend to have net long positions in the currencies in which they maintain due-from accounts.

Even if a bank is completely square except perhaps for modest, working due-from balances, the absence of a substantial net position does not end the international bank's foreign exchange exposure. Since the net position limit concept assumes a liquidation of all foreign currency assets and obligations, the factor of time also must be considered by a separate view of the bank's foreign currency position. A substantial foreign currency loan maturing in the future could be offset by an identical amount in a demand deposit, for example. Although the net position in this currency would be square in this example, withdrawal of the deposit could cause a substantial net long position to appear any time before the maturity of the loan.

In this situation, although the net position is square, there exists a timing gap between foreign currency assets and liabilities. A summary by days, weeks, or months of net positions of all accounts by each currency could produce, in fact, numerous gaps of substantial magnitudes, although the total net position in a currency could be square or slight. For this reason, in addition to total net positions by each currency, long and short, banks with large transactions over periods of time also establish gap limits. Gap limits recognize that the cost to cover or hedge between foreign currency positions during various time frames may be less than the loss resulting from a periodic devaluation or revaluation of the currency that could occur between the gaps. With appropriate gap reporting and gap limits, at least, consideration can be given to hedging or eliminating gaps.

Obviously, speed is of the essence in producing information on net positions and gaps for use by foreign exchange dealers to protect and earn profits for the bank and by management to control and change limits on the basis of their knowledge. Accordingly, the larger the foreign exchange operation and the more quickly the foreign exposure changes, the sooner and more often information is needed. In a small international unit, net positions and gaps may not change substantially for weeks, except for the due-from accounts. In large operations, exposure could vary tremendously in minutes. Therefore, any management that approves doing business in foreign currencies has the duty to assure that record keeping and reporting are adequate to control this area. Otherwise, inordinate risks will be assumed and losses surely will result. In some operations with extremely low foreign currency activity, hand-posted records will suffice. In most units, however, machine-prepared or computerized records are necessary.

FUNDING INTERNATIONAL LOANS

Funding international loans really is more than a procedure, even in the broadest sense of this concept, and we shall deal with only a few facets of this subject here. Funding is a process or function common to both domestic and international commercial banking and usually fits into the broader topic of asset and liability management. In essence, asset and liability management involves the matching or allocating of assets and liabilities, taking into consideration income, the cost of funds, and the difference, or net interest margin. Usually, asset and liability management covers foreign exchange risk and maturity gaps for all currencies, as well as the net interest margin.

Accordingly, profitability and pricing are closely related to this process. In fact, parallel to the credit decision, funding goes to the heart of lending and deals with managing the net margin or difference between the prices for lending funds and the cost of borrowing funds. If funds at low enough cost are not available for loans involving reasonable risk at market rates, then obviously the bank does not have raw material to conduct its business at a profit.

In banking, the gathering or purchasing of funds is analogous to the acquisition of raw materials or the purchasing function in a manufacturing concern. In a manufacturing concern, however, certain products have obvious limitations. Certain metals go into the car engine, body, and frame; glass is used for lights and windows; and plastic, leather, or fabric, for seats and interior finishing. However, money is fungible, can cross borders, and through foreign exchange contracts can even be changed from one currency into another. Hence, the allocation or use of funds is not so limited or obvious in banking as compared to the manufacturing enterprise. The decision on use of funds in banking can be quite arbitrary or even political within the organization. This involves serious consequences for the international division in smaller banks.

In order for the decision-making process to be as rational as possible, the total bank plan must rank markets by priorities. Potential profit must be measured against potential risk. If international loans as a category are viewed by management as less profitable or more risky than domestic lending opportunities, then few, if any, funds ever will be allocated to international lending. If all income

streams and total expenses for foreign relationships are not compared with all income and expenses for domestic accounts, then,
funds use or allocation decisions will be made on the basis of only
some and not all the facts.

For these reasons, relationship analysis must consider all income
streams and nonfunds expenses to weigh with risk factors. Then,
decisions must be made to undertake business contingent upon
allocating funds whose costs fit within the projected profit structure.
Should higher and higher cost funds be taken to fuel the bank, then
loans at increasing rates and correspondingly higher risk will result.
Care must be taken to avoid the obvious dangers in this situation. In
addition, risks can increase as money is shifted internationally from
various markets. Capital controls or laws can be imposed by each
country to impede the continuous flow of funds. For these reasons, it
generally is safer to take funds from the market being served.

Following this general rule with regard to Eurocurrency lending,
of which the largest component is now in Eurodollars, involves
taking funds from the Eurodollar market for funds loaned in
Eurodollars. In many banks, especially U.S. regionals, it is often
argued that U.S. dollar sources of funds are less expensive than
Eurodollars. Should this be the case, it would decrease profits to take
in Eurodollars as deposits merely to fund Eurodollar loans. However, to the extent that the international division has not funded
itself entirely with its own deposits, it is using domestic bank funds in
its international operations.

Assuming that the bank in question has the credit standing to take
in Eurodollar deposits to match its Eurodollar loans, but is not
permitted to do so by the asset and liability policy of the bank, then it
is reasonable to allocate funds internally to the international division
at the Eurodollar cost of funds. Under these circumstances, the
international division would earn only the spread or margin over the
LIBO rate, and some other unit of the bank would earn the difference between its actual cost of funds and the LIBO rate. In the
event that the cost of funds of other units exceeds the LIBO rate, the
international division should have the option to obtain Eurodollars
and, hence, indirectly force the other units of the bank to find other
uses for more expensive funds or stop acquiring them.

The better view in most international banks, especially larger banks and Edge Act banks, is to match each Eurodollar or other Eurocurrency loan on the date of each rate fixing for each loan. In this manner, the margin over LIBOR is locked in until the next maturity date. To fund short always presents the risk of the cost of funds increasing before the end of the rate-fixing period, which could cause a diminution or total elimination of any funding advantage achieved during the earliest part of the period.

In many banks designated personnel are responsible for asset and liability management decisions, either on a full-time daily basis or on a policy-level committee basis. Most larger international banks staff this function on a full-time basis, headed by senior personnel with extensive international experience or at least a global viewpoint. However, even in the smaller or regional bank dominated by domestic or local market considerations, it is important to have the international viewpoint well represented so as to prevent mistakes in connection with funding decisions for foreign loans.

12

Credit-Related
Procedures

Credit Package Preparation / Annual Review Procedure / Credit Review
Process / Country Analysis / Country Limits / Industry Analysis /
Pricing Systems and Relationship Analysis

T his chapter discusses several detailed procedures and basic
techniques most commonly used to manage international
assets resulting from the extension of credit. The main
objective of portfolio management is generally stated as earning
profits by accepting reasonable risks. This objective is accomplished
in several ways, including diversification of bank assets according to
various principles. Specifically, excessive concentrations should be
avoided in individual borrowers, in particular nations or parts of the
world, in various currencies, and in specific industries.

Although the consideration of different countries and currencies
is peculiar to international banking, as was pointed out in Chapter 2,
the other two factors are common to managing most other portfolios
of domestic assets. In addition, all the elements involved in assessing
the quality of any borrower or user of credit, domestic or foreign,
naturally come into play.

Diversification should not only minimize actual losses attributable to problems of a customer, country, currency, or industry but also have a positive aspect by leading to wise selection of successful borrowers in prospering nations and lines of activity. Working with leaders in growing areas should maximize return on assets and make the best use of the commercial bank's resources. Healthy customers pay back extensions of credit, increase deposits, use more services that produce fee income, and often lead the bank to other profitable opportunities.

Materials used to make decisions on credit extensions must be collected, analyzed, and processed in a systematic and consistent manner. All credit extensions should be reviewed regularly and procedures should exist to assure that this is done. In addition to the credit approval process, which was introduced in Chapter 2 and involves the credit committee as discussed in Chapter 6, a separate and independent credit review committee should review all major credit extensions. This after-the-fact review serves to enforce bank policies and often helps spot future difficulties, preferably while remedial action is still possible.

Country and industry analysis parallel the approach taken for reviewing credit extensions to each customer. Most domestic banks and many other institutions use analysis of different industries or lines of activities, but country analysis is unique to the international field. Several different approaches have been taken to country analysis. These are referred to as free-form essays, ranking, scoring or grading systems, and the checklist approach. Closely related to country analysis and diversification is the subject of foreign exchange risk. However, for the sake of convenience, this topic has been dealt with already in Chapter 11.

To assist in loan pricing, various grading or ranking systems also have been applied by some banks to individual credits, including occasional systems that attempt to bring in the country risk factor. These systems seem to have serious drawbacks when used for this purpose, since they can lead to the rigid application of mechanical formulas. Accordingly, the best approach for most banks involves balancing all factors, with ratings or rankings used only as rough guidelines, and stressing account profitability or relationship analysis.

CREDIT PACKAGE PREPARATION

A *credit package,* as used in this chapter, refers to the internal bank documents used to summarize information about a user of credit for the bank's own credit approval process. The standard cover form, or top sheet in a package, is variously called a credit application, line mat, or credit or loan recommendation sheet, among other names, by different banks. Although such forms and packages usually are used uniformly throughout a banking organization for both domestic and overseas credit extensions, the increased number of facilities and worldwide locations often complicate the process in the typical international division.

Preparing a credit package for an international customer consists in listing all services involving extensions of credit provided by the bank, whether domestically or overseas, with amounts or limits for each service or unit of the bank. When financial and other information about the customer, along with explanations of the specifics of new or unusual transactions, is combined with the listing of services, this entire package of information is presented to the credit committee for approval.

This preparation may be done by a foreign branch, subsidiary, or affiliate for approval within the limits of the preparing unit's credit authority or for forwarding to the bank's overseas regional office or the bank's head office, if the total amount involved exceeds the unit's authorized limit for granting credit. For locally owned customers within the foreign office's country, all preparation is completed by the overseas office. For example, this would include a German-owned company that is the customer of the Frankfurt office of a U.S. bank.

For foreign-owned local customers, the preparing unit would concentrate on describing the specific transaction under consideration and pass its credit package to the bank's approving unit, which may or may not be the head office. This other unit then would be responsible for completing certain information, adding any other extensions of credit to the package, or reworking the information in the package to combine it in a larger package, and granting approval. An illustration of this situation would be a U.S. corporation's German subsidiary dealing with a U.S. bank's Frankfurt office. All credit approvals for the U.S. corporation's worldwide operations generally would be centered in the U.S. headquarters of the bank.

A more complicated situation in a highly decentralized, U.S.-headquartered bank might involve the bank's Athens office sending the package recommending credit extension to a German corporation's Greek subsidiary for approval by the U.S. bank's Frankfurt branch. In this bank all decisions for German-owned companies worldwide would be handled by the Frankfurt branch, where the relationship between the German company and U.S. bank is centered. If total credit extended to the particular German company were to exceed the Frankfurt branch's authority, then it would have to apply to the U.S. headquarters with a credit package.

As a general rule, a credit package for every significant international borrowing relationship in a bank should be prepared at least once a year. This package would then form part of the annual review process discussed in this chapter. However, customers cannot always time their requests for new or modified borrowing to coincide with the annual review. Thus, the need to prepare new credit packages can arise anytime during the year. In practice, therefore, lending officers are constantly preparing credit packages for their customers throughout the year, either for routine annual reviews or for new or modified transactions.

Because much of the information for a credit package remains the same year after year, it is often useful to store the contents of the main part of the package, called the credit recommendation sheet, in a form that can be used in word processing machines. This form could include a magnetic card, floppy disk, or a tape, for instance. Design of the recommendation sheet should take into account placing all basic or historical information, which does not change frequently, in a position on the recommendation form that does not affect other parts of the form. Use of word processing machines and their related storage devices is particularly useful in credit extension to banks, which involves numerous money market lines or other types of credit that change most often only with regard to amount. A listing of some of the most common forms of credit extension to banks appears in Appendix E.

Almost every bank uses standard forms for credit packages to simplify the summarizing of information and to encourage decision making on a consistent basis for all credit extension. The combining of standard line wordings with standard forms also permits the best use of personnel in information gathering for processing credit packages. More junior persons or trainees can work with collection and arranging data, and more senior persons can concentrate on analyzing the data and participating in the credit decision process. Obviously, filling out every part of the form does not assure a proper credit decision. When special questions arise, additional explanations and data may be required for a sound decision and should be added to the package.

On the other hand, copies of detailed supporting documents as a rule should not form part of the package, since this defeats the goal of summary and uniform treatment. When the round-robin credit approval procedure with circularization of the credit file as described in Chapter 6 is used, every member of the credit committee has the opportunity to read beyond the credit package materials routed on top of the file and examine the entire contents of the credit file.

The face of the credit recommendation sheet that usually is the first item in the credit package contains at the top of the sheet basic information such as the name, address, and line of business of the customer, along with the date of the recommendation and the originating office or unit of the bank. Most of the remainder of the top part of the first sheet is available for describing the amounts and types of credit being extended. In global annual reviews for major multinational customers, where such a listing might run into many pages of lines or facilities, this front space can be used for a summary of all facilities by types of credit risk, and the detailed lisiting can form an attachment to the page.

Amounts and currency of each facility should be clearly set out on the left-hand part of the form, and the middle and right-hand parts of the form should clearly describe the nature of the facility being extended. Wording for identical transactions should be identical from recommendation sheet to recommendation sheet and from customer to customer to aid the credit committee in determining the degree of risk involved and in comparing facilities granted for the same customer from year to year and to different customers. Standard wording also eases the transition to computer or other machine applications for summarizing data for other purposes, such as the central liability ledger, which was discussed in Chapter 11.

Standard wording usually identifies the type of transaction by short title or purpose and then indicates which unit of the bank is administering the facility. The body of the description then permits a more detailed description of the facility, including rates, fees, repayment provision, and security arrangements, if any. Appendix F illustrates facility wordings for some usual transactions involved in approval of credit for international customers other than banks.

Next in order, on the remainder of the first page of a typical recommendation form, blanks or boxes are provided for listing actual amounts outstanding, by type of facility and historical usage of credit. This usage could include high points and low points, or clean-up periods when no credit was used, as well as volumes or days of usage, or all these items, depending upon the type of facility involved. Information on actual and average demand deposits and time or other deposits is usually also included somewhere on the front sheet.

It is imperative that both total outstandings as of the date of the recommendation and the total of all credit facilities being recommended in the package be clearly indicated. In spite of the various degrees of risk involved in extending credit, all credit exposure, as we have noted before, is additive in the last instance. Thus, total potential exposure and actual outstandings are of great importance to the credit committee. Forms or presentations that are unclear or attempt to avoid these key totals, contrary to expediting approval, perform a disservice to the members of the credit committee. Total average deposit balances, unless hypothecated, are relevant, of course, not to decreasing or mitigating credit risk, but only to pricing considerations.

The reverse of the credit recommendation front sheet often is left blank by most banks as space for a written narrative. However, to expedite the use of word processing machines, information on this sheet should follow a standard checklist or outline, with the most historical information and other matters least likely to change at the beginning or top of the reverse sheet. The customer's business activity should be described along with the history of growth and change in this activity. Following this should appear the history of the bank's relationship, the range of services provided by the bank, and the goals and likely changes in the relationship in the future.

With such background completed, the narrative then should analyze the customer's business not only on the basis of financial statements but other relevant factors, such as market conditions, competitive position, industry trends, and technological developments. For new or modified facilities, the specifics of significant aspects of the transactions at hand should be dealt with in the remainder of the narrative. These could include the purpose or mechanics of the transactions, as well as any special security or documentation involved, and any other relevant factors.

Finally, at some point, perhaps at the end of the narrative section, total country exposure is summarized by some banks. Total approved lines or loans and actual outstanding could be broken down by various maturities or types of customers, such as government agencies, banks, and private corporations. Obviously, in some cases this total narrative might require more sheets than the reverse side of the credit recommendation sheet. Extra plain sheets should be added, but in total pages no more than one or two sides at most should be used for most relationships, since a summary viewpoint is required. Typing this information from the bottom to the top of the sheet on the reverse sides of recommendation sheets makes reading files easier when materials are held in the file at the top of each sheet.

To the recommendation sheet and any additional narrative pages, most banks add balance sheets and income statements for at least three years on the bank's standard analysis forms, in both the currency of the borrower and the currency of the bank's head office. Indication of whether the statements are audited or not, whether the opinion is qualified or unqualified, and the translation rate between the two currencies are included on these financial statement forms. Any qualified opinion, of course, would require additional comment and explanation at some point in the total package, perhaps in the narrative section. The initials or name of the person spreading the financial statements on the bank's standard form are usually also contained somewhere on the standard form spread sheet.

To complete most packages, where the customer has several bankers, banks usually require summaries of current credit investigations from a representative sampling of banks or, in other cases, investigations from suppliers or other entities that deal with the customer. Some banks include all materials related to financial statement analysis in a separate document, in which case the narrative portion of the credit recommendation sheet could be shortened considerably. The better way, however, is for lending officers who prepare the narrative to include financial analysis in the context of all other factors that enter into the credit judgment for an international customer. To see it in total context is particularly necessary in international lending where accounting standards and financial statements might not always reflect accurately the credit capacity and circumstances of the customer.

When the information from the credit package is to be presented to the board of directors, some further summarization may be necessary to save the time of the board members. Financial information usually can be compressed to eight or ten asset, liability, revenue, and income captions and a few ratios. Narrative also can be shortened considerably and the credit investigation results eliminated. In this manner, two sides may adequately summarize the package with additional points to be covered as answers to specific questions.

ANNUAL REVIEW PROCEDURE

The lending officers of the commercial bank's international division prepare credit packages not only for any new or modified extensions of credit but also for all existing credit extensions, even if they are not changed, at least once a year. Accordingly, in order to make certain that all credits are reviewed at least once a year, usually as promptly as possible after receipt of audited annual financial statements, all credit extensions are scheduled on monthly sheets by customer or group name. Each lending officer or area lending section maintains a running schedule. For control purposes to insure that good housekeeping standards are maintained, an independent person in the international division or overseas office often retains a copy of each officer's review lists or a master review schedule for all customers. Computerized tickler systems help the lending officers perform this function at many banks.

Ideally, every customer is reviewed on the same anniversary every year. However, several factors work to defeat this objective. Customers' credit requirements frequently change between annual reviews, which occasions special or interim reviews. Some customers occasionally make accounting changes between a calendar year and a fiscal year or adopt different dates for ending their fiscal year. Therefore, in order to have fresh financial information for the annual review, it is necessary to adjust the review date.

A few credits, including problem loans, may require more than one review per year to monitor developments and make changes in terms, when necessary, such as during restructurings, or because each transaction takes less than a year and the lending officer wishes to commit the bank for only one transaction at a time. Also, adjustments in the schedule may be necessary to even out work flows of financial analysts and credit committee members. If most customers are on a calendar year, for example, final audited annual financial statements will arrive in waves sufficient to drown most banks by the end of the first quarter or beginning of the second quarter of each year.

In order to even out such seasonal workloads, review of the soundest credits should be deferred, so that the most critical credit situations can be reviewed immediately after receipt of financials and, if necessary, be scheduled for a special review on the basis of the next interim financials. Well-known and highly rated correspondent bank lines and facilities for other high-quality customers can be handled last and farthest from the time of receipt of the annual financials. Review can even be done on the basis of older audited annual financials plus unaudited interim financials.

Occasionally, a bank will declare that as a policy all reviews must take place within a set number of days after the close of the customer's year. When statements are not received or workloads are too heavy for processing all at once, such a system then compounds the paperwork and record keeping by increasing the routings to credit committee members for extensions, pending completion of the annual review. Naturally, extra work occurs during the midst of the peak period, and credit quality is not improved, since reviews do not take place but are merely postponed. Such a system is bureaucracy at its worst, since paper moves and builds up in files only to prove that a rule exists.

The problem of stale financial statements is complicated further in some countries, especially in certain Western European nations, where company laws often require that the general assembly of shareholders approve the annual financial statements and distribution of profits before financial statements can be released. If such meetings are held late in the first quarter or even in the second quarter or later and translation, printing, and mailing times are added, it may be the third quarter or even later in the calendar year before final financial statements are received by U.S. banks. This seems especially true for many European banks, even those of major size.

To solve the entire problem of spreading, analyzing, and processing lines of credit for banks, new specialized services in banks and nonbank organizations are being developed to sell their work to banks needing such information on a timely basis. For example, Chase Manhattan Bank, with a service called Bankroll for U.S. banks, is one of the pioneers in this field. Manufacturers Hanover in London and Steven Davis Associates, a London consulting firm, are offering a service for analyses of European banks. Libra Bank, London, a consortium-owned bank specializing in Latin American business, announced in late 1979 a similar service for information on leading South and Central American banks. These and similar other services yet to be launched undoubtedly will revolutionize the processing of credit reviews for credit extensions to major banks around the world.

Such services provide useful comparisons betweeen banks in the same peer group and often provide more analytical information than otherwise would be available to most banks. Ratios or numbers that appear out of line or at variance from the norm can be useful for further questioning or research by calling officers. Thus, rather than reinvent the wheel at each bank and prepare repetitive work, these services provide the opportunity to rise above the routine and become more analytical and selective with less basic work. This development, although coming somewhat late to commercial banking, should be no surprise, since the investment research units of organizations managing equities and bonds have been using numerous, analogous, analytical services in their field, at least in the United States and Europe, for years.

In order that an annual review system may function properly, it is necessary that the officers who handle the account make the review. This is so even when materials are used from special services previously mentioned. By making reviews themselves, account officers exercise self-discipline to insure that they are completely knowledgeable about their customers and that their accounts are performing properly from the standpoint of safety for the bank, receiving proper servicing from all parts of the bank, and producing maximum profits for the bank. Annual review time provides an opportunity to be certain that customers have been visited, that customers' financial results are satisfactory, and that the customer's industry or business is not experiencing previously overlooked problems or missing opportunities.

Preparation of the relationship profitability analysis is usually scheduled to coincide with the annual review date. The credit file index or header sheet and loan documentation also should be put in order at this time, if necessary because of any changes in basic facts or methods of operations. For these reasons, the round-robin credit committee system, with the routing of the credit recommendation package attached to the credit file, is preferred by most banks. Credit committee members can determine from the condition of the credit file, among other materials, much about the quality of the credit in the context of the total relationship.

For a complete picture, it is necessary that all facilities for all related customer names be brought together at the time of the annual review. In this regard, the example of the multinational corporation with some 100 facilities around the world, as discussed in Chapter 2 under the topic of credit approvals, should be recalled. It cannot be overemphasized that this annual review process is carried out by the regular account officer. The annual review process should never be confused with the credit review committee or process that is carried out for a different purpose by entirely different personnel.

CREDIT REVIEW PROCESS

The credit review process is somewhat analogous to the work of a hospital's board of review. All of an officer's or an area's credit extensions are examined periodically, usually once a year, from the standpoint of quality control, meaning, in banking, probability of collection of all sums owed without incident, and especially loss. Unlike the process conducted by some hospital boards of review, this credit review process should be conducted by entirely independent persons, not those responsible for lending or staff members with some role in the original credit approval process.

To function properly, the credit review committee should be composed of persons who are in no way responsible for the origination or administration of credits. Obviously, this would rule out the international division's senior credit officer. The work and policies of this officer, as much as those of the actual account officer, are the subject of the review. If the senior credit officer chairs the credit review committee, for example, this defeats the entire purpose of the review.

One of the difficulties involved with the credit review process is finding qualified personnel with lending experience who are not actually involved in credit extension. Former successful lenders are ideal candidates for the review committee, but care and planning are needed to assemble a qualified panel. Most successful lenders enjoy their jobs and often wish to continue extending credit and working with customers. In order to obtain such persons, temporary assignments of a few years may be arranged.

Personnel with overseas credit experience may be rotated back to headquarters or regional offices where review committees operate. Such an experience, especially with credits from a different area, can be broadening and at the same time give a former lender depth by permitting an examination of the credit extension from the perspective of distance or standing back from the process. Other good candidates for credit review work include domestic auditors, former foreign branch auditors, and persons whose job might involve handling problem or workout loans.

Since the credit review committee performs its duties on an after-the-fact basis, it is necessary that the committee state its conclusions in some type of written report, Furthermore, since the credit review process involves an across-the-board look at a geographic or specialized area of borrowing customers, it is important that the committee point out any observations with regard to trends inside or outside the bank, lending areas, or special industries. Often this committee with its unique perspective may be the first to note warning signals of future danger resulting from particular bank policies or marketing strategies.

The format of credit review studies can vary from the credit recommendation package or follow the same style with emphasis on different factors. What really matters is that the review is performed by experienced but independent people, who work from original bank records and not only the credit file. For example, information on the timeliness of interest and loan repayments from the loan administration area of the bank is useful for the review process.

The reports of the credit review committee should be passed up the line to senior management and the board of directors. The international lending officers, including the senior lending officer, should see the credit review studies or summaries prior to their appearance before the committee. This not only prepares these officers for their appearance before the committee but allows an opportunity for correction of any factual errors, which may result when persons not generally familiar with the particular credits, files, and other records prepare the basic summaries for the review committee.

The final report will be of use to all of the international officers involved, who obviously should have, if necessary, an opportunity to reply to the report in the manner of an audit reply, since, in essence, the credit review process is an audit of individual credits and credit policies. For this reason, some banks include the credit review as part of the audit function, where it is certainly not out of place. The trend to include the credit review function as part of the auditor's work is more pronounced in those institutions that are taking a broader view of the auditing functions and including review of the formulation and functioning of systems, policies, and procedures as part of the audit responsibility.

COUNTRY ANALYSIS

Sound country analysis starts with the collection of timely, accurate, and comprehensive information. In this regard, the existence of an adequate international library and the development of good reading habits are indispensable. Materials related to all major world powers and any country or region of the world where the bank does business or might do business in some future year should be collected and grouped by countries, regions, or specialized subject topics to form a library. Open shelving permits and encourages maximum access and use of materials that are free standing. Covered files or folders can be used for loose or floppy items, including newspaper clippings and magazine articles.

Correspondent banks, central banks, and other financial institutions usually prepare and distribute free or at nominal cost economic studies and statistics on nations in which they are headquartered or have extensive dealings. The major international public accounting firms around the world provide general background information on doing business, local commercial laws, and accounting practices in countries where they maintain offices. Government agencies, embassies, commercial offices, and chambers of commerce are additional sources of information.

Regional bodies, such as the Organization for Economic Cooperation and Development, and international institutions, such as the World Bank Group and the International Monetary Fund (IMF), probably provide the best material, because it has been developed on the basis of consistent systems, which facilitate comparisons between periods and between countries. In this regard, *International Financial Statistics* and *Direction of Trade*, two publications of the IMF, are without equal, and the World Bank has pioneered in its compilation of *World Debt Tables*.

When these sources are supplemented by a selective sampling of subscriptions to leading international, regional, or local journals or publications, such as the *London Financial Times, Asian Wall Street Journal, The Economist, Business International, Euromoney,* and *Institutional Investor*, and by a regular program of purchasing hardcover books, the international library should be sufficient for preparing brief, basic research papers on individual countries.

Country analyses or studies as currently being performed by international commercial banks may be grouped for the convenience of our discussion here into three general categories. These consist of free-form essays, comparative ranking or scoring systems, and checklist-type studies. The free-form, essay-style research, as its name implies, follows no set outline. Comparisons between reports on different countries or even between reports for different periods on the same country are not facilitated. Each author has complete literary license to discuss any factors deemed relevant, with the only direction being to come to some conclusion about whether to do business in the country in question.

Free-form, essay-style reports tend to be found in banks with less international experience and a relatively lenient approach to written procedures and established systems. In the United States, reports in this form tend to be "for the files" to placate auditors and examiners or to comply with some vague directive from senior management. Such undisciplined research rarely seems to be used for conscious decision making, but more as a written rationale for what has been or is being done after making country lending decisions on some other basis.

At the opposite extreme is found, usually in several of the larger, more experienced international banks, extremely complicated systems of weighing various factors or ranking or scoring countries against each other, often by letter grades or combinations of letter and number grades. If the free-form essay makes country analysis the province of the amateur, these more complicated systems tend to limit country risk research to the confines of experts, often to the exclusion of bankers on the line and out in the field, where practical expertise resides.

Unfortunately, in at least several of these more complicated systems, results often have not been commensurate with the effort in creating and operating such systems. In fact, communication between home-based experts and bankers on the scene may have been impeded and the thinking of all concerned convoluted by the jargon and complexity of the formulas involved. Common sense and "gut feel" warning signals may have been overlooked as money was poured into some nations by bankers lulled into a false sense of safety and security by overrefined analysis systems. Almost every author in the field of country analysis cautions that especially in this area international banking is an art and not a science. It seems doubtful that economic events, which are so frequently influenced by political decisions and other social changes, ever will be reducible to formulas the way engineering problems can be solved with application of calculus or a handy differential equation.

Most international bankers seem to be avoiding the two extremes just discussed and concentrating on a checklist approach to country analysis. This approach facilitates comparisons between different countries and within the same country at different times, even if the reports or studies are done by different authors. At the same time, flexibility is allowed under this approach to cope with the very real differences between completely different types of economic and political systems. Depending upon the importance of the factor being considered for the country in question, a great deal or a relatively small amount of discussion can be provided, but all the same factors are covered for all countries.

Moreover, the checklist approach to country analysis permits work to be done piecemeal on each study. This is an ideal system for smaller banks without an entirely separate group of research personnel or economists. People with other duties, usually lending officers, can work on country analysis when time permits. Moreover, the specific topical listing of the checklist approach encourages discussion between different persons in the bank about each factor and increases the opportunity for a significant contribution by personnel in the field who can add their comments topic by topic. A representative checklist with brief explanations used by one regional bank is shown in Appendix H.

In each international bank, it is important to evolve a system of country risk analysis that matches the capabilities and resources of the bank and balances the type and volume of international business carried on. At the World Bank, some fifteen or more economists, separate from the lending staff, may study only one country. At the other extreme, a small international commercial bank may have brief, one- or two-page country studies prepared by its lending officers. The problem with lending officers preparing their own studies for the countries in which they lend is that invariably they rate the country more by business development opportunities than by objective outside criteria. Few lenders over the long run are likely to cut off their bread and butter by severely downgrading a country they work with. Yet, in most organizations, the lenders in the field or account officers traveling their territories usually have the most valuable on-the-spot and up-to-date experience and contacts to develop information on trends behind the published numbers or statistics.

To temper lenders' judgments, some banks involve the lending and country officers with their economic staff to produce a final country study. Even in a bank with a small international department, reliable work can be produced on country analysis by using even one experienced person to vet drafts of country studies prepared by the country desks. Many services, such as the quarterly *Economist Intelligence Unit* for countries and groups of countries, are available at reasonable prices to supplement the *IMF International Financial Statistics*, other data, newspaper and magazine articles, and, of course, the results of visits with key officials and other leaders in each country.

COUNTRY LIMITS

After country reports have been prepared and a determination has been made that business may be conducted within particular nations, the next task is to define what types of business may be conducted and how much of each type. In some banks a cover sheet is prepared for the country study to summarize the limits for each type of business. This sheet is analogous to the recommendation or line mat form used with individual credit packages. In fact, some banks use the same form and, in effect, prepare country packages, with the country study attached in place of a customer's financial statements and other information.

In setting limits for types of business, it is useful to recall the concept of classifications or degrees of risk discussed earlier in this book. Other useful categories of business are bank to bank, government or private corporate risk. Also, a bank's level of experience in a particular country should be balanced with the country analysis. Most banks generally consider bank risk or government risk to be safer than private corporate risk. But there are exceptions, for in some countries it may be preferable to deal with private banks or corporations than with the government. On the other hand, the nature of some economic and political systems limits the type of business that can be conducted, almost by definition. In socialist nations, for example, only state entities or perhaps only one foreign trade bank may be permitted to deal with outsiders. In this situation, the decision merely boils down to the appropriate level for the usual short-term transactions and, possibly, how many years and an amount for term business.

In addition to these considerations, market conditions must be taken into account and limits established to balance risk with opportunity. Country limits should never be new business goals; yet, limits should be flexible to permit reasonably prompt review if more than the originally established level of business materializes in countries that are considered good risks. Recent changes in the U.S. Comptroller of Currency's examination process provide for a percentage-of-capital test on the basis of the Office of the Comptroller's view of each country. According to its formula, if X country rates only a 10 percent exposure, credit exposure amounting to more than 10 percent of capital in country X requires a write-up in the examination report to advise the bank's board of directors of a potentially dangerous situation. It is then for the bank's board to determine whether the bank has sufficient experience to conduct such a level of business with the nation in question.

Most banks that prepare country studies and establish country limits review each country and its limit at least once a year. More frequent reviews usually are occasioned by deteriorating economic or political situations, which call for consideration of lower limits, or by improving economic and political conditions and successful marketing efforts in highly rated countries, which necessitate study of larger limits.

Persons involved in the country review process and in approving country limits vary from bank to bank. In some banks, the same people involved with approving individual credits approve country limits. For tightly self-disciplined organizations with experienced personnel and good track records, this approach presents no problems. However, with the rapid deterioration in economic conditions and evident political changes in several parts of the world during the last few years, most banks are moving to create some kind of check-and-balance system for country limits. A separate committee composed of various management representatives and the bank's economist or economists may be selected to approve country limits.

Or the bank's most senior policy committee, including the president or the chairman or even the board of directors, may handle approval of country limits. In a few banks, which have outside international advisory boards, this body may be involved in establishing country limits, as noted in Chapter 6.

Regardless of the approval committee or body, the majority of international banks believe that it is imperative to have some system to periodically review the economic and political conditions of the nations where international commercial banking activities are conducted and have some consistent rationale for the levels of business conducted in each nation.

INDUSTRY ANALYSIS

Many banks have not yet established formal industry limits, either domestically or worldwide, However, increasingly, information is being generated to report on credit outstandings by industrial categories. In the United States, the federal government's Standard Industry Classification (SIC) code system or the bank's own system can be applied quite easily to the central liability ledger concept to produce information by industrial or commercial line of activity. Several drawbacks are readily apparent, however, with regard to the industrial classification system.

On the one hand, some banks have made a conscious decision to specialize in certain business lines as a result of the customer mix in their market area or in order to be in strong and growing industrial areas. A major bank may have specialized personnel and expertise in serving the energy or mining industries, for example, whereas a regional bank may serve jewelry or precious metals dealers in its area. Export of agricultural commodities may be significant for another bank, and so on. In addition, some entities are difficult to categorize. Corporations involved in foreign activities, whether shareholder-owned multinationals or foreign government holding companies, may be genuine conglomerates and hence hard to place in any particular classification.

Nevertheless, with recent worldwide difficulties in shipping, shipbuilding, steel production, synthetic fibers, and various other lines of activity, to mention only a few, most banks are placing more emphasis on understanding the international dynamics of the various key industries that are now tied together in worldwide cyclical performance. The economics departments of most banks are becoming more closely involved with the planning process on an advisory basis, not only with regard to general economic conditions, but also with regard to performance in specific industrial sectors.

This is probably the best way to assure a continuous interaction between bank economists and others in the bank, including lending officers, who may often have a feel for certain situations but may be unable to explain precisely the reasons for their conclusions. Because a great deal of economic material is produced in the United States and other developed countries about specific industrial outlooks in connection with investment in equity and fixed income securities, it usually is not necessary for the economics department or international division to produce a great amount of original material. A system of selective reading, routing of important materials to key personnel, and good dialog among various parts of the bank should be sufficient to enable the economics staff to produce periodic conclusions about dangerous trends and new opportunities.

Obviously, the earlier this type of conclusion can be brought into the planning process, the better for all parties concerned. However, another possibility is to route to the bank's economists the international division's monthly management report materials on outstanding credits by industrial classifications. This should provide a formal opportunity for a written response by the economics staff and over the long run allow the economists to have their say in pushing the international division and the entire lending effort away from the shoals and reefs and out to smoother seas. To complete the picture and permit this function to be performed, the economics staff also should receive industrial outstandings from the domestic units of the bank, as well as from the international division.

PRICING SYSTEMS AND RELATIONSHIP ANALYSIS

Although we have stressed that pricing considerations should not cloud the credit decision, it generally is more convenient in most banks to make the pricing and credit decisions at the same time.

Also, the same people make both decisions in most banks. This is not always the case, however. In one extremely successful regional bank with extensive worldwide activities, all pricing information is deleted from the credit package on materials seen by members of the credit committee. Account officers and the international division are responsible for profitability, and if they "give the bank away," another matrix in the organization remedies that problem.

Most banks have neither the courage to so completely separate pricing and credit nor a sufficiently developed profit center system to operate this way. Therefore, in most banks there is a constant pull between credit and pricing, and some credit committees spend more time discussing pricing than credit. Fortunately, for strong credits, only time is lost by such extended discussions. However, once pricing starts to dominate the discussion of weak credits, then the bank may be opening itself up for loan losses. Front-end fees, which are quite common in some types of international lending, including syndicated loans, should be viewed either as compensation for extra work actually performed or else as interest paid in advance. Unfortunately, the front-end fee is often billed as a selling point to reluctant credit committees.

One situation in which relatively large front-end fees are often justified, however, occurs in lending to Eastern European or other socialist countries. The central banking officials of these nations often think they can dictate to the world's bankers the maximum rate of interest their nations will pay. In response, pragmatic trade enterprises needing foreign equipment or materials with related financing then offer higher front-end fees to adjust the total package cost to world market borrowing rates. When such fees must be approved in advance of payment by the central bank in question, there seems little risk to the international banker. The adjustable fee merely lets the central bank save face and believe it is holding rates. Packing the front-end fee into the product cost or taking payment from sources outside the borrowing nations is a clear danger sign for the bankers, however. Such an arrangement could indicate that local laws are being violated, which could taint the entire transaction including the financing and the international banker.

To handle pricing and credit decisions simultaneously, but separately, many banks regularly prepare relationship profitability analyses, at least at the time of the annual review. These analyses are particularly important, since most international relationships involve many different services and sources of income, including fee income. In many banks, such as U.S. regional banks, for instance, domestic representatives on the credit committee tend to view all relationships from a compensating balance viewpoint. This approach not only overemphasizes the sometimes low level of demand deposits in comparison to domestic credits, but totally ignores any offsetting effects of other income streams. Hence, a total relationship profitability analysis, especially if used throughout the domestic and international credit approval process, could put all credit extensions on a comparable footing and thus present a more accurate picture for pricing considerations.

One of the main difficulties of administering objective relationship analyses involves the need for an information system to pick up all income and noninterest expense associated with an account or group of accounts. Systems design, as well as administration, requires personnel and computer or machine expense. Yet, it would seem that no bank could afford not to know which of its accounts are profitable and which are not. Income and volumes for international transactions can be captured by specific income accounts in the international division for foreign exchange, letters of credit, acceptances, collections, and payment orders. Breakdown for individual customers may be developed from subsidiary records maintained within the division.

13

Office Management Procedures

Clerical Positions and Rotation / Secretarial and Administrative Duties / Office Machines, Equipment, and Flexible Working Time / Filing Systems and Libraries / Language Laboratories and Translators

For several reasons, clerical functions and office routine must be better organized in international banking than in domestic banking in order to accomplish similar amounts of work on a timely basis. In spite of modern communications methods, the distances involved in international activity still affect the time factor. Telephones and telexes transmit messages quickly, but some parts of the world are asleep while others are awake, and the time zones for other continents do not overlap much each day. Also, some foreign language items must be translated, since not all international staff involved in handling various transactions can read or write every language. Finally, functions not found in domestic banking, such as country analysis, foreign currency dealings, extra subledgers, and different accounting and legal systems in each country, all require additional work that is not encountered in domestic banking.

267

To maintain momentum under these circumstances requires high-velocity activity and quick turnaround time on communications, issuing letters of credit, examining documents, and processing credit requests, for example. In addition, heavy travel usually keeps a portion of staff out of the office at any one time. Foreign trips require more time than domestic travel to cover distances and gain transportation economies by making more stops during each trip. Yet, mail arrives, telephone calls continue, and the office work of the travelers continues in their absence; some processing, decisions, and action often are required to maintain customer service. Thus, remaining staff often have to shoulder to some extent a double workload.

Coping can be made easier by better organizing all routine office functions in order to maximize the contribution of clerical staff, secretaries, and administrative assistants. Office machines and equipment can replace human effort and save time and money. Uniform filing systems help one person find materials filed by another person with no wasted time. Libraries can handle general information for quick reference, and language laboratories can help bring the teacher to the students by means of taped cassettes, which saves wear and tear on busy people with heavy travel schedules. When volume warrants, translators can move words while bankers move money and make credit decisions.

The manager of any size international office who ignores office routine is not only beset by internal problems, errors, and unhappy staff but also is easy prey to the competition. Banking is a service industry and people still provide most of the service. The more that each person down the organization line can do to provide fast and accurate service, the more customers should return with future business, the more the profits of the bank and its customers should grow, and the more satisfied employees should be with a job well done.

CLERICAL POSITIONS AND ROTATION

Starting positions are as important for clerks, messengers, and secretaries as for officers. In fact, clerical turnover usually is higher than officer turnover, and total clerical, secretarial, and messenger staff usually outnumber officers, especially in developing countries. New and often inexperienced staff need well-defined positions where they perform effectively with minimum orientation and supervision and, yet, still prepare for more responsible positions. Accordingly, a number of starting positions and a general pattern of rotation and development are necessary for office staff. Then, when people move up the organization, salary levels do not become a problem, and the chances increase that over time the highest paid employees will be the most productive workers.

In developing countries where checks and local communications must be collected and delivered outside the bank, messengers or driver jobs are typical starting positions. With a few hours' training per week in banking or even a nonlocal language, messengers can be developed for eventual transfer to inside work as file clerks, telephone operators, or junior clerks. Even in developed countries, someone must sort, open, and deliver mail internally. Such a task provides an ideal opportunity to learn the people, office routine, and some basics about international banking and work flow in the office. With the growing use of word processing machines to replace the standard typewriter, the centralized word processing unit also offers a good way to start in the international banking office.

Movement from messenger, driver, mail clerk, word processor, and other similar starting jobs generally should be upward toward general clerical, junior accounting clerk, secretarial, and administrative positions. File clerk positions, depending upon the number of files and complexity of the operation, also could be starting jobs. Secretarial work in some organizations always has been a starting position.

Another example, the telex operator's position, especially in smaller operations, is an ideal way to start in international banking, especially for the first-time employee or recent clerical graduate. Clerical skills such as typing can be applied immediately, the importance of detail work and accuracy can be learned quickly, and the international perspective can be gained while contending with distant places, different time zones, and unusual names. The sending and receipt of messages quickly introduces the newcomer to all the people and sections of the department and also prevents the newcomer from being lost in a corner. Reading the messages for content in addition to accuracy should provide a basis for solid discussion, including questions and answers, with a patient supervisor, who should be experienced, at least to some degree, in all the workings of the department at a general level.

Movement upward from the telex operator or other starting position will depend upon the balancing of the clerical openings in operations or other parts of the banking office and the abilities, interests, and job performance of each employee. Possibilities include secretarial positions anywhere in the office, as well as positions in operations areas with functions that are relatively easy to master, such as funds transfer, bookkeeping, or collections. It is probably better to transfer persons to openings in sections dealing with foreign exchange, letters of credit, and systems, procedures, reports, and control only after training and experience in other areas of operations.

As for transmission of telex messages, banks in most nations of the world now have the option of using conventional telex channels or joining the Society for Worldwide Interbank Financial Telecommunications (SWIFT), which requires a separate telex machine and special equipment for authenticating messages. The SWIFT system is used exclusively by member banks that become shareholders of the organization and gain cost and other advantages associated with expressing all similar messages in uniform styles. Not only payments but foreign exchange, Eurocurrency transactions, confirmations, and even statements of account activity, among other types of transactions and information, eventually will be sent through the SWIFT network.

With the advent of SWIFT the successful telex operator more than ever becomes an excellent candidate for the next opening in the paying and receiving or funds transfer section. By necessity, the telex operator has had interface with the authentication process and hence understands the need for the signature control function and test numbers for authenticating messages.

A rough rule of thumb for clerical starting positions in a particular operation is that the turnover rate should approximate the time needed to completely master the job and provide several months of relatively unsupervised or lightly supervised performance. Thus, to continue the telex operator example, if there is a turnover of two employees per year in a total operations section of about twenty persons, each year a new telex operator would occupy the entry-level position for about six months. If turnover increases or remains at the same rate for a large, expanding operation, then additional entry-level positions should be defined.

SECRETARIAL AND ADMINISTRATIVE DUTIES

Because of the foreign travel schedules of supervising officers on the lending or account administration side of the international division, more duties and greater responsibility usually are delegated to secretaries in those areas. In the absence of the supervising officer, other officers must fill in and do double duty, which means that secretaries often take up additional routine work. In this capacity, some organizations use administrative assistants whose duties fall somewhere between the work of a secretary and that of an officer.

Secretaries in well-organized international units usually do more than organize incoming mail, take transcription, type correspondence, and send out mail and materials to be filed. With an international travel schedule and a supervisor away from the office for extended periods, secretaries control their supervisor's schedules by making appointments, planning itineraries, and booking travel arrangements, including international flights and foreign hotel reservations for future trips. An efficient international secretary knows the supervisor's whereabouts when he is traveling abroad, can handle expense accounting for travel and related entertainment in foreign currencies, and maintains follow-up files to bring up pending matters on a timely basis when the officer is in the office. Replies to routine correspondence are drafted or composed in final form, and material for filing is marked clearly for proper handling by file clerks. In addition, the international secretary can work with foreign telephone calls and handle incoming and outgoing telexes, including making certain that outgoing telexes are transmitted or delivered to personnel responsible for transmission.

International protocol usually requires a like reply, or a telex reply for a telex and a letter reply for a letter. Furthermore, detailed subject references are required on most correspondence to facilitate proper routing in other organizations. Also, file indexes and especially address lists are more necessary in international banking. Account officers or division heads in most international banks exchange annual reports each year and send individual letters to announce organizational changes, new offices, or additional or changed international services. Annual reports and, increasingly, interim financial statements to correspondent banks especially need cover letters to assure direction to the proper officers who will arrange for spread and analysis of financial information for considering annual renewals or extensions of credit and also to make certain that their bank's annual statement is mailed back to the sender, so that reciprocal lines of credit can be prepared for renewal.

Because annual reports are usually the most comprehensive and expensive international pieces prepared by most banks each year, as well as the basis for line renewals with correspondents, it is important that care be taken all year long to keep the international mailing list up to date and accurate. Even with such care and frequent visits, some personnel changes always are taking place in some organizations, and, on the basis that letters require letter replies, much valuable information is often received in exchange for the annual report cover letter. Of course, nonbank customers, foreign lawyers, and other contacts also should be sent annual reports.

Many banks prepare economic data, information on doing business in their country, and articles by members of their management. An efficient secretary with a current address list can keep all of this material flowing unless the bank has a centralized mailing unit for such work.

Because of the heavy travel schedules and increased delegation of routine work to secretaries and administrative assistants, it is imperative to keep clear the signing authority of international staff. As a rule, only officers should sign letters, other materials going outside the bank, and instruments or agreements that bind the bank. This is the duty and responsibility of an officer and cannot be delegated. However, the preparation of such materials by nonofficers for review and signature by the officer is customary and is an ideal training method for junior staff preparing for greater responsibility in the future.

It is not unusual in international banking for one officer to prepare correspondence for another officer, sometimes of higher rank, but not always. For example, an important matter related to an operations transaction may be prepared by an operating officer for the signature of an account officer who deals most frequently with the foreign customer or correspondent bank. Such a chain effort involves the rule of maker, checker, and signer. By this rule, one person prepares a piece of correspondence or item of work, and at least one other reviews and signs the item.

In the same manner, in operations units it is customary in most banks to have two or three separate persons involved in each ticket or entry to the bank's records, each review of documents under letters of credit, each settlement of a collection, or similar item. In applying this rule, the least experienced person prepares the book-keeping entry or investigates the background to answer correspondence. A more experienced person, usually a supervisor or potential supervisor, reviews the work, and an officer, presumably the most experienced person of the three, signs the item. Although this three-level process may seem tedious, it minimizes errors, teaches by doing, and saves the time of the higher-paid staff in the long run.

MACHINES, EQUIPMENT, AND FLEXIBLE WORKING TIME

Machines other than the typewriter generally have been slower to enter the office than the factory. With inflation, increasing employment costs, never ending paper flows, and the pressing need to increase office productivity, however, the pace of applying machines to banking, among other forms of office management, is accelerating. The telex machine now is used often with an attachment capable of preparing a punched tape. Thus, a message may be prepared for transmission by making a tape without having the telex hooked up to its destination. After the tape has been completed, proofread, and corrected, it can be fed at a faster rate for lower cost during transmission. At night the tape attachment can be left on to provide a backup for incoming messages, which might be garbled, overprinted, or otherwise illegible because of machine problems. The new SWIFT organization, whose members use separate machines, private telex lines, and special encoding devices to transmit payments and other international messages, also will speed up the processing of most routine telex communications between banks.

Word processing machines are computer-driven typewriters with the capacity to store data on tapes, disks, or magnetic cards and handle editing or revisions by retyping only the words or letters that need to be changed. These machines have the capacity to take the time, drudgery, and expense out of preparing routine credit recommendation sheets, credit packages, country risk analyses, other reports, and even statistical materials, as well as memorandums, letters, letters of credit, loan agreements, and other documents that may have to be drafted or even redrafted repeatedly with minor modifications.

Because the greatest part of the cost of these machines is related to the computer, savings can be achieved by purchasing or leasing combination units with multiple cathode-ray-tube (CRT) screens and printers. Some banks have purchased software programs for use on their main bank computers and then set up CRT screens and printers at various terminal stations around the bank. With compatible systems between offices, telex messages can be sent to the computers on initial typing, checked by CRT, and then released for transmission without reprocessing. When linked in this manner with the telex machine, additional savings are possible because telex messages need not be retyped again on the telex machine.

Microfiche has reduced the need to store bulky pages of computer printouts and other voluminous information. Most banks now maintain their lists of authorized signatures on microfiches, and this alone can reduce shelves of hard-to-handle books and related filing to the size of a few shoeboxes. The central liability ledger and other subsidiary ledgers also can be reduced to microfiche when bulk and costs warrant.

The use of mini- or desk-top computers should not be overlooked for regional banks and smaller offices. Simple programs can be written within the international unit for special applications such as foreign exchange accounting or handling collection records. Hand-posting foreign exchange records, for example, is difficult to justify now except in developing countries where labor costs are extremely low. Not only can the foreign exchange accounting system be automated on these mini-computers for the smaller international operation but collection reports, record keeping for acceptances, and numerous other uses can be devised.

Although machines can speed up office work and make it easier, the attitude of employees toward using machines often makes more difference in productivity than the actual machine selected. Accordingly, as much care sometimes must be taken in dealing with staff as in shopping for the best equipment bargain. This is especially true with word processing equipment, toward which the attitude of managers and staff using the machines is critical. The machine operators and managers must work together to devise machine applications and often change work methods to gain maximum economies of scale from these machines.

Flexible working time (flex-time) is another area in which worker attitude is more important than the machine involved. In flex-time, a clocklike machine activated by plastic pegs permits workers to log actual hours on the job, but to come and go in accordance with a time schedule agreed upon between supervisor and worker. Late starters can start late and leave late, early birds can get home early, long lunch hours can be taken, or personal errands and appointments accomplished during the day, so long as certain core hours are observed and details are arranged in advance with the supervisor, who must balance all staff requirements. Invented in Germany in 1967, this idea has swept through offices throughout the world, and the system is easily applied in banks. Employees, however, are more or less on an honor system, and pressure is on managers to plan work, arrange schedules, and manage despite all the hustle and bustle of international comings and goings. For many banks, flex-time is an ideal method to permit all staff to participate in flexible schedules on a fair basis to all.

FILING SYSTEMS AND LIBRARIES

In addition to *credit and statement files* mentioned in Chapter 8 in connection with the activities of the credit department, the international division should have several more filing systems to function effectively. Again, because of travel schedules and the increased numbers of people using international records and correspondence, the common objective for all international filing is to get materials out of individual desk files and into collections or file systems to which all appropriate personnel have access. To increase access, each system that is established should have an index and some designated person responsible for maintaining the files and filing materials in them.

A uniform system of marking materials for filing or use of file stamps is indispensable for assuring that materials get to the proper file. Obviously, more than marking the word *file* on some letter or document is needed for this purpose. The filing system to which materials are directed should be clearly indicated. Besides credit and statement files and *loan documentation files,* the international division could have *operations files* for routine correspondence that relates more closely to specific, repetitive transactions than the credit standing of the customer. Materials for these files can be routed to account officers for their information on the way to the files, if the account officers have not signed or seen items involving their customers. *General* or *management files* can contain information by subject matter or function, or for organizations or entities for which credit extension is not a factor.

Files for functions would include audits and examination reports, internal and external reports, activities of foreign branches, subsidiaries, and affiliates, planning, budgets, personnel policies, and capital expenditures. Entities for which credit extension is not a factor would be organizations and associations to which the bank or division belongs, accounting, law, and other service firms, as well as organizations such as the World Bank, regional development banks, and specialized government agencies, or private entities that assist the international bank or its customers. In addition to designing the appropriate filing system and clearly marking the individual file name and geographic location where applicable, file stamps or rules for filing can even specify the proper section of the file, if it has more than one section, and the retention period for the materials being filed.

When all personnel know the different filing systems, have copies of indexes for each system and uniform file stamps, understand the ground rules for filing procedure, and follow these rules, then filing becomes a communications function. New staff can be started in file clerk positions, and time is saved by secretaries and officers alike in locating needed materials.

Because of their importance, it is imperative that all credit files should be included within an index system so that a shelf-by-shelf search does not have to be conducted to determine whether a credit file for a requested name exists. Once it has been determined that a file exists, reference can be made to a drawer or shelf in which the file should be located, or a card will indicate to whom the file was delivered on a certain date.

No more than one credit filing system should exist for each bank location. If each headquarters department, for example, starts its own file for the same customer, the communications function of the credit file system is defeated. One of the most important purposes of a central credit file is to put all information concerning customer contact, calling, and business development, as well as credit information, in a single file, which international as well as domestic department personnel may use for reference in planning, decision making, preparing for future calls, and obtaining basic information.

Although the functioning of the credit file system is vital to the daily work of the lending and lending-related areas of the bank, this system is seldom, if ever, even briefly reviewed or spot checked, let alone audited by most internal or outside auditors because of the press of more urgent matters. A poor filing system without audit or control leads many a secretary or junior officer to despair, since in many banks few seniors ever directly summon a file and can seldom be convinced that a filing system is not functioning properly.

Another common problem with many credit filing systems is the rapid and mountainous accumulation of material in the most used files. A bursting file or numerous volumes for one name defeat the advantages of one, compact, and easy-to-use central repository of orderly information. The first items to come out of the bulging credit file are financial statements or annual reports, which are often confined to separate *statement files* organized parallel to the credit file system. If statement files or more than one volume of a credit file exist, the header sheet of the credit file should so indicate by cross reference. Material for routine or repetitive transactions can be consigned to general files or operations files, again with some notation in the credit file for easy reference.

Perhaps the most obvious, but also most tedious, solution to overweight credit files is to clean them out periodically. A good time to perform this chore is during the annual review process. If junior officers are expected to clean out files, some ground rules should be given, or seniors should at least review the materials recommended for destruction. To aid in periodically cleaning out credit files, a file stamp may have a place to indicate the number of years an item should be held or whether it should become a permanent part of the file.

For statistical materials and general credit information that is received from central banks, foreign governments, accounting firms, as well as newspapers, magazines, periodicals, books, and other materials that can stand upright or be stored in piles, it may be more convenient to place materials in a library rather than in filing systems. Whether the library is a few shelves or a room, some order of arrangement is necessary. Since many of the materials more suited for a library are used in connection with country analysis, one of the most common international banking arrangements is by country order or regions of the world.

To supplement the country order, statistical series and similar materials can be grouped together, reference books and directories can form another unit, and textbooks and other explanatory materials can create still another grouping. If newspapers, journals, and magazines are separated from the books and permanent materials, a simple arrangement exists for the smaller library. More elaborate topical systems, common in major libraries, are used for the libraries of larger banks. For economies of scale in the largest banks, it may be appropriate to combine international division materials with a bankwide library.

Furthermore, centralization of materials and responsbility for library materials and subscriptions provide more effective control of costs and monitoring for receipt of purchased materials. The international division budget for newspapers, magazines, statistical and other information services, and books from around the world represents a substantial investment, and these working tools must be maintained in good order to be used efficiently. Moreover, because of the high cost of foreign subscriptions and other printed materials, it is necessary to use routing lists extensively so that more than one person may have the opportunity to read current materials on a timely basis. In addition to handling the budgeting and ordering and receiving materials, an efficient librarian can maximize use of library materials by tailor-made routing slips for each subscription or type of material.

LANGUAGE LABORATORIES AND TRANSLATORS

Some of the largest commercial banks with extensive international activities have full-time language instruction programs. Language instructors are engaged permanently or on contracts, and bank training or conference rooms are in constant use for teaching languages. Other banks rely on outside schools and services, which can become extremely expensive for individual instruction or classroom tuition. Accordingly, for many banks, establishment of language laboratories represents a more economical and efficient way to handle language instruction.

Depending upon the particular student and language, some formal study may or may not be needed to supplement the language laboratory materials. But in almost every case, the language lab can save wear and tear on the working banker student and money for the bank. To properly equip the bank language lab, consultation with a school or university is recommended. Special tape playing and recording machines are relatively inexpensive, but, more important, the taped materials and corresponding textbooks must be selected with some expert guidance. This is especially true when different levels of the same language are involved, so that the student may progress satisfactorily to increasingly more difficult work on a consistent basis. In many countries, taped materials can be reproduced with the publisher's prior permission and agreement to purchase textbooks for restricted use by the bank.

In smaller international divisions, foreign language translations are handled on an ad hoc basis by those knowledgeable in the particular language, or are sent outside the bank. If volumes are not great, this does not impose too great a burden on personnel whose primary responsibility involves other work. In larger banks or when volume in particular languages increases in the smaller bank, it is necessary to arrange for language translation on a more formal

basis. In the more formal arrangement, all material sent for translation should be time-stamped upon delivery and return, translations
should be typed and filed with the original item after use, and copies
of any replies also should be filed with copies of translations sent in
response.

At some point in the large-volume translation process, it becomes
necessary to lay down firm ground rules for division of labor.
Otherwise, bankers may spend too much time translating and not
enough making banking decisions. Accordingly, the general rule is
that all material important enough to merit reply, used by others,
and placed in a file must be completely translated by translators,
unless it is so brief that the person handling the item can write the
translation and reply in a few sentences. On this basis, even those
gifted in languages are not bogged down with translating and following up to make certain that files are completed.

In addition, the time of bankers is used according to the level of
their banking ability and not merely because they are also skilled in a
particular language. Furthermore, as many of the bank's routine
matters can be handled by form letters, the translation unit quickly
becomes adept in developing specialized replies and responses to
common situations. This is the key to a good translation unit in any
international bank. Soon, even the translators become bankers with
language skills rather than language experts who work for a bank.

In the event that customers ask the bank for assistance on
banking-related translations, it is important that a clear understanding be worked out in advance to avoid liability on the part of the bank
and that some method of paying for the bank's time be arranged.
For many large importers and exporters, almost all items to be
translated are quite routine. Therefore, many banks make no separate charge for translation work in this circumstance but consider it
to be part of the total package so as to obtain and keep large and
profitable volumes of business, such as letters of credit, for example.
However, it is still necessary to maintain accurate records on the
amount of such work and make certain that the customer is aware
that such work is part of the relationship and the profitability
analysis for the account.

PART IV

Problems

14

Integrating International and Domestic Functions

Traditional Development Pattern / Serving Multinational Corporations / Delivering Commerical and Retail Services / Combining Various International Operations / Dealing with Foreign Investors

T his chapter and the two subsequent chapters combine knowledge of organization, services, planning, people, and procedures in international commercial banking to deal with three problems that will continue to challenge most international banks during the early 1980s. Although these problems may be viewed as challenges, they also represent tremendous opportunities. The international banking organizations that most successfully handle these three areas, without doubt, will outpace their competitors. In addition, in the United States market, both domestic and foreign banks will be dealing with these matters in the face of new and evolving rules and regulations as the United States continues to reform its outmoded banking laws.

The subject of this chapter is the evolution of the international division as more and more of its functions are combined with other units of the commercial bank. This process occurs in order to better

283

serve the bank's customers, especially the multinational corporation. However, individuals increasingly require personal financial services at the international level, and foreign investors are becoming a special category of multinational corporate customer in many nations, both developed and developing.

In the process of integrating international and domestic functions to serve multinational corporations outside the home country of the commercial bank, amalgamation of some previously distinct functions usually occurs. To serve individuals, certain commercial customers, and foreign investors, creation of new specialized units becomes necessary. Integration of other functions such as money market activities, foreign exchange, and other operations, on the other hand, involves greater centralization and a degree of autonomy from the remaining functions in the international division.

Because of the importance of working with the multinational corporation, Chapter 15 is devoted to dealing with the multinational treasury department. Chapter 15 emphasizes the working relationship between commercial bank and corporate treasury department staff, and the present chapter approaches the multinational corporation from the standpoint of internal organizational changes within the commercial bank to better serve the corporation. Finally, Chapter 16 deals with international problem and workout credits, which seem destined to be with the commercial banking industry in greater volume for the next several years than in the past because of the difficult economic conditions and turbulent political changes taking place in many parts of the world.

TRADITIONAL DEVELOPMENT PATTERN

Historically, in most banks, all services with any international connection started or at some point were concentrated in the international division or foreign department. All foreign exchange transactions, from a million U.S. dollar forward sale of Swiss francs to purchase of a bank note for 1,000 Spanish pesetas to collection of a check for 20 Canadian dollars by a U.S. bank and a 10 million Eurodollar term loan for a foreign subsidiary of a multinational corporation, were the responsibility of the international staff. And in many banks this is still the case today.

In many U.S. banks, for example, any letter or correspondence from a foreign address is still sent by the mail department directly to the international division, and, of course, telex machines usually are located near the international staff until a separate bankwide communications department and wireroom is established. At least in the beginning, such arrangements make sense, because only the international staff usually know how to cope with such transactions. Expertise is not sufficiently diffused throughout the banking organization to handle international work in any other way.

However, with the passage of time and as the volume of international business builds, it becomes inefficient for the same person to open a personal checking account, next approve a sizable overdraft for a correspondent bank, then consider the provisions of an agreement for a large and complicated corporate loan, and finally answer a telephone inquiry about purchasing travelers checks, all because the transactions in question relate to France or French-domiciled persons. Over time, work on international transactions can be delegated to people with different specialized skills and levels of experience and can be organized by type and size of customer and importance and difficulty of transaction.

We already have seen in Chapter 2 that initially international commercial banking functions generally divide into at least two subunits of the international division, one handling operations and the other account or lending activities. In Chapter 10, the trend toward international correspondent banking was noted. In addition, personal international banking has been separated from the account administration and lending functions in other banks. As a bank develops its international activities, this process of separating special functions continues until, at some stage, specialized international functions begin to be combined with what were once considered purely domestic activities. From mainly a geographic matrix, the bank moves to a functional matrix or to a mixture of the two more heavily weighted toward a functional division of work for international transactions.

Such a trend occurs in an effort to improve service and gain economies of scale by increasing specialization, as well as relate to customer developments and needs, especially for the multinational corporation. But at the same time, certain clearly identifiable and often predictable problems arise as each different commercial bank wrestles with this evolutionary process. Sometimes, customer service improves, but at other banks, customers become so confused that even the key treasury staff of the largest worldwide corporation cannot determine who the corporation's account officer really is in the newly reorganized international bank.

Furthermore, in recent years, especially in U.S. commercial banks, frequent organizational changes have followed in relatively rapid succession in an attempt to cope with competitive and market developments. In some organizations, this involves more than industry specialization, although separate units have existed in many of the largest banks for years to deal with central banks and foreign governments, international institutions and development banks such as the World Bank, and specialized programs at government agencies, such as the Export-Import Bank and the U.S. Agency for International Development, among others.

SERVING MULTINATIONAL CORPORATIONS

As corporations have become more international in conducting their activities, the traditional division of the bank into lending and account units for international activities, for national corporate business or specialized industries, for commercial, and for retail or personal banking, usually conducted through branches, has tended to break down. Building upon the general concept of the specialized industries division, more than ten years ago, several large U.S. money center banks moved toward structures with world corporation divisions. In this type of unit, worldwide relationships of multinational corporations were supervised, while totally domestic companies remained with the national or regional divisions. Within the last few years, many U.S. regional banks have followed this pattern or some variation of it with the creation of their own world banking or multinational banking departments.

Identifying this trend, however, does not explain the variety of organizational combinations now being used in an attempt to better serve the multinational corporations. Nor do the skills of the officers in these newly created units always keep up with the demanding requirements of the multinational corporation. This problem further accounts for some of the different organizational approaches taken, especially by the U.S. regional banks. But non-U.S. banks are by no means behind in this trend and many foreign-owned banks and branches in the United States have established corporate finance or other departments in their U.S. offices to single out the multinational corporation for special attention and expertise, at least at the marketing level.

To illustrate and better understand the extreme range of possibilities that exist for organizing the international commercial bank to serve the multinational corporation, let us consider two hypothetical commercial banks, Bank A and Bank B. Later we will introduce two other banks, Bank C and Bank D. Let us assume, for convenience here, that all these banks are full-service U.S. commercial banks.

At Bank A the international division or department is relatively new, having been established between five and ten years ago, and is combined in a group with the bank's trust, investment, and marketing services divisions. The international division is staffed at the senior officer level almost entirely with personnel who came originally from outside the bank. Thus, many of the staff are new to the organization and to the bank's market area. In addition, the international division is in a location physically separate from the rest of the bank, that is, an entirely different building, and the division maintains its own operations, procedures, and subsidiary ledger accounting records, although the general ledger interfaces with the rest of the bank. Moreover, this international division has its own credit files for U.S. customers, conducts its own calling program to obtain business from U.S. customers, and has only limited contact with the rest of the bank.

Bank B, on the other hand, has an international division that is more than ten years old and is combined in a group with several other wholesale commercial banking divisions, which are generally organized by industry and U.S. geographic lines. Bank B, in fact, applies modern matrix techniques to manage the bank from at least three different aspects, including geographic, industrial, and product or service line.

Bank B is staffed mainly with people drawn from inside the bank. All of the domestic calling staff have extensive or at least some working experience in dealing with almost all types of corporate customers in the United States and abroad. During calls, these domestic officers discuss with their corporate customers or prospects not only cash management, short-term investment portfolio opportunities, and domestic lending, but also letters of credit, overseas collections, international paying and receiving, foreign exchange, acceptance and trade finance, and export or project lending, among other matters. When calling, the domestic officers always inquire about the international activities of their corporate customers and over the years have encouraged some originally totally domestic companies to enter the export market or obtain raw materials and services from outside the United States. Often the bank has assisted with introductions and other ideas in this regard.

Bank B's international calling officers share a floor of the bank with domestic corporate calling officers, and international operations are closely integrated with the systems, procedures, and accounting systems of the entire bank. One set of common credit files is used throughout the bank, and there is frequent contact between the international and domestic calling officers, who are able to take marketing of specific transactions quite far before bringing in the specialized international experts, who are responsible for various areas of the world or particular international services.

At this point, let us consider which bank would provide the best service to its customers, which bank derives the most profit from its business, and which bank would be the best employer for the prospective international banker. Obviously, Bank A offers some distinct advantages, such as direct access to the international division, since that unit conducts its own calling program. However, Bank A might not be doing as well as its competitors with regard to net income, because it could be missing cross-selling opportunities, which also make it easier for the corporate treasurer to function with fewer banking appointments.

At Bank B, on the other hand, the calling officers might have to work harder, be a more experienced, and know about more services, techniques, and developments around the world. A calling officer position at Bank B would be a more challenging, demanding, and interesting job. On balance, most persons would quickly select Bank B for providing better service, greater profit, and better employment opportunity. Moreover, most observers probably would agree that Bank A needs several changes to become more effective.

These examples deliberately show two extremes, one situation probably representing the ideal, and the other, much less than the worst reality. Short of the ideal situation, there are several ways that can be devised to handle a situation, which would fall somewhere between these two extremes. One solution might be to create in the international division, in the domestic corporate banking function, or perhaps somewhere in between a unit composed of internationally experienced officers who would call on U.S. customers and prospects to provide international services. Either of the three variations — that is, with this unit in international banking, in corporate banking, or entirely separate — would require a great deal of coordination between the units or departments involved.

To carry this example a step further, let us assume that at a third bank, Bank C, an entirely new unit is formed with at least fifteen officers, all of whom are experienced in corporate calling, overseas duty, or both. With this number of qualified staff, a significant dent could be made in the total U.S. market, certainly at least on a selective basis. Calls could be made alone by officers from the new department or in tandem with domestic corporate calling staff.

The Bank C solution represents one of the more typical multinational banking divisions, and has both advantages and disadvantages. A large investment in personnel and management is required. Customers still are dealing with several calling officers from the same bank, one for domestic, and another for international. A great deal of communication is required of the corporate treasury staff, both within the bank and, often overlooked and probably harder to control, within the corporation.

However, this multinational banking department probably does the job well. Given some time to make a sufficient number of calls, cross-selling more than likely occurs. Business and profits are generated as the staff of the new department is introduced to or meets with existing customers and also proceeds to reach new prospects for the bank. This probably is the most traditional multinational banking organization in most U.S. banks these days, but not the only solution possible. Keeping in mind the organizational structures of Bank A, Bank B, and the multinational department of Bank C as a frame of reference, another possible approach to multinational banking exists, which will be described here for Bank D.

Let us assume that Bank D has an excellent core of proven multinational customers, a larger list of prospects, and wants to move slowly without the Bank C type of investment and disruption from a mass transferral of account relationships to new officers. In essence, Bank D wants to make certain that its U.S. customers are being adequately provided with international services, which otherwise might not be possible without sufficient personnel trained in international banking to cover customers in the United States and customers in countries outside the United States.

Moreover, let us assume further that at Bank D the overriding goal is to tie together existing international customers, loans, and services, and other customers in the bank's own market area in the United States. By providing international services for domestic customers, Bank D believes it can be of more service and keep these customers in the bank at the same time it attempts to cross-sell and increase income from building more banking services for each corporate relationship. Accordingly, at Bank D, the new multinational banking division consists of the domestic corporate banking function serving large corporations with international activities, all of the previous international division activities, and a correspondent banking section that is responsible for all banking relationships, in the United States and throughout the world.

All these general patterns and several additional variations on them have been or are being used by different U.S. banks. The degree of success with each formula depends not only upon the formula, but also upon the human and management resources that particular banks can devote to their effort to serve the multinational corporation. In some regional bank markets without intense competition, the mere emphasis of any type of service for the multinational is enough to gain market share, regardless of organization form. In other cases and especially if competitors promptly make similar moves, it is difficult to measure any gain in market share, but results might be measurable in terms of improvement in internal efficiency. In any event, it is safe to assume that further experimentation, change, and reorganization will occur in both regional and money center banks over the coming years.

Perhaps the most extensive organizational change of this type was announced by Citibank during late 1979. Under the terms of this reorganization, which is still being implemented, almost all traditional commercial banking services have been divided along market lines for delivery by two main groups, one to serve individuals, and another to serve nonindividuals or institutions, including governments, corporations, and other businesses and nonprofit organizations. One goal of this reorganization is to better prepare Citibank for greater penetration of both U.S. and non-U.S. markets to serve the banking needs of individuals and at the same time permit delivery of efficient service to continue for multinational corporations and foreign government units, which have been the bank's main foreign market for more than two decades. Should Citibank's efforts be perceived as successful after some period of time, it is likely that other large banks, both inside and outside the United States, could follow this pattern.

DELIVERING COMMERCIAL AND RETAIL SERVICES

As discussed here, reorganizing the international bank to better serve the multinational corporation in most banks today means creation of a new integrated structure. This usually involves combining international and domestic functions, especially for marketing efforts, account administration, and lending decisions, and therefore represents to some extent a greater degree of amalgamation or even centralization. The recent trend for handling international commercial (in the sense of trading) and retail services, on the contrary, is toward decentralization.

Commercial relationships with emphasis on trading at the international level usually involve lending and many different domestic services of the bank. However, as already mentioned in Chapter 8, for commercial customers involved heavily in international trade, namely, exporting and importing or providing related services, the largest volume of daily business with the international bank often centers on international payments, collections, foreign exchange transactions, opening letters of credit or negotiating documents under letters of credit, or acceptance financing. Under these circumstances, commercial customers, especially firms with relatively small numbers of management staff in relation to volume of business and frequency of transactions conducted, need banks that are located convenient to their places of business.

If a firm is close to the headquarters-based international division of the bank, there is no problem, of course, and the firm's employees handling banking matters have no problem in coming frequently to the bank. However, for firms outside the central banking or downtown bank headquarters perimeter, the journey involved may become a hardship. Therefore, many banks have set up international units in branches throughout important commercial cities or even throughout nations. Among others, the European and Asian banks have pioneered in this effort, but leading banks of some South American, Middle Eastern, and African countries are by no means behind. Offices capable of handling international transactions may be in branches near seaports, airports, industrial park areas, or wherever enough customers, perhaps even one important customer, can provide volume sufficient to warrant staffing international units in locations outside the international division headquarters.

At these branches or regional centers are account and lending officers with responsibility for relationships in the region, usually up to some limited amount of credit extension. In the United States, on the other hand, this decentralization effort has been much slower except in a few major banking centers and key exporting states. Under the U.S. banking law, the Edge Act banks carry out the function of an international branch or regional center within the United States, away from the bank's headquarters international division. Many U.S. banks are now establishing chains of Edge Act offices across the nation. The International Banking Act of 1978 permits the establishment of branches of Edge Act banks, instead of entirely separate entities. This eases the capital requirements and legal housekeeping to maintain separate entities. At the same time, chains of Edge Act offices permit U.S. banks to better prepare for nationwide banking.

Analogous to such developments to bring appropriate international services closer to the location of commercial firms is the effort to provide international services for individuals at retail or domestic branch offices. In Chapter 8, the task of domestic branch personnel in providing international services and leads to international services was considered within the context of supporting the international division. A domestic branch network staffed with personnel trained to handle routine international transactions is not only more convenient to customers but also builds volumes for the international operations unit of the international division. Assuming such volume can be handled without large or any staff additions, this volume should help spread overhead and hence increase profits. In addition to these results, moving the more routine international transactions out to the branch offices tends to free international division personnel to concentrate more of their efforts on more complicated transactions or on corporate wholesale business, which generally involve greater monetary amounts per transaction and the principle of management by exception.

The most resistance to moving international services out to branch offices arises in regional banks or banks with newer international functions. Major money center banks and those with decades of international experience in the United States, for example, usually have one or more persons in each important branch capable of handling routine foreign transactions. European banks usually do not consider buying and selling foreign currency and cashing travelers checks as international business, but just another retail service to long-standing customers, travelers, and tourists.

To overcome resistance within the smaller bank, it is usually necessary for the international division to make some direct effort at handling retail business and to demonstrate that it is profitable and often necessary for competitive reasons. A start in this direction usually involves moving a specialized foreign teller to the retail banking floor of the headquarters office branch. This teller can be responsible for over-the-counter sales of international funds transfers and foreign banknotes and also can handle bank note sales and general inquiries from other domestic branches.

By maintaining statistics on which branches provide the most foreign activity, a priority list can be established for training personnel at other branches to provide international services. This effort becomes particularly important when key officers of multinational corporations, either domestically based or traveling from abroad, are able to execute international transactions such as exchanging foreign currency or cashing travelers checks at a randomly selected branch office instead of making their way to the bank's headquarters-based international division. Improving retail foreign services thus may be an entree to building the bank's wholesale international business, especially foreign exchange.

One major money center bank in the United States attacked this problem by establishing a complete branch office for personal international transactions on the ground floor of its headquarters building. Staffed with multilingual personnel, the office was doing a thriving business within a short time after opening. With the new office, it was no longer necessary for customers to ride elevators to do business at the limited counter space in a corner of the international division. A bank that makes a smaller start in this direction by placing only one specially trained international division teller on the main office banking floor may hope that in time the teller and others at additional branch offices could become part of the branch or retail banking staff. The foreign exchange teller, foreign teller, note teller, or teller in charge of all miscellaneous functions is the starting point for international services in most banks with extensive branch operations. These tellers are usually more experienced, can handle payment orders, drafts, and foreign currency, and are trained sufficiently to contact appropriate international division personnel by telephone in the event of questions or problems.

For a bank starting out to provide international services at the retail level in only one or a few domestic branches, foreign currency or foreign checks may be accepted against simple receipts from regular customers with accounts on a collection basis. After application of proper exchange rates and receipt of good funds, the customers' accounts can be credited.

As international business develops at retail branches, it is important for experienced international staff to monitor distribution and use of the foreign services manual that was described in Chapter 8. Use of this tool with its sample forms, instructions, applications for international services, and explanations expedites delivery of foreign services and facilitates questions between branch office and international division personnel to solve problems and improve services for customers who deal with the branch office.

COMBINING VARIOUS INTERNATIONAL OPERATIONS

At some point in the development of a major international bank, the basic international operations activities, such as foreign exchange, Eurocurrencies, funds transfers, international collections, and letters of credit, outgrow their original home in the international division. That time may be at hand when several hundred staff are involved in these functions and senior officers with years of experience and technical expertise have been developed over the years in each of these areas. At this stage, personnel matters, space requirements, and similar considerations of scale outweigh factors such as specialized knowledge and proximity to the remainder of the international division for close coordination and backup supervision.

When international operations reach this stage, they constitute well-defined and large businesses in their own right. The problems of management are different. New techniques plus automated equipment, including word processing machines and other hardware, may be required to move the workload each day. Several years ago Citibank went outside the field of banking to hire a well-known executive with manufacturing experience to run its international and domestic operations. In short order, the entire operations function in its own separate building in downtown New York City was running according to the management concepts of an automotive assembly line, several miles away from the international and other divisions at the bank's midtown headquarters.

If something is gained by such sweeping changes, something also is often lost. The problem of quickly locating specific documents or transactions for follow-up or status reports in such high-volume operations becomes almost more difficult than actually carrying out the transactions. No or little information is available to the customer until the final results roll off the assembly line at the end of the transaction. Tailor-made servicing or special reports for individual customers are difficult and expensive, if not impossible, to produce on a timely basis. Staff of the customer seldom deal with the same persons in the bank. Before recently changing banks, one important U.S. exporter sent routinely each month one of its key staff to another city for at least a day at a time to visit its bank and determine the status of pending outgoing international collection items. It is within this context that smaller banks in major cities, Edge Act banks in the United States, foreign bank branches, and even inland regional banks can provide quality service.

As banks grow in size in international activity, foreign exchange and Eurocurrency functions are often consolidated with the domestic investment or funding functions in the bank. Again, this makes good sense if volumes warrant and qualified senior-level staff with knowledge of these functions exist. However, controls and related accounting for foreign exchange involve entirely different criteria than those used for domestic transactions. Thus, the cost and effort for relatively elaborate accounting systems and procedural changes make integration of the foreign exchange function fairly unusual for most banks. It is far more likely that as foreign exchange volumes expand, an entirely separate unit for this activity alone will be created.

Although the Eurodollar function is more often combined with domestic investment functions, especially in the smaller U.S. regional banks, this also can create more problems than it solves, depending upon the size of the bank. If other Eurocurrencies are handled in addition to Eurodollars, there is the same problem with transfer of foreign exchange accounting controls to the investment area. Moreover, because of the basic similarity in the techniques of contracting, basic paper flow including confirmations, accounting, and control for foreign exchange and Eurocurrency functions as compared to other investment operations, these activities often are combined in small-volume operations. Breaking off part of the workload, assuming, for example, that in a U.S. bank only Eurodollars and not other Eurocurrencies are involved, may render uneconomical a previous concentration of labor.

If any lesson can be drawn from this, it would seem to be that continuous or periodic review of all international functions is needed as international activity expands. An almost continuous search must be under way to discover possible economies of scale from combining what may at the time be viewed as separate international and domestic functions. For example, communications, consisting of all telex, wire, and facsimile transmissions involving movement of money or related information, is another function that often warrants combining.

This trend, as it approaches its logical conclusion, often leaves little of the original international division in recognizable form. If international operations move to an assembly line administered by the same division of the bank that has the ultimate responsibility for check processing and similar functions, if the overseas money desk merges with the domestic investment function, and international corporate banking becomes part of a multinational unit, then the remaining international division consists mainly of those responsible for handling international correspondent banking relationships, administering foreign branches and other offices, and coordinating certain activities between various other units of the bank, such as credit approvals over certain limits. One trend, however, has developed recently to break this orderly evolution of redeployment of international division work in the United States and elsewhere where foreign investment plays a dominant role in the domestic economy. Thus, organizing to better serve the foreign corporation doing business in the home country of the bank has now become a major challenge for many banks.

DEALING WITH FOREIGN INVESTORS

Logically, it would be assumed that banks with multinational banking units would place responsibility for relationships with foreign investors with these specialized units. However, review of the origins of most multinational banking units, especially in the smaller and regional U.S. banks, indicates that staff from this part of the bank is charged primarily with responsibility for selling international services to domestic-based corporations doing business around the world. Even at the larger banks, the world corporation departments concentrate on a global approach to banking, regardless of the customer's home country.

However, with reverse investment, a new dimension, or at least greater emphasis on what previously was a smaller part of a total picture, has been added. The foreign investor often establishes or takes over by acquisition an almost entirely domestic business operation of some kind to expand a share of its market in the home nation of the international commercial bank. Exporting from the new entity or other international activity may play only a small part in the new business. For most foreign investors, especially those coming to the United States in the last few years, the U.S. market is the main part of their business, if not the total objective.

These new businesses in the United States are staffed by only a few key foreign personnel, if indeed the operation is not totally staffed by U.S. personnel. The emphasis by the treasury officers of the new business is on domestic U.S. financing and money handling techniques. Only the shareholders of the new firm may be foreign; otherwise the entity is American. Cash management services, lease financing, and special programs to provide tax holidays or financing at tax-free rates, among other techniques, are the services most sought. The foreign and local staff want local contacts and wish to quickly become part of the local scene. Yet, especially key foreign staff or representatives of the foreign shareholder may not be entirely comfortable with totally domestic-oriented staff of the bank.

The challenge to serve these firms has existed for U.S. banks for several years now, and certainly will increase well into the 1980s with the weakened U.S. economy and dollar relative to other nations and currencies. The fact that the challenge has not always been well met by U.S. banks is evidenced by the rapid growth and obvious success of foreign banks, which have expanded the number of their locations not only in the coastal and major money centers but also throughout the heartland of the United States. These foreign banking operations are serving an obvious need by bridging the distance between the foreign company's treasury staff, well known to the banks at home, and their customers' new U.S. operations.

As U.S. banks overseas once led or sometimes followed the U.S. multinational abroad, the foreign bankers are now leading or following, as the case may be, their homeland customers to the United States. Although the emphasis here is on U.S. techniques of domestic banking, the credit risk may well be foreign, regardless of whether actual or foreign guarantees are involved. Here again, the foreign bank, with greater knowledge of its native customers and better contacts and introductions, may be more aggressive than the U.S. bank in extending credit. Furthermore, the U.S. office of the foreign bank may put forth greater effort in providing other services for the foreign-owned U.S. company.

To counteract these efforts by foreign banks, some U.S. banks again may have to reorganize to modify the responsibility for or alter the approach of the existing multinational unit or other similar departments. It is clear that a great deal of coordination will be required between any totally domestic units of the bank handling any part of the relationship and those with knowledge and experience gained from working with the foreign parent or investor. The bank in the nation of the direct investment, however, has one natural advantage. Generally, it is advantageous for the new entity to become a part of the local scene to the greatest extent possible. This means working with local management, suppliers, and customers, as well as local accountants, lawyers, and bankers.

Moreover, as the local operation of the foreign investor grows, more and increasingly sophisticated banking services will be required from the commercial bank. For example, administration of employee benefit plans in accordance with U.S. laws is but one area where U.S. banks doubtless will excel for some time vis-à-vis their foreign bank competition in the United States. With time, however, it is only logical to assume that foreign banks will begin to provide a broader range of services and move to compete on more fronts with U.S. banks. This indicates a trend of increasing competition between U.S. and foreign banks for both international and domestic banking business. This is especially likely, since a higher percentage of significant new capital investment in the United States is from foreign sources.

15

Working with Corporate Treasury Departments

Acquisition of most international commercial banking services is controlled by members of corporate treasury departments. They not only select the types of services to be supplied by banks but also decide upon the particular banks to provide services, and pay the banks for their work. Accordingly, the banker must work with the treasurer to conclude a sale and obtain payment for services. The purpose of this chapter is to examine the relationship between international commercial bankers and treasury officers or treasury departments of customers.

Although the words *corporate treasurer* are used in this chapter, the concepts discussed here apply in broad outline to many other noncorporate organizations encountered by the international banker. Officials of finance ministries, central banks, development finance institutions, and state holding companies, to mention only a few examples, usually will consider the international banker in basically the same way as the corporate treasurer will. Moreover, interchangeable use will be made of the terms *corporate treasurer, treasury personnel,* and *treasury department staff,* since international bankers, especially when working with far-flung multinational organizations, deal not only with the treasurer but also with his assistants and various staff members.

In working with the treasury staff of each customer, it is necessary to understand the organization of that corporate treasury department within the context of the entire corporation. Also, it is important to understand the main functions of the treasury section and the priority given to each function. Further, the banker must know exactly where his own bank fits into the overall corporate banking picture of the customer and what approaches the corporate treasurer takes with his bankers in general and with his own bank in particular.

Although all treasurers tend to consider international financial matters in accordance with certain basic principles, each treasurer and organization is unique. Accordingly, the final decision or way a matter ultimately is handled is based upon the history, characteristics, and personalities of the organization and key treasury department members. Individual bankers assigned to particular customers must know these customers well, work with them long enough to know the details of each customer's business and industry, and understand how each customer reacts through its key decision makers under different economic conditions and circumstances.

Based upon the perspective of how the treasurer views bankers in general and his own bank in particular, the international banker then can develop a calling program in accordance with his bank's international marketing strategy. During the course of implementing this calling program, the banker will learn more about the customer and specifically how his bank might provide useful services and ideas to the customer. At the same time, the customer learns more about the caller's bank, especially its key personnel who can serve the customer's organization, and its strengths, which distinguish it from other banks.

To maximize return to the bank for all the information, ideas, advice, and various different banking services that are supplied to different units in complex organizations around the globe, the relationship analysis is indispensable. This analysis, which summarizes all work done by the bank in association with all related income and expenses, must be prepared at least once a year, if not monthly, and then must be reviewed jointly by the banker and the treasurer. On the basis of this review, the mix of services, fees, and other compensation will be modified from time to time to assure a long-term relationship of mutual benefit to the customer and the bank.

TREASURY DEPARTMENT ORGANIZATION

In most nonbanking organizations that use international commercial banking services, the treasury or international financial unit tends to be relatively small in comparison with other units of the corporation. This is true not only when comparing numbers in line activities but also in staff units. In most manufacturing organizations, for example, production personnel vastly outnumber the financial personnel concerned with treasury duties. Sales personnel of most customers also tend to be more numerous than treasury staff. But even when comparing one staff unit with another staff unit, legal personnel in many corporations, for example, vastly outnumber the staff of the treasury section.

As a consequence, the treasurer's staff is often hard pressed to keep up in detail with developments throughout the corporation. If the raising of funds from outside the organization is of high priority, treasury people may spend more of their time with outsiders, namely bankers or other financiers, than they do with people from within their own organization. It is not surprising, therefore, that often they are not fully aware of the details of recent developments or future plans of their organizations. Many large corporations provide regular quarterly meetings for treasury personnel, not only to improve communications within the treasury department, but also to update treasury staff on significant corporate activities and trends.

This problem of information or knowledge of developments within the corporation is particularly pronounced in the large organization operating worldwide, the multinational corporation. In situations where the treasury staff is not sufficiently aware of total corporate activities, the bankers may find it useful to develop contacts with key personnel responsible for international activites, including planning, development, mergers, acquisitions, administration, and sales, or even various operating units. Care must be taken, however, not to go around the treasurer, as in some cases it is difficult to distinguish between what the treasury staff does not know and what the treasury staff does not wish to reveal to outsiders, including bankers.

Another characteristic of the treasury function in some larger organizations is the internal rivalry, potential competition, or overlapping jurisdiction between treasury and accounting functions. Many corporations have met this problem head on by combining both treasury and accounting under one financial officer. However, many organizations still struggle with a split in this area, and the results appear in many different ways.

For example, in dealing with new projects, acquisitions, or mergers, a small treasury staff may work closely with accounting staff or other designated personnel in order to develop financial projections, assumptions for these projections, and alternative financial plans. On large and sophisticated projects, the banker sometimes can obtain more information in terms of both quantity and quality from the accounting personnel assigned to the project than he can from the treasury department.

To obtain sufficient facts to render sound advice, the banker must deal with well-informed personnel, and sometimes such persons are outside the treasury function. The helpful treasury member will recognize this situation and, if possible, become more knowledgeable in order to satisfy the banker's proper inquiries. As an alternative, the treasury official could prepare an accounting or other expert, who may not be experienced in working with bankers, to meet with the banker and the treasury representative.

Perhaps one of the most difficult situations encountered by international bankers occurs in connection with larger multinational customers that may have relatively weak or inexperienced treasury personnel assigned to a particular function or project. Even in activities involving vast sums of money, treasury personnel may have only limited knowledge and little authority, or perhaps only the power to make recommendations up the line. In these cases, the international banker often can incur great cost and expend valuable time to no avail if proposals are not submitted up the line or are given only cursory consideration.

Worse yet is the inexperienced treasury official who takes the unique ideas and detailed creative thinking of an international banker and then uses such work as a pattern for competitive bidding by a flock of other bankers to gain a fraction of a percentage point advantage so as to impress his superiors. Once on the receiving end of such treatment is warning enough for the banker, who has no patent on his technology as do engineers, or monopoly on his relationship as do lawyers. A corporate treasurer who does not know enough of market prices to accept reasonable offers but must shop continuously for bidding and rebidding to the nearest fraction of a percent not only lacks confidence in his own judgment but soon lacks bankers to bid for his projects. Eventually, of course, others outside the treasury function in the customer organization discover the problem and new treasury personnel have a chance to rebuild banking relationships.

Interestingly, it is often in engineering or construction organizations, where complaint is loud and acrimonious if one of their customers uses detailed engineering or feasibility work to solicit competing tenders, that this plagiarism frequently occurs on the financing proposal side. Competition is welcome among bankers, but when extensive preparation of creative financing or assembling of syndicates of bankers is involved, the corporate treasurer has certain ethical limits to not broadcast and call for rebidding. Likewise, the banker has an obligation not to take undue advantage of lack of knowledge on the part of the customer. To charge more than the fair market price may lead to the first transaction for the banker, but not to repeated business opportunities, when the corporate treasurer eventually becomes more knowledgeable.

Another common situation arises in smaller organizations, especially in smaller overseas operations of even large corporations, where separate treasury and accounting personnel cannot be justified, even though this may be the general rule for the corporation. In these situations, a controller often is asked to do double duty and handle treasury functions, including raising finance and dealing with bankers. If both accounting and treasury functions are under common headquarters or regional control, no serious problems are likely to arise or remain unresolved for long.

More often, however, coordination between the two functions within the corporation occurs only at a relatively high level, often back in the headquarters country. The controller, for instance, may report on a straight-line basis to headquarters accounting officials but only on a dotted-line basis to the headquarters treasury head. This, obviously, is another potential trouble area for the international banker, and the best results can be achieved only by a totally coordinated approach between bankers serving the headquarters treasury and fellow bankers dealing with the overseas operation. Otherwise, the only real loser in the showdown between the treasury and controllership functions that inevitably occurs is likely to be the international banker, who all in the corporate headquarters agree is the real scapegoat, as the treasury and controllers departments at last reach harmony after the fact.

Because of the specialized nature of international financial activities, many major corporations and other organizations having extensive dealings with international bankers may divide domestic and international treasury functions in some manner. For these organizations, the chain of command is clear for the international banker, and many of the problems of the type already mentioned may have been resolved long ago.

Furthermore, success by the banker in one overseas situation often may be repeated easily by the international banker for other foreign operations and lead to an expanded overall relationship. However, in order for this success to be recognized properly, once again, close coordination is necessary between the bankers dealing with the head treasury officer in charge of international financial activities and the bankers serving units in the field. Otherwise, senior home-office personnel may not know or could overlook the importance of effort provided by the bank far away from headquarters.

TREASURY DEPARTMENT FUNCTIONS

Because we are concerned in our study with the relationship between the international banker and the customer treasury department, we will not make an exhaustive study of the entire corporate treasury function. Instead, we will focus only on areas of international importance. Naturally, the more the international banker knows about all of the banking services provided by his entire bank for the corporation or other customer, the more effective he will be in maximizing the bank-customer relationship at the international level. A helpful concept to keep in mind in this regard is that the corporate treasury department functions as the internal bank of the corporation and thus performs many services the commercial bank provides. The commercial bank is an extension of the treasury department function and must work closely with it to benefit both parties. Moreover, although the international work of a treasury department parallels its domestic activities to a large extent, it can be broken down into about half a dozen broad areas that may be related to the corporation's balance sheet for purposes of our study.

1. *Cash management.* As its name implies, the treasury department is concerned with cash or, more properly, bank accounts and management of money. This involves selecting banks to hold deposit accounts and establishing and monitoring desired or target balance levels to avoid excessive idle funds and overdraft charges and yet also pay for services rendered by achieving the set average balance levels. Money constantly flows in and out of corporate accounts as the corporation sells its goods and services, collects for it sales, meets payrolls, and pays invoices for goods and services acquired. The corporate treasurer controls this flow and depends upon the banks to safekeep the balances in the accounts.

The well-known object of cash management is to collect monies due as fast as possible, pay out monies only when due, and keep no more idle balances on hand than necessary. Excess funds can be marshaled or concentrated in key accounts for investment or greater ease in handling payments. Success in this effort depends on good forecasting and fast and accurate information, which is coordinated promptly and used properly. The international banker is a key to good results in many of these areas and is indispensable for carrying out instructions to move balances from one bank account to another upon proper instructions from the treasurer or his designates. For treasury personnel inexperienced in moving money internationally, unclear or incorrect instructions often set off chains of circumstances that cause delays in routing money though the international banking network and, hence, loss of interest earnings. Accordingly, it is imperative for international bankers to work closely with their customers before the inception of large money transfers to assure that proper instructions prevent costly problems that necessitate lengthy investigations and explanations.

Examining the detail behind the corporate balance sheet should show cash balances at various banks and short-term investments resulting from inflows of payments for accounts receivable and other items reduced by the outflow of expenses, accounts payable, and other similar items. What is not clearly shown on the home currency balance sheet is the foreign exchange exposure of the corporation. Detailed records must be referred to for this information. Thus, the second main international responsibility of the corporate treasurer is to manage this foreign currency exposure. Although the domestic treasury function also is involved with cash management, foreign exchange exposure is unique to the international treasury function, since a purely domestic operation would have assets and liabilities only in one local currency.

2. *Foreign exchange management.* Foreign exchange exposure arises from any asset or liability being denominated in a currency other than the currency of the home office of the corporation. If the entire operation of the organization were frozen in time and liquidated, the gain or loss resulting from converting all accounts of the corporation into the currency of its home office would be the total net foreign exchange exposure of the organization. Since most operations are managed as going concerns, this concept of total net position upon liquidation is not too helpful to the managers of an ongoing enterprise. Hence, foreign exchange exposure is defined in terms of net position, currency by currency.

All Deutsche mark or cruzeiro accounts, for example, are set off against each other to produce a total net position in marks, another in cruzeiros, and other net positions in each other currency in which the corporation does substantial business. Amounts of *de minimus* size may not be worth trying to manage. Accordingly, the first task of managing foreign exchange is to define exposure and the size of exposure that will be managed.

Next, an information system must be set up to gather data regularly on foreign currency transactions and asset and liability account balances. With this information in hand, it is often possible for the corporation to match forecasted foreign currency needs with anticipated receipts in the same currency. Whenever requirements can be matched, the possibility arises of avoiding the need to purchase or sell foreign exchange with parties outside the corporation. Amounts can be maintained in foreign currency accounts and used by other parts of the corporation with only internal accounting. Foreign exchange differentials and commissions for purchases and sales will be unnecessary.

It must be noted, however, that the accounting profession by its rules and by the laws of some countries requires certain prescribed treatment of foreign currency transactions. Furthermore, special rules might exist for the methods and timing of revaluing foreign currency accounts, converting their values to the home currency, or translating and bringing back gains or losses from this process to the home country through the corporation's income statement. The international banker helps corporations with information about such rules, requirements, and changes in the value of individual currencies. Should risks exceed limits established by the corporation, the bank can then assist with arranging for sales of unwanted currencies or purchases of needed currencies by means of spot or future foreign exchange contracts.

The degree of exposure in each currency that a corporation deems acceptable and the methods agreed upon for use in reducing exposure to these limits constitute the foreign exchange exposure policies of the organization. The international banker must know each corporation's policies and be aware of changes in policies that could provide an opportunity for foreign exchange services. Because of the potential for abuse in this area, analogous to a broker churning a customer's investment portfolio, most banks separate the functions for providing information and advice on foreign currencies and for supplying service to actually purchase or sell foreign exchange. Chemical Bank, among other banks, is noted particularly for its high standards and good service in this respect.

3. *Credit management*. Continuing down the balance sheet to understand treasury department international functions, the third area of importance involves the approval of all credit risk, since credit extension leads directly to accounts receivable on the corporation's books. In addition, credit risk arises not only from the sale of the corporation's goods and services to its customers but also from entering into contracts with suppliers, especially for construction or similar services. If one of these suppliers or contractors should fail in completing its contract for credit or related reasons, the corporation could be seriously injured. Specific illustrations could include relining a kiln of a cement producer or completing a vital expansion of some other process plant facility.

Credit-approving officers of the corporation may be organized by geographic, product, or service areas, or by combinations of these. In large organizations, bearing in mind the analogy of the internal bank, this function may be staffed in much the same way as the international division of the bank. In working closely with these persons in the treasury department, the international banker may make a major contribution to the success of the corporation's sales efforts by supplying information on country risks and foreign exchange developments, as well as answering routine credit inquiries. In attempting to serve the corporate treasurer in connection with this function, the international banker should seek constantly to provide credit information before credit is actually extended by the corporate customer and to assist with collection problems on accounts receivable.

4. *Borrowing and financing*. In addition, from the frequent contact in connection with marketing these services the banker may become aware of future financing needs, which could be satisfied by providing bank services ranging from buying receivables, discounting notes, or moving to grant credit directly to foreign purchasers of the corporation's goods or services, or suppliers to the corporation. Thus, from credit and collection work arises the fourth main area of the corporate treasury function, namely, the raising of financing. International financing may be sought to convert corporate accounts receivable of foreign customers into cash, to enable overseas corporate customers to pay the corporation in cash, to start or expand activities of the corporation's offshore subsidiaries or

affiliates, or in some cases to raise money in foreign markets for use by the corporation in its home country.

Working with accounts receivable usually involves application of the various techniques of short-term trade financing. These techniques include issuing or confirming letters of credit, creating bankers' acceptances, and discounting or purchase of trade acceptances or promissory notes. Exports of equipment, machinery, or entire process plants may involve medium- or long-term financing for international customers. Financing overseas subsidiaries and affiliates can involve both short-term and long-term finance, as well as other specialized techniques. Raising money internationally for the use of the home corporation could involve loans from the Eurocurrency markets and especially from the Eurodollar market for U.S. and other corporations.

5. *Financial planning.* The fifth major area of corporate treasury responsibility concerns the entire functions of financial planning and review of investment proposals. A great deal of this work is largely internal by its nature but also involves extensive working associations with house and outside counsel, internal and public accountants, as well as various tax experts, to investigate assumptions for future plans, prepare realistic feasibility studies, develop and consider alternative financial plans, and arrange contractual relationships to organize various parties to carry out large undertakings. Especially in considering new projects, the international commercial banker may play an important role in assisting the corporate treasurer. Information on business conditions in countries well known to the bank and introductions to key contacts, including foreign lawyers and government officials, may be extremely useful in helping the corporation in this regard, even before the actual financing stages for the project or investment are reached.

6. *Country exposure management.* Finally, a sixth area of growing importance to major corporations, country exposure, is being assumed as a treasury responsibility in some organizations. Over and beyond foreign currency risk, country exposure concerns the questions of whether a corporation should have any activities within a country and, if so, what the nature and level of these activities should be. This task requires close coordination with the corporate planning, risk management, or insurance and economic functions, as

well as the international department or overseas product or service sales functions, depending upon the corporate organization chart.

Occasionally, sales, project-oriented, or some planning personnel in a corporation may become overenthusiastic about the market or prospects for a particular developing nation or region, including areas of relatively long economic and political stability where trouble or sudden change may be imminent. On the other hand, insurance experts or economists, if the corporation has any, are sometimes too specialized in their particular fields to act as impartial and practical risk evaluators on an overall and ongoing basis. Accordingly, in more and more organizations, the treasurer's function now includes at least some role, if not total responsibility, for general country exposure.

The treasurer's role may range from setting and monitoring permitted levels of accounts receivable, and hence channeling or redirecting sales efforts, to determining whether corporate funds should be invested directly in some nation where the corporation has no previous experience. The international commercial banker is often in a position to make a significant contribution to his customer in connection with country risk and direct investment. With frequent and repeated contact with the treasury staff, the international banker can rely on his own experiences and those of his more specialized associates to keep the treasurer up to date with current developments in areas where the corporation does or is considering doing business.

The contents of country analyses in whole or in part can be supplied to the treasurer, and specific inquiries can be answered, all in the framework of specialists who have worldwide perspective and experience in evaluating changing conditions in many countries throughout the world. It is true that much of the analysis work performed by the bank is aimed at the bank's own purposes rather than for use by customers. However, with slight modifications here and there, a great deal of this detailed work has direct application to the corporation or other institutional customer. Different factors must be emphasized for determining country levels for short-term receivables versus a long-term equity investment for a mine or manufacturing facility, for example, but much of the basic information is common to the entire range of corporate decision making and to international banking.

TREASURER'S CLASSIFICATION OF BANKS

The treasurer's main goal with regard to the international banker is to obtain satisfactory bank services for the corporation or other organization in order to carry out the functions enumerated in the last section. Success in this regard is measured in the eyes of most treasurers by whether the organization receives quality service at reasonable prices from a bank, which fits into the organization's overall plans for development of banking relationships. In short, the treasurer's first priority is to select banks his organization will deal with, and this is a jealously guarded prerogative.

Next, the treasurer wishes to approve the terms and conditions of all important arrangements made with a bank prior to the conclusion of any agreements. Although it may not be necessary for the treasurer to approve every minor detail in advance, he must know eventually all details and arrangements. This is particularly important in international banking when corporate operations may be conducted at locations far removed from the headquarters or even a regional office that has treasury personnel. In this situation, the treasurer might be operating by remote control, and the banker may be closer to the nontreasury corporate officer or employee. Under these circumstances, the banker must take great care to assure that the treasurer is informed completely of all developments with the bank.

Knowing clearly the treasurer's goals and plans for developing banking relationships greatly simplifies the tasks of the banker. If the bank may never fit into the corporation's plans because of quality, size, location, or some other factor, this should be known. Then the banker may decide whether to continue his calling or business development efforts, which almost always involve greater expense in international than in domestic banking, on the basis of a hope of change in the corporation's plans or key personnel within the treasury function. On the other hand, most corporate treasurers wish a demonstration of consistency from a potential banker and will often suggest how often the candidate should call.

One of the most challenging tasks for the international banker in trying to help the corporate treasury department carry out its functions efficiently is obtaining sufficient knowledge about the customer's activities to be of genuine assistance. If the banker wears down the treasury personnel of his customer in the course of collecting the information he needs to propose useful services, he may wear out his welcome. Yet, the banker often runs a risk of offending some members of the treasury department if he works too closely with other units of the corporation, as we have noted earlier.

Furthermore, treasury staff often inadvertently neglect to inform the banker of some activity to which his bank could make a real contribution. To overcome this knowledge problem in most large corporations and other organizations, international bankers have no choice but to cultivate as many contacts throughout all levels and every location of the organization as possible. At the same time, all bankers must remember that the treasury department in most organizations controls the relationship between the organization and bankers. Therefore, all leads to new business opportunities must be fed back through the officer of the bank closest to the appropriate treasury official for action.

As the international banker calls on customers and potential customers, obtains treasury approval for any agreements and arrangements, and develops increasing sources and amounts of information to be better able to serve the corporation, it is important for the banker to know how his customer classifies its bankers. The treasurer's classification of a particular bank is conditioned to a large extent by how he characterizes the bank on the basis of the past history, if any, of the bank-customer relationship. At least four classifications can be identified in this regard.

First, the treasury department may think of the bank in terms of a *line bank*, meaning one with which the customer has a permanent relationship involving the supply of funds, whenever the customer needs to borrow money. Obviously, such a permanent relationship is the highest form that can exist between a customer and bank, and a line bank also is a major depository or bank of account for its customer.

Second in position would be those banks from which the customer occasionally borrows but are not necessarily included in every borrowing, and banks that are depositories of funds but not major depositories. Such *secondary banks* may be occasional lenders or have smaller accounts or be both periodical lenders and holders of smaller accounts. Smaller as opposed to general deposit accounts may be necessary in locations remote from corporate headquarters for payrolls and other special purposes or even at the bank's head office for subsidiaries, affiliates, or other activities, For example, oil, mining, and other resource corporations often have temporary accounts for geological or exploration personnel. Other organizations may need temporary accounts for short buying or sales campaigns in different countries. Construction projects or movie production may require temporary accounts for months or several years.

Corporate treasurers are becoming much more sophisticated about using such secondary banks in international activities. For example, a regional bank with a payroll account or other special purpose account that is used by a domestic plant or other local operation of a corporation may be requested by the corporation to participate to a limited extent in an export financing or major overseas financing, which helps the corporation. The regional bank then must quickly consider whether it has been adequately compensated for services rendered in connection with the account over the years or whether the corporation has built up merit on the bank's slate of reckoning. Also, the chance of moving up a notch in the corporation's banking picture must be considered along with increased account balances or other increased fee income opportunities.

After the secondary banks in the treasurer's mind come the *odd-job banks*, which have for various reasons over the years performed some specialized service, perhaps on and off, but cannot be considered as secondary banks. Often both parties are quite satisfied with such an arrangement of fair compensation for each service when performed, whereas for some reason or another, a secondary-level relationship even at some future date does not appear possible. Banks with only limited geographic coverage or highly specialized services come to mind in this regard.

For example, whenever the corporation ventures out into the bank's part of the world or requires its specialized services, contact is reestablished. But both sides realize that a permanent relationship will not result, unless the corporation undertakes some extensive new activity in its area of expertise, perhaps involving direct investment as opposed to occasionally selling to one of the bank's local customers, for example. Banks used for letters of credit, collections, or foreign exchange in nonmajor currencies are examples of this type of classification.

Finally, the last category or classification in the treasurer's heirarchy is the *calling bank.* All banks, with or without relationships, call upon the corporation, of course. However, if a bank has no relationship but continues to call on a corporate treasury department, it may be referred to as a calling bank. Calling represents its only tie with the organization and distinguishes it from other banks that do not call on the corporation. Calling banks' officers stop by periodically to see the corporate treasury staff and try to sell their wares. Usually the treasury officer establishes the frequency of such calls, such as annually, semiannually, or quarterly. For foreign banks whose travel schedules permit only such periodic calls, the treasurer may tell a banker to call whenever he is in town, knowing full well that at most this will involve only one or a few calls per year.

Calling banks in the treasurer's eyes are usually in some stage of relationship development or else are being kept on tap in the event some activity or project develops within the bank's territory or area of expertise. The challenge for the banker in this situation is to determine why the corporate treasury department wants to see the bank's representatives. Repeated questioning, discussion, and mention of services and places of business activity usually can develop the treasury department's goals. On the basis of such interest, eventually the calling banker will be given some task to perform, or information about some specific subject will be requested. Then the bank has moved up to the odd-job category, and future sales of services may be possible.

TREASURER'S APPROACHES TO BANKERS

Most treasurers do not take on new banking relationships lightly. Two or three years' calling effort by many officers from the bank, involving different corporate officers at various levels, is considered minimal. Sometimes, fifteen years of international calling effort is not uncommon before a corporation establishes a direct relationship or asks a bank to participate in or provide a major financing. Such a calling effort involves a long, steady effort from the standpoint of time and the travel budget. Some banks do not have the staying power, patience, or funds for such programs. For these banks, international business, except on a very limited basis, probably should be avoided.

Although a corporate treasurer's approach to the banker is greatly influenced by the bank's ranking within the corporation's classification system, that ranking is not the sole determinate of the treasurer's approach. The treasurer's style, either personal or corporate, also determines to a large extent how the banker will fare in obtaining business. Each organization and treasury department is unique, as each bank has individual characteristics, but certain general approaches or styles of dealing with bankers can be identified.

First is the *handout approach*. This style, although not confined to international banking services, is particularly prevalent on the international side largely as a result of the various levels of country risk that are found in the field of international commercial banking. Bankers and treasurers often perceive the same countries in the same way with regard to degree of risk. Hence, it takes some salesmanship to find bankers willing to take on what most in the international community recognize as unattractive or unreasonable risks. The best way to move off such risks in the eyes of some corporate treasurers is to discuss only these difficult situations during a call.

Sometimes treasury personnel will contact the bank first by inquiring whether the bank does business in this or that country. Usually, of course, the treasury staff do not mention their view of the particular country. Any admission of inferior risk could weaken the corporation's bargaining position with the bank. When making an inquiry for financing to assist with a sale by the corporation, for instance, the treasury people may stress the importance of the sale to the corporation or the urgency of obtaining a firm financing commitment.

Occasionally, however, some corporate treasurers will imply or promise that future business in better locations will be available for the bank that takes on its share of difficult assignments. Unfortunately for the bank trying to work into a new or increased relationship, it seldom, if ever, hears about the supposedly attractive opportunities from the treasurer working on the handout approach. Often, the best transactions go only to major line banks, whereas inferior risks are handed out, bite by bite, to eager aspirants. If one or more of the risky situations become problem loans, however, the bank that has done "its share" by taking such difficult assignments may be in no condition to entertain new business from any customer for quite some time.

The second general approach of treasurers' staff might be termed the *cafeteria approach*. Although this approach is preferable from the banker's view to the handout approach in many cases, it is really only one step away from the handout approach. The corporate treasurer spreads out several opportunities in front of the banker and offers to let the banker make a selection if any of the places, risks, or proposals are of interest to the banker. Coincidentally, it seems quite often that none of the selections is truly appealing. Partly from truth in some cases, and partially in order not to weaken his bargaining position in most cases, the treasurer explains that he knows that different banks have different appetites and he realizes that certain country limits may be full or close to full for many international banks.

Sometimes that is the situation. Bankers do not always react in the same way to each country risk or type of transaction. But more often than not, the fate of these difficult transactions is well known by both parties in advance. If a corporation seems overloaded with unattractive financing opportunities, the international banker still may be helpful. The first possibility to be explored, of course, is whether otherwise unacceptable risk can be eliminated or reduced to an acceptable level.

Use of special programs from institutions such as the Export-Import Bank of the United States (Eximbank) or the Foreign Credit Insurance Association (FCIA) in the United States, for example, or equivalent programs that exist in many other nations, should be considered. Other imaginative proposals might be considered, including political risk insurance by private insurers, through insurance brokers in some cases.

If by chance the banker knows of correspondents or other banks willing to entertain such risks on the basis of special knowledge, expertise, or techniques, he might consider referring the corporate treasurer to these banks. Some banks in nations with different foreign policy and economic considerations might be able to handle credits to Eastern European nations, the Soviet Union, or other communist or socialist nations, for example. Bringing in other banks obviously might increase the banker's competition, which must be weighed against any merit obtained from the corporate treasurer and the receiving bank for arranging such an introduction.

If no acceptable financing method can be devised, the corporate treasurer is not willing to pay the price for minimizing such risk, or if no correspondents or other banks come to mind, it might be useful to provide country risk information and explore further why the corporation is seeking business in countries that seem unattractive to the banker and, often if the truth be known, to the treasurer also. In such circumstances, it is possible that the sales department or some other part of the corporation may be determining policy without proper reference to the treasury department or after ignoring treasury advice. Usually, corporate effort is wasted as much as a bank's risk is increased in these difficult cases.

Often the treasurer may welcome the banker's assistance in supporting his attempts to keep his company out of higher-risk situations. Country studies, other information, and advice from the banker sometimes can be instrumental in changing corporate directions. This is especially true if, after learning the details about the company's products, services, or marketing strategies, the banker can arrange introductions or steer the company through the corporate treasurer to more attractive places to do business, as well as arrange financing.

Third and last is the treasurer's approach, which is total. Most often this approach is enjoyed by line banks, but not exclusively, since the candid treasurer may take this approach with any bank that he truly respects and may wish to deal with on a continuing basis, regardless of the present level of the relationship. By such an approach, the treasury staff attempts over time to fully inform and educate the banker about the corporation's operations in all corners of the globe. Existing line banks and sometimes their areas of expertise or services and problems are revealed.

In the *total approach*, the types of new business opportunities being generated are discussed, and the interested banker is invited to stand by for one of these. Formulas or patterns for dealing with banks are laid out, and the rules for bringing in new banks are explained. The fairest thing to all banks is to add new banks for expanding business and in return for useful ideas, which help the business. All bankers can live securely with such a corporate treasury style, although all must work hard every day. Every international banker must look continuously for ways to help the organization expand or improve, and, occasionally, if required for large credits, the corporate treasurer can bring banks together to carry out together what none may be able to do alone.

Obviously, the style of the total approach is consistent with the line bank classification, although neither banker nor treasurer needs to wait for the achievement of the line relationship to implement this style. If after a few calls some tendency toward a total approach cannot be discerned, the banker involved probably will not be able to deal effectively with the corporate treasurer as a line bank. Calling should be kept to a minimum until events or personnel change. Handouts or cafeteria selections should not be entertained unless they truly fit the bank's book, represent reasonable risks, and are profitable transactions in their own right without implementation of future promises.

BANK CALLING PROGRAMS AND PROCEDURES

Development of any bank's calling program to obtain, maintain, or increase its international business with any customer must be based squarely upon the bank's international market strategies. These strategies, as we have seen, are the product of the detailed planning process that was analyzed in Chapters 3, 4, and 5. Although these strategies may change from time to time, the calling programs that implement these strategies may change more frequently. Every call should provide valuable intelligence about the customer and simultaneously point the way for any future calls by indicating information, ideas, and services to be developed further.

After a few reconnaissance calls to determine whether a calling program is warranted, a calling program must be designed for each customer or similar groups of customers on the basis of the bank's marketing strategies and how the customer views or is likely to view the bank. This view includes the treasurer's probable or known classification of the caller's bank and the treasurer's likely approach to the bank. Useful information in this regard often can be gleaned from conversations with other bankers and from various publications, including announcements of syndicated loans.

Every calling program, as opposed to random reconnaissance calls, should be based upon the bank's strategies, and no call should ever be made without adequate preparation. A random call may involve minimal preparation, since possibly a well-developed credit file might not exist. However, once it is decided to visit a potential customer on a regular basis, which is the definition of a calling program, then preparation includes the gathering and study of information before starting the visits. Annual and quarterly reports, if publicly available, are the usual starting point for any credit file, until reports on calls and internal memorandums and other materials can be developed.

Newspaper clippings, magazine articles, and credit information from specialized services should supplement the credit file. It is the duty of calling or account officers to make certain that the customer's annual report is obtained and placed in the credit file on a timely basis along with articles, clippings, news releases, and other information that crosses the officer's desk and is routed regularly to him. Many organizations often are willing to add bankers to their mailing lists for annual reports, news releases, internal company magazines, newsletters, or sales literature. Technical brochures and product descriptions are especially important for corporations that manufacture sophisticated technical items, provide engineering or construction services, or license patented technology.

After making the appointment for the call, preparing by reading the bank's credit file, and reviewing the details and costs of any particular services that might be emphasized during the call, it is important that the banker appear for the call at the appointed time. Next to being on time to start the call, the banker should be on guard to leave at the agreed upon time or, lacking such agreement, to establish that goal early in the visit.

Following routine introductions and the usual polite conversations that may vary in length from culture to culture, the heart of the call should consist of an exchange of information about the organizations of the bank and the customer. From call to call with the same customer, care should be taken to develop different subject matter or greater detail on any matters covered previously. Copies of call reports from previous calls are indispensable for this purpose, and it is important to be certain that any promises made in earlier calls have been kept with regard to supplying information or handling other matters. In this respect, bank calling does not differ from sales calls for other products and services. Preparation and enthusiasm are the keys to any selling effort for a sophisticated, personalized service, and international commercial banking is no exception.

Some calling officers always make it a point to leave the customer with some useful literature or memento of their visit, and this is appropriate if it fits the banker's personality. Interesting and useful are the key words here. News, information, or ideas also can be left with the customer, with follow-up to come in written form by mail or telex if the treasurer expresses interest. After each call, a thank-you letter from the banker for the visit, along with any timely information or appropriate enclosure, is usually standard procedure. Bank newsletters, specialized mailings, annual and quarterly reports, and bank directories or similar items are useful to keep contact with the corporate treasury staff until the next call.

After each call, a written call report should be prepared to summarize the persons met, along with titles, time, place, and length of call. Matters discussed should be noted, and each call report should reach some conclusion about the caller's overall impression of the customer or potential customer, the role of the bank, and a list of points to follow up. Each call report not only recaps the substance of the meeting but attempts to light the way for future visits and areas to explore in preparation for the next meeting. Obviously, any problems or opportunities should be handled immediately, and some might require a telephone call or visit before the banker leaves the customer's city. At this point, the banker has gone past a formal calling program and is providing banking service, which is the goal of every calling program.

A banker with so much regular and profitable business to handle that he has no time for a formal calling program is fortunate indeed. However, even if new, high-quality customers are walking in off the street, it is still imperative that the banker visit his customers on their own premises, tour their own operations, including offices and plants, and be competely informed about their activities. Even with a solid and profitable customer mix, some calling on potential customers is necessary to keep abreast of new developments, be aware of competitive moves, maintain broad perspectives, and expand horizons. No international bank account officer can afford to sit in his office for prolonged periods. Call reports should be prepared not only for calls outside the bank but also to summarize meetings that take place within the bank, or inside calls.

Next to actually providing services, calling, and writing call reports, the international account officer's best use of his time probably is reading the call reports of other officers. From studying their efforts he can find possible interconnections with his work and customers. The best solution to one corporation's problem is often to introduce the treasurer or, through the treasurer, other appropriate corporate personnel to another customer of the bank. Two competent organizations with complementary activities often can earn more money working together on a common activity than can each working alone. Any resulting banking business for both is more likely to stay with the bank that brought them together.

Furthermore, reading call reports of others often gives an officer ideas for his own calls, for his own further reading and study, and might suggest ideas to be sent back to the original calling officer. Therefore, all call reports should be routed to appropriate peers and working associates as well as up the line to more senior officers in the bank's hierarchy. A standard routing list or lists is a starting point for periodically sending batches of call reports to others in the bank, but special situations may require that extra copies of single reports be routed directly to other persons in the bank from time to time. Copies of all call reports should be filed in the appropriate section of the credit file for use in starting the entire cycle over again with preparation for the next call and for reference by other interested parties in the bank.

BANK RELATIONSHIP PROFITABILITY ANALYSES

In Chapter 12 dealing with credit-related procedures, the importance of developing a method to collect and analyze information on the profitability of each individual customer relationship was discussed. Whereas the thrust of that discussion related to pricing considerations,the results of relationship analysis along with other information are used in working with the corporate treasury department. Regardless of whether or not an account relationship exists, it is necessary for the calling officer to periodically list in summary form for the corporate treasury official all of the services performed by the international bank at all locations.

If an account relationship exists, an analysis of the account or accounts is the obvious starting point for the relationship analysis. Information on the basis of average book balances, collected balances, and debits and credits by average transaction amount and volume is relevant to determine the profitability of the account or accounts. In addition, all services provided should be summarized as to frequency or transaction volume and monetary value per average transaction. Activities such as international payments, foreign exchange contracts, collections, letters of credit, acceptances, loans, advances, bills discounted, and all other forms of credit extension should be detailed. Records for these transactions will be obtained from the various operating sections of the international division and foreign offices of the bank. Income streams and various expenses are integrated into a format that produces a bottom line. In some banks this information may be produced largely by computer programs.

Information about account and loan balances and income and expense items should not be the limit of the relationship analysis, however. From the credit file and especially by reference to the call reports, the experienced and thorough account officer will develop further listings of many other miscellaneous services, such as credit, country, or other information supplied and special tasks performed for the corporate customer. With time, cost accounting, and computerization, it should be possible for most banks eventually to quantify such items as credit inquiries, foreign exchange, and country information. Until such a system is in place, all such matters should be summarized in the best form possible in listings that will supplement other routine and more numerically oriented account relationship information.

In export financing, for example, proposals that are prepared and submitted, but not utilized because of contract awards to competitors of the customer for other than financing considerations, are especially relevant. Much work and effort, including preparation and presentation of credit committee packages and possibly assembly of syndicates composed of other banks, might have been involved. Yet, no entries would appear in the accounting records of the bank since expired commitments would have been removed from the appropriate ledgers.

Only the credit file would contain records of these past proposals, commitments, and many other tasks performed by the bank. If the total history of all items is not extracted from the credit files, as well as other bank records, and summarized, neither the appropriate bank officers nor corporate treasury officials will know the extent of the bank's efforts on behalf of the corporation. In addition to summarizing information by account and by type of banking service, it is sometimes helpful to list activities by countries, foreign offices, or regions of the world, by corporate subsidiary, division, or unit, and by officer or employee of the bank involved in working with the corporation.

When this information is presented and reviewed with senior corporate treasury staff, results in terms of furthering the relationship are often significant. First, corporate staff has an opportunity to see at one glance all of the bank's efforts for a period of time and to assess the bank's commitment and consistency in serving the corporation. Often in the absence of such summaries, the treasurer, financial vice-president, and other senior corporate officers may not be aware of the extent of the bank's activities or may have forgotten significant events in the history of the corporation's relationship with the bank, in the press of other activities, Second, and more important, compensating balances may be increased and specific new business leads may be directed to the bank to serve as an incentive to keep up the good work. Finally, as a result of such reviews, future additional business and other tasks to further the relationship may be more likely to be assigned to the bank.

Relationship profitability reviews should be conducted at least annually and more often, if necessary. The banker should not hesitate to pinpoint unprofitable situations and negotiate for improved terms and conditions or substitute business if some activity cannot be made profitable. Enlightened treasurers wish to treat their bankers fairly and neither underpay nor over-reward them. In addition, all banks and corporations are constantly changing their mix of activities, which may necessitate a change in the mix of services that the bank can provide profitably and competitively to its customers.

The annual relationship profitability review usually is the best time to discuss major changes in the relationship from the standpoint of both services and personnel. With a total relationship analysis, the banker is well armed with his record, and the treasurer who values his banking relationships is likely to speak frankly in ranking the quality of services and to make adjustments, as necessary, to maintain a mutually beneficial relationship for the corporation and the bank.

16

Handling Problem and Workout Credits

Origins and Early Warning Signals / Definitions and Collection Responsibility / Information Gathering and Fact Finding / Foreign Counsel and Asset Searches / Study of Possible Solutions / Nonaccrual, Recovery, or Write-Off

M
ost lenders, whether international or domestic, are uncomfortable with bad credits, which also are referred to as problem, workout, and nonperforming credits in this chapter. This uncomfortable feeling results whether or not the lender was involved with the original decision to extend credit. Problem and workout credits are unpredictable and involve increased risk of loss to the bank. Lending officers take pride in developing new business, building loan portfolios, and helping to create new or enlarged enterprises and projects. Loan fees are received and interest earned; deposits are obtained and other banking services provided. But if difficulties develop with a credit, less experienced lenders and managers may be uncertain how to react, let alone anticipate future events. Careers may be in jeopardy, and tensions usually develop within the banking unit and perhaps up and across the lines of the entire banking organization.

Nonperforming credits by definition are not repaying as agreed, and must be collected. Collection work requires action, usually difficult and unpleasant action, by the banker, often with the assistance of lawyers and others from outside the bank. The banker must protect the interest of the bank's depositors and shareholders and will be under closer than usual scrutiny from inside and outside the bank while working. Although handling bad international credits involves most of the techniques encountered in dealing with nonperforming credits domestically, some additional factors are involved. If there tends to be a greater variety of problems on the international level, however, usually there also are more varied solutions possible.

This chapter will review some of the ways bad credits originate in international commercial banking. Errors in conducting international operations activities, as well as approved extensions of credit, can result in bad credits. For this reason, the term *bad credits* is used as well as *bad loans*. Most operating errors can be prevented or minimized by following sound procedures, and most potential bad loans give early warning signals. Moreover, throughout the process of handling bad credits, decisions must be made and sometimes reversed as to whether the credit is merely a problem credit that will not interrupt the permanent bank-customer relationship, or is a workout. A *workout credit* by definition implies an end to the relationship.

After identifying and defining a nonperforming credit, responsibility for future handling must be assigned. This assignment can take place before or after the information-gathering and fact-finding stage, or responsibility can be changed after this stage. However, at some point, a decision to assign responsibility must be made on the basis of the special skills of the personnel, the need for any assistance from outside the bank, the level of the bank's experience in a particular market, and the stage of the economic cycle with regard to the market, among other factors.

After examining documents and materials in the bank's possession, determining the exact status and condition of the debtor, engaging and working with outside or special counsel when necessary, and searching for any available assets, one must weigh various alternatives for possible solutions and decide upon a course of action. After the plan is selected, it must be implemented or a changed plan must be developed and carried out. The plan will either correct the problem and recover the total amount of the credit or result in a loss of some amount. Also, at some stage during the collection process, the question of placing nonperforming credits on nonaccrual status must be addressed, regardless of whether the debt plus interest is ultimately collected or not.

ORIGINS AND EARLY WARNING SIGNALS

Although most bad credits result from loans, in addition, foreign exchange contracts, international funds transfers, documentary collection transactions, letters of credit, Eurocurrency placements, and even due-from accounts with failing correspondent banks can create bad credits. A pattern of recurring bad credits, which originate from unauthorized extension of credit in operating sections of the international division or unit, may require new procedures or better trained personnel or both. A few detailed illustrations may prove instructive.

In a forward or future foreign exchange contract, knowledge of failure or inability of the other party to perform before delivery date still permits the bank to go back into the market to cover the contract on or before delivery date by making another exchange contract with some other party. Depending upon any fluctuation in the exchange rate between the dates of the original and the second contracts, the bank could earn a profit, break even, or suffer a loss. For most currencies at most times, any loss usually would not be a large percentage of the total contract, perhaps on the order of only 10 percent to 20 percent, or even less. However, should the other party to an exchange contract fail to deliver its side of a contract after the bank has paid its part of the contract into the other party's account at another bank, then the entire amount of the foreign exchange contract will be lost, if no recovery is made.

This latter situation occurred at many banks, especially U.S. banks, that were dealing with the Herstatt Bank of West Germany in late 1974. Herstatt's accounts on the books of its correspondents were credited during U.S. working hours with monies owed to Herstatt for one side of foreign exchange transactions, when the

West German Central Bank intervened on European time to take charge of Herstatt Bank's books and affairs in West Germany. However, the German Central Bank intervened before Herstatt had credited the bank accounts of its correspondents with Herstatt's side of the transactions. The risk of the other party failing to deliver its part of a foreign exchange transaction after the bank has delivered its side often is referred to as clean risk at liquidation. This risk can be quantified by a sublimit, sometimes called an overnight limit, which is less than the total amount for all exchange contracts that may be outstanding under the foreign exchange line for any name. Although most banks in the Herstatt situation eventually recovered substantial portions of their outstandings, these bad debts were collected only after a long period of time, substantial loss of interest, and, in some situations, lengthy and expensive court actions.

Unauthorized extensions of credit and subsequent collection problems may result from clerical errors in transmitting payment orders. For example, extra zeros inadvertently added to payment instructions may send several million instead of several thousand dollars to a payee in a distant nation. If the payee is unwilling to return the excess amount, legal action may be required by the bank to obtain recovery of monies involved.

Incoming collections coupled with careless use of guarantees for missing airway bills may result in uncollectible loans, as mentioned in Chapter 2. Likewise, errors on outgoing collections can create unauthorized loans. In a recent situation, the employee of a U.S. bank typed the post office box number of the purchaser of goods instead of the post box number of the collecting bank on the envelope used for mailing an outgoing collection. Instead of a Central American correspondent bank receiving the documents for delivery against payment by the purchaser, the purchaser received the documents in its post office box and used the title document enclosed with the collection instructions intended for the bank to obtain possession of the merchandise without payment.

Letters of credit provide numerous opportunities for mishandling by banks or misuse by the parties, with resulting unauthorized extensions of credit and consequent difficulties for banks. Even Eurocurrency placements or due-from accounts can result in losses if, for example, such accounts are with failing banks, such as the

Herstatt Bank, already mentioned in connection with foreign exchange risk.

In approved extensions of credit, especially loans, in addition to
the reasons that may cause any business to fail, domestically or
overseas, such as poor management, inadequate financial controls,
or industrywide problems, in international banking there are a host
of problems that can arise from national or international economic
and political problems. On the economic side, these problems range
from economic recession or depression to unfavorable balance of
payments conditions, or shortages of foreign exchange. A borrowing customer in a foreign nation may be literally put out of business
as a result of its government's own measures to counteract balance of
payments problems, if such measures shut off raw materials crucial
to the borrower's business, for example. Or a foreign customer may
operate profitably and deliver loan repayments in local currency
promptly in accordance with local laws to its nation's central bank,
which because of a shortage of foreign exchange is unable to deliver
to the lending bank the original currency of the loan.

Political events that negatively affect borrowers can range from
severe social and even religious changes to civil war, revolution,
invasion, or war with neighboring countries. Sudden changes in laws
not only in foreign countries but also in the lender's nation can cause
increases in risk or losses, also. The 1979 freeze of Iranian assets by
the United States government, for example, may have helped those
U.S. banks with deposits in excess of loans but not necessarily those
U.S. banks whose loans exceeded Iranian deposits, especially in the
case of loan repayments, that were under way within the U.S. banking system at the time of the freeze. Visits, reading, and other
sources of information, coupled with experience and background,
usually provide the alert lending officer and country specialist with
warning of adverse developments. The goal of the country analysis
procedure, discussed in Chapter 12, is to prevent economic and
political surprises of such a severe nature as to disrupt debt servicing
by the country's borrowers.

A breakdown in communications between the international bank
and its foreign borrower often presages credit difficulties. Whether
a borrower seeks to avoid embarrassment or deliberately tries to
hide bad news or unfavorable developments, the banker soon be-

comes hard pressed to assist his customer and loses creditability within his own bank if he is constantly buffeted by surprises and does not have up-to-date information, which usually only the borrower can supply. To prevent or remedy a breakdown in communications, international lenders should regularly visit in person with their customers, tour their offices, plants, or facilities, and talk to key people in the borrower's organization, as well as others who have contact and deal with the borrower.

Financial statements, of course, can provide early warning of deteriorating situations. Time delays and distance factors in international banking often make it necessary to request financial information more frequently than for similar domestic credits. Even internally prepared and unaudited information in between delivery of regular audited statements can be of some assistance, especially in new projects, start-up situations, or significant expansions. However, there is no adequate substitute for frequent personal visits with the borrower in international banking.

Slow payments and requests from the borrower for rescheduling are probably two of the latest early warning signals before actual nonpayment. Accordingly, it is imperative that every slow payment that appears in the daily past due report should be investigated immediately by the account officer. It is only possible to be certain that a payment was slow after payment has been received. Therefore, it is safer to assume that any past due payment is a nonpayment rather than a slow payment.

On the other hand, in certain parts of the world, borrowers are habitually late in making payments because of general lack of punctuality or delays largely beyond their control and inherent in their local banking systems. In such cases, if borrowers cannot be convinced or coached to change their own ways to initiate timely payments or extend lead times for processing within their nation's banking channels, it may be better to end relationships, while the bank is not in trouble. For without a steady pattern of on-time payments, the banker loses one of his most important warning signals for possible trouble. Lending under these circumstances is analogous to letting a surgeon operate without any equipment to provide information about the vital signs of the patient on the table.

Correspondent banks, frequently in the lender's own country, especially overworked money center banks, often cause unpredictable and inordinate delays. Therefore, the best borrowers build up balances in their accounts at the lender's bank in anticipation of payment dates. In this way, one large, last-minute, closely timed payment is not the cause of an adverse notation on the borrower's repayment record. In addition, the banker enjoys a few days of probably well-deserved extra demand deposit balances and is saved needless worry and unnecessary investigation involving the borrower's name in a search for incoming funds at its correspondent banks.

DEFINITIONS AND COLLECTION RESPONSIBILITY

The distinctions between problem credits and workout credits relate to timing and the banker's attitude toward the customer. A problem credit is perceived to be a temporary situation with an identifiable solution in sight. More money, more time, patience, or changed conditions, sometimes even outside the control of both the debtor and the creditor, or a combination of these factors, usually will resolve the problem. Problem credits might involve a deterioration of financial ratios as a result of readily ascertainable causes of a nonpermanent nature. A sudden and severe currency devaluation, such as occurred in Mexico in 1977, is a typical example. Earnings capacity usually is not impaired in such situations, and the assets, management, and organization of the borrower remain intact to earn enough in due course to repay creditors. More local currency earnings will be required, however, to repay foreign liabilities that were contracted at the earlier rate of exchange.

Moreover, in the case of problem credits, banks wish to keep rather than abandon their customers. Some observers, including nonbankers, say it is under these circumstances that bankers do their real job and earn their pay. Most bankers, however, prefer as a rule to extend credit in order to finance readily ascertainable timing differences between payment and receipt of funds by their borrowers. Surprises are not considered part of the routine and, therefore, problems generally are viewed with varying degrees of alarm by different parts of the commercial banking organization. Lending or account officers who made the credit decision usually wish everyone to be calm. They do their utmost to supply up-to-date information and to assure everyone in the bank that the situation is under control and that workable solutions exist and are under execution. Most others in the bank almost always are not so sanguine, and neither should they be. Many questions are asked and alternatives explored. Satisfactory answers and sensible solutions only decrease worry. Continuous questioning and intensive monitoring, including periodical special reports of all problem loans, are necessary until the borrower's health is restored or the problem causing nonpayment is corrected.

Workout credits are a different situation entirely. The bankers do not intend to stand by their customers that may have been dealt a mortal blow or been proven to be below the standards of the bank. Limited cooperation may occur between creditors to the same debtor and between the debtor and the creditors, but only to the extent required to maximize recovery of the debt. From time to time, every problem credit must be reviewed to determine whether it should be viewed as a workout or continue in the problem classification. Over the life of some loans, the classification may change back and forth several times from problem to workout credit. If the debtor regains full health and the relationship has been salvaged, while the banker has outstandings, only a problem loan was involved. All other situations clearly are workouts. The distinction between problem and workout credit must be made carefully and always kept in mind by all parties to the decision-making process, since a classification can influence heavily the type of actions to be taken by the bank.

At least two major issues are involved in assigning responsibility for handling any nonperforming credit. First is the decision of whether to end the responsibility of the regular account officers and assign the credit to other specialists in the bank, or work on some joint basis as opposed to keeping responsibility solely with the regular account officers. Second is the decision of whether to bring in experts from outside the bank, usually lawyers, to assist the account officers or the others handling the credit.

In international banking, there is more of a tendency than in domestic banking for regular account officers to keep working with problem and workout credits. Remote locations, language skills, specialized knowledge, and experience often tend to keep the regular officers on the case. In foreign branches, affiliates, or subsidiaries of even the largest banks, and especially in regional banks or those with smaller or newer international divisions, there is unlikely to be sufficient personnel or those with the skills necessary to gain economies of scale by assigning personnel to handle only nonperforming assets on a full-time basis.

If the original lenders who made a loan or personnel who created the situation are gone, the most important remaining consideration is whether the regular account personnel have sufficient time to handle bad credits, as well as existing relationships and business development. If it is planned to decrease marketing efforts because of world conditions, bank policies, or other reasons, existing lenders and account officers often can handle the nonperforming credits. If new business is expanding, existing business is time consuming, or personnel are stretched thin, the extra workload of bad credits may cause new problems. Then, either attention to collection efforts or new and existing business could suffer.

The main advantage of making a special department totally or partially responsible for bad credits is that priority is given to these situations. If ordinary officers are not experienced with difficult credits, satisfactory results may be achieved faster and with less effort by specialists. If the legal department is given responsibility for bad credits, there is still the matter of creating a clear division of authority between legal decision making and business decision making, unless the legal or other special department is given authority for all decisions. Lawyers are not necessarily skilled in making business decisions, although as part of their job they always must carefully define legal and business decisions and differentiate between the two.

Personnel from inside or outside the bank, other than those originally involved with the soured credit, may bring greater objectivity as well as specialized experience to nonperforming credit situations. This in turn raises the question of whether outside consultants or lawyers should be hired to bring their experience to bear on bad credits. Usually, if these experts are well known and respected by the bank's management, such outsiders can be effective and save time and effort of regular personnel, who can concentrate on existing and new business. If the outsiders have little or no creditability within the bank, however, no amount of skill, objectivity, or sound advice is likely to be of much value.

With the difficult economic conditions now prevailing and expected to prevail for the next several years in many parts of the world, it is likely that more workout loan specialists will find work on a case-by-case basis in spite of the tendency for most banks to keep the skeletons in their own closets. Some investment bankers already have moved into this field, although they more often tend to represent borrowers, especially government borrowers, rather than commercial banks. Former commercial bankers with extensive experience probably make the best workout specialists for most banks, since they are familar with the regulatory and internal considerations necessary to deal effectively with the management and different units of commercial banks. Various law firms and lawyers also have gained a great deal of expertise in this function and also may be able to work well with bank management, as well as with the international unit.

Certain economies of scale sometimes can be achieved by having a strong lead bank assume the bulk of the workload for handling problem credits in the case of group or syndicated loans. All the other bankers or lenders then are given a chance to review and approve the lead bank's work. To expedite a solution, the reasonable leader usually bends over backward to be fair to all parties. Difficulties can arise, however, if the lead bank does not have the largest portion of the credit, if all lenders do not participate exactly in the same credit risk with regard to terms and conditions, such as repayment dates and security, or if the most resourceful individual lender involved in the group is not from the lead bank. More often, in such cases, common sense prevails and the best solutions are adopted, regardless of origin. Sometimes it may be easier and less expensive for other banks to allow one bank to do most of the work, including developing facts and creating and proposing solutions. The other banks then have the luxury of reviewing and even second-guessing the work of the first bank with little risk and effort, if the bank taking the initiative has basically competent and dedicated staff.

Another common occurrence involving multiple lenders also should be mentioned here. Often, a group of banks, or banks and other lenders, will stop extending credit in a situation where additional funds are needed in order to protect the total credit granted. Lack of working capital for an otherwise complete project is one example. Delays or cost overruns or both may have exhausted the patience and resources of the original lenders. In such a case, the last lender that extends the funds necessary for an otherwise sound project to succeed may obtain attractive rates, solid security, and a lifelong customer. The original banks that have exhausted their staying power may fade from the scene, sometimes after having taken the greatest risk and having done the most work early in the project.

Furthermore, it should be mentioned that certain parties, especially outside accountants and examining or regulatory authorities, must be informed of developments about bad credits, but they make little or no positive contribution to handling difficult situations. It must be recalled that this is not their function. Such outsiders have their jobs to do more in the role of judges or referees. If the banker allows the goals and objectives of such outsiders to influence the handling of bad credits, wrong decisions may result. The banker must concentrate totally on doing what is best to maximize recovery for the bank in order to protect depositors and shareholders.

Sometimes the workings of the law, accounting principles, and outside authorities in doing their job properly actually make the work of the banker more difficult in handling problems. When the spotlight of publicity or disclosure magnifies problems out of context to the layman, the result might be to increase the leverage of the borrower rather than the bank. If such a situation develops, the banker must use all his ingenuity and resources to keep the pressure where it belongs, on the nonperforming borrower, and to deflect the pressures brought against the bank to settle quickly, compromise unnecessarily, or take a loss in order to end a problem rather than maximize recovery over the longer run.

INFORMATION GATHERING AND FACT FINDING

After responsibility has been assigned for handling the problem or workout credit, the next step is to gather information and marshal all facts that will help in considering various solutions to resolve the difficulty. Four separate activities usually are involved in this step. These are (1) examining all documents and records in the bank's possession; (2) visiting and learning as much as possible about the borrower and the borrower's condition, with particular emphasis on comparisons with earlier visits; (3) determining what legal and other experts may be available to assist the bank in obtaining facts and helping in other ways; and (4) searching for and identifying all of the borrower's possible assets, with or without help from lawyers or other outside experts.

In addition to the bank's credit files, all the documentation from the transaction giving rise to the bad credit must be examined. The loan agreement generally is the most important document to be reviewed, especially clauses relating to covenants, warranties, default, acceleration, giving of notices, and choice and application of law. Required balance sheet ratios, duties to provide financial and other information, prohibitions against or permission required for merger or change of business often are covenants of particular interest. Also, clauses concerning payment of reasonable expenses for the bank to enforce its rights, including reimbursement of legal expenses, are relevant. Guarantee agreements, mortgages, and other documents creating security interests must be examined also.

The documentation for project lending often includes a separate contract, known as a project completion agreement, or perhaps there is a project completion clause in the loan agreement. Most project completion agreements or clauses provide that as between the project sponsors, usually shareholders, and the creditor or several creditors, the sponsors have a duty to provide funds until the project is completed. Completion usually involves meeting a two-pronged test. First, completion may be defined in a mechanical sense, meaning that all parts of a plant or project must be assembled. In more complex activities, mechanical completion often involves the achieving of some rated capacity of product output or ascertainable level of performance as measured by objective physical standards. The fact that engineers or technical personnel are required to define the test in the agreement and determine whether the level has been reached during certain test periods often creates complicated problems in interpreting agreements and conducting the test. Second, the completion formula usually contains a requirement of

adequate working capital after mechanical completion and successful performance tests. Working capital may be defined as some
specific amount of money, as some level of current ratio, or by some
general expression containing reference to adequacy.

The main difficulty with most completion agreements or clauses
arises in their enforcement. Some lenders are reluctant or lack the
will to invoke the agreement, and often completion arrangements,
even when clear on paper, are almost impossible to enforce without
litigation when project sponsors believe they have good legal defenses or mitigating circumstances. One way to minimize difficulties
in enforcing a completion agreement is to set up the completion
agreement or supplement it in the form of a separate equity and loan
agreement, with a definite amount, rate, term, and designated
provider of funds, usually a shareholder, for each set of circumstances and a clearly defined duty to provide additional equity or
subordinated debt or both. Sometimes this document is called an
overrun agreement, and by its terms the flow of funds is triggered by
a call from a creditor or group of creditors that unilaterally make the
determination the project needs more funds in order to be considered complete in their opinion.

After a study of all bank records and documents, a detailed inspection of the borrower must be undertaken to determine the exact
nature of the problem or problems causing nonperformance and
also the borrower's true condition, which may be better but is often
worse than indicated by financial statements. In some cases, especially when fraud or other dishonesty is involved, it is impossible to
learn the borrower's true condition or even make a visit. The borrower in such cases has no intent to cooperate or even communicate
with his creditors.

In other cases, such as those involving national economic crisis or
severe political change, on-site visits may be of little or no use and
perhaps even unsafe or dangerous for the international banker or
others from outside the borrower's country. Effective communication in these cases sometimes can be established through representatives, agents, or others in third countries or even the lender's home
nation. This is especially true for government risk credits, since
almost every country in the world is anxious to preserve its ability to
borrow and to protect its reputation even under the most difficult

circumstances. For these reasons, most government credits are merely problem loans and not workouts, although once burdened with a problem credit, some banks elect to stay out of certain nations, at least for a period of time.

In most situations, of course, it is possible to visit the borrower, and numerous previous visits usually have established a detailed pattern of information that can be used as a framework for comparison of current conditions. Some preliminary work may have been done already, to separate national economic or political problems from purely business or management reasons for existing difficulties. During the visit, the banker mentally moves through a catalog or checklist of factors, while constantly searching for safer grounds to protect the bank's interest and ways to bring together the bank's strengths and the borrower's situation. Perhaps the bank knows and has known the borrower's problem or problems and has been working to correct the situation. But now, the bank, with or without other creditors, has reached a turning point in its relationship.

Problems of a technical nature or relating to raw material supply or marketing often can be solved more easily than management problems. With time, technicians, engineers, and experts can usually make a plant or project operate, although some white elephants dot the landscape of international finance. Often the problems center on the cost and timing of various alternatives for correction. Raw materials usually can be found, if at a price, or sometimes another project might be started to make a first one work. New markets with less competition might be opened instead of those originally planned, or terms of sale, including sales financing, might be offered to penetrate stiffer marketing competition.

Management problems usually are more difficult in international lending, especially in less developed countries or other locations where management expertise and modern management concepts are in short supply. Financial controls and accounting systems, especially cost accounting to use for pricing decisions, can be developed with help from outside accountants and selected key employees. However, modern ideas of planning, organization, delegation, decentralization, or selection, motivation, and remuneration of employees sometimes cannot take hold within the time frame for a project in many medium- or long-term loan situations.

Specific management problems are often hidden from both local and foreign bankers for relatively long periods. Local bankers in the borrower's own city may not know as much as a lending office in a distant bank that has worked with the borrower for a number of years. Local and long-established banks in many countries also may be slow in applying modern management methods and objective criteria for credit decisions. On the other hand, local offices of large international banks may have all the modern methods available but often stretch their key personnel resources too thin and turn over their knowledgeable staff at too rapid a rate. This situation alone largely explains why some smaller and regional banks with a sustained effort, qualified staff, and lower turnover have established and maintained well-defined markets in various corners of the world under varying economic conditions.

Vital clues about the level of a borrower's management ability may usually be found by the alert international banker. These often transcend language and cultural barriers and can point the way to further questions and investigation. A chief executive officer, for example, might sign every check for a relatively large company, and no payment of any sort can be made without his specific approval. The chief executive personally authorizing every payment of a large company is not wrong per se, but such practice should lead to some other questions. Often there is no backup management in such organizations and little delegation of duties and responsibilities.

Managers in less-developed countries or other areas where entrepreneurs and managers are in short supply usually work harder and longer each day than their counterparts in the industrialized world of modern management. This tends to stretch capable management quite thin. The rapidly expanding economies of the Middle East or busy centers of Asia come to mind immediately in this regard. It is not unusual in these areas of the world for one man to operate numerous businesses, handling import or local assembly of dozens of diverse products and services from different nations, serve on several large company boards, such as banks and airlines, and also be the working mayor of a large city and active head of the local chamber of commerce. In such pressure-cooker business environments, many successful new managers blossom forth each year. But the learning curve is short and steep for the survivors, and in many of these countries foreign managers are being imported in increasing numbers until adequate numbers of local nationals can be trained.

In other parts of the world, such as South and Central America, or parts of Africa where industrialization is increasing significantly in once almost totally agricultural nations, modern management also is indispensable. However, the relatively slower pace of economic growth and more tradional social patterns in many parts of these areas mask the need for quick accommodation to new management techniques. One-man enterprises and tightly controlled family empires often appear able to maintain old methods and attitudes. Some salesmen and a few plant operators are hired from outside to staff a modern project. Specialized and experienced personnel to apply modern accounting standards, especially cost accounting, to the purchase of raw materials with technical specifications and to sell highly technical products often are considered superfluous.

The business, under these circumstances, is not run by departments with qualified section heads who advise the chief executive and coordinate their activities with other heads. Each man follows the leader's instructions, or leaves. Outside accountants, lawyers, and a board of directors, or any kind of committee structure to set policy, participate in major decisions, or make certain that the business is run along modern lines are all nonexistent. Failure of management under these circumstances often means that the banker, along with other creditors, must take responsiblility for changing management, if management cannot adapt quickly enough.

FOREIGN COUNSEL AND ASSET SEARCHES

During the investigation phase of handling a nonperforming credit, local counsel in the borrower's country should be consulted and supplied with copies of bank documents, files, and other information on the borrower. If local counsel prepared or approved original documentation, this task is relatively easy and consists mainly in assuring that local counsel is up to date on all information and developments. If local counsel must be initially engaged at this point, it may take considerable time before a law firm is selected, all documentation and information is supplied to the firm selected, and the firm has reviewed all material and researched various points of law.

Moreover, at this stage, other creditors may be seeking counsel to advise on their rights in the same case. In a smaller city or nation, most of the local law firms experienced in working with foreign clients might be utilized in a large credit involving numerous different foreign lenders. For obvious reasons, prudent bankers, therefore, select local counsel and work with them in preparation of documents and investigation of other legal matters before granting and funding a loan. As discussed in Chapter 9, this pattern of selecting and dealing with foreign counsel not only minimizes but also prevents future problems in many situations.

It is important when dealing with foreign counsel about nonperforming loans to establish clearly the terms for employment in advance. In some legal systems, the customary practice is to be paid on a contingent fee or percentage-of-recovery basis when handling cases involving collection of bad debts, with or without litigation. For large credits, it is usually more advantageous to the bank and not unfair to the lawyers to pay in accordance with an agreed upon hourly billing for actual work performed plus out-of-pocket expenses. Payment by the hour plus expenses also is customary for any advice rendered or work done in connection with a rescheduling or reorganization.

The foreign or other law firm engaged should be asked to render its opinion on the various remedies available to the bank in accordance with the documentation and local law. To save time and expense for foreign counsel, the bank's in-house counsel may define issues and pose specific questions for reply by foreign counsel. In addition to rights and remedies available to the bank, foreign counsel should give its opinion on the condition of and any problems with the documentation, the likelihood of success in applying various remedies, and, perhaps more important, the estimated timing of each of the various legal alternatives available.

Outside counsel also may be engaged to conduct a search for potential assets of the borrower in addition to those known by the banker. Assets and the existence of mortgages or other security interests may be discovered through detailed examination of various court and public records. In smaller nations, local counsel may have valuable knowledge of the condition and assets of the borrower through other means, as well as a feeling for the borrower's attitude and willingness to repay debts.

As the international banker investigates the borrower and searches for other assets, either with or without assistance of outside counsel, the banker at this stage must keep in mind the strengths and capabilities of his own organization. Some international commercial banks, for example, have developed over the years highly specialized skills in developing raw land or other real estate-related assets, such as apartments, condominiums, and commercial or industrial buildings.

International banks have developed rural lands taken in settlement of bad debts into luxury resort plots and urban land for use as middle-income housing and retail businesses. Bank customers or others known to the bank or new customers may be able to use a borrower's assets and create a source of repayment for the bank. Products may be sold at distress prices or in new markets. Most such solutions to problem or workout loans, however, involve substantial time on the part of numerous bank personnel and may require full-time bank employees to be located in the country where the assets or businesses exist.

In searching for assets that could be used to secure or repay a loan, the banker must keep in mind that other creditors may have done or be doing the same thing. In the event of bankruptcy, the laws of most jurisdictions require that certain payments, transfers of assets, or granting of security interests be upset or disregarded, if they took place within a certain period of time prior to the date of bankruptcy. For this reason, especially in project finance, it is advisable to obtain all mortgage and other security interests at the beginning of the lending relationship or simultaneously with actual extension of credit so as to be in a priority position with regard to other creditors.

Assuming that interests in security or unencumbered assets can be obtained at a later date, however, the most logical method to search for assets is to start down the asset side of the borrower's balance sheet. Although most borrowers probably will be out of cash at this point, it might be possible to obtain cash from assignment of sales proceeds or accounts receivable, use some to service debt, and return the balance to the company for working capital. This method might be used, for example, in connection with the proceeds for ore sales from large mining projects where mines are developed and financed with foreign funds and are also sold outside the borrower's nation. Sales proceeds could be deposited directly in accounts at one of the borrower's foreign banks. If future problems are anticipated because of foreign exchange shortages in the borrower's country, this is another device to establish at the beginning of a loan. However, the same type of solution sometimes can be applied after the fact. Assignment of accounts receivable or the proceeds of specific letters of credit might offer solutions mutually agreeable to lender and borrower.

Security interests in or control of inventories — raw materials, semifinished or finished goods, or all inventories — might be useful to the banker in some circumstances. In this regard, field warehousing should not be overlooked. In the bank's attempt to obtain security or improve its position, all secured lending devices should be considered. Mortgages on lands and buildings or chattel mortgages on equipment and machinery, of course, are common terms of security, but other asset accounts also may yield forms of security or eventual repayment. Investments or shares in other companies or properties might reveal ultimate sources of repayment or lead to discovery of assets outside the main business. In the event that guarantees exist or are available, a detailed examination must be made of the value of these guarantees, the assets and liabilities, and the overall condition of the companies or entities that provide or might provide such guarantees.

Finally, some assets may not appear directly on the balance sheet. Some lenders have been repaid from insurance proceeds when assets were destroyed by insurable events, regardless of whether the insurance was assigned or not. Furthermore, in many nations, various government agencies or special programs insure against selected risks to encourage their nationals to engage in foreign investment or exporting. In the United States, a U.S. government agency, the Overseas Private Investment Corporation, conducts programs to insure U.S. investors and lenders against the risks of war, nationalization, and lack of foreign exchange. The Foreign Credit Insurance Association, a private organization of U.S. insurance companies, insures U.S. exporters or their assignees, which can include commercial banks, against loss from certain specified political and commercial risks.

STUDY OF POSSIBLE SOLUTIONS

After reviewing all documents and bank files, gathering up-to-date information on the borrower, guarantors, other assets, and security interests, consulting with local lawyers or other experts where necessary, and perhaps discovering previously unknown assets, it is time to consider the various alternatives available for handling the bad credit. At or immediately after this stage there also may be another change in the assignment of responsibility for handling the problem or workout loan. Problem loans, as noted, are more likely to remain with existing account officers, whereas workout loans, especially if litigation will be involved, tend more often to be assigned to the legal or another special department outside the lending area.

Until the last few years, an entire generation of international lenders had grown up in many countries, especially the United States, without extensive bad debt and collection experience at the international level. Therefore, in this section we shall consider a brief checklist of some of the possible solutions for handling nonperforming credits. These solutions may be available to the bank acting alone or may require all creditors to work together. The bank or all creditors may continue to work with the debtor as a continuing entity or it may be necessary to end the borrower's legal existence. Some of these alternatives may be used alone or used in combination with one or more other solutions.

1. *Additional funding.* Some borrowers, especially in the case of new projects, literally run out of money before the project can reach the level necessary to generate sufficient cash flow to repay debt. A significant number of projects fail to meet completion or production schedules or else overrun estimated costs, or both. Even with experienced and sophisticated sponsors, unforeseen events, such as labor problems, government interference, natural disasters, or accidents, can cause significant overruns. Without completion agreements or other readily available funds to complete the project, lenders may face a choice of supplying more funds to save monies already ad-

vanced. If a shortage of working capital is the main or only problem, the bank, with or without other creditors, may be well advised to provide additional funds. Rates and terms might be attractive on balance for an otherwise completed project ready to turn the corner.

On the other hand, a bank, even if it wishes to carry on, often may have reached its prudent or legal lending limit or because of previous reschedulings be unable to provide new monies without increasing assets which are or will be criticized by bank regulators. In this situation, another bank may rescue the original lender with the money needed. A few banks specialize in gaining major relationships and fees after others have worked to their limits with a project from the beginning and taken more of the indeterminate risks. If more than money is required, no new lenders are likely to appear on the scene, however.

2. *Rescheduling debt.* Rescheduling of existing indebtedness is another form of providing additional funding. If debt that is past due is put on a new schedule for future repayment, this really amounts to the same as lending the borrower new funds to repay the previous debt. Accrued and past due interest often is capitalized or added to future principal repayments. Rates and other terms and conditions usually are modified in reschedulings. Care must be taken with regard to various security interests and especially guarantees, since by law in most jurisdictions guarantors will not be held liable for debts modified in any respect without their concurrence.

3. *Additional security.* With additional or better security, a lender may be willing in some cases to provide additional monies or grant longer repayment terms. Accordingly, this alternative is found almost always as part of other solutions. However, if more than one creditor is involved, it usually becomes difficult to gain security at a later stage, since rights of other creditors may be adversely affected. Difficulties may exist in stretching available security to cover the debts owed to all lenders.

4. *Restructuring debt.* Restructuring involves more than merely changing repayment dates or rescheduling. Amounts of repayments may be changed, as well as interest rates and other terms, including the form of security and the relationship or ranking of creditors vis-à-vis each other. Different levels of debt by maturity and priority or security may be created or rearranged, or some debt, especially

that of shareholders or sponsors, may be subordinated to build equity.

5. *Reorganizing borrower/Bringing in new owners or management.* With or without court assistance, supervision, or protection, the borrower's business may be changed in basic respects, above and beyond working with the debt section of the balance sheet. Old shareholders may be bought out, new shareholders may be brought in, or some creditors may become shareholders to the extent of some or all of their loans. In the solutions discussed up to now, usually no loss other than extra time and effort by the banker has been involved. Now loss by shareholders or creditors or both may be experienced. As a general rule, if creditors take any loss, shareholders should lose all their interest first. Often when ownership is changed, it is necessary to change management, although this is not always so. When outside managers are brought in, it is advisable to spell out in detail all rights, duties, and obligations in separate contracts, which provide for substantial, if not total, control by the bank or creditors. All incentives and compensation to new managers and owners should be fully disclosed.

6. *Merger/Nationalization.* As an outgrowth or a special form of reorganizaton, it is often possible to merge a business experiencing problems with another stronger business. This could be a competitor (horizontal integration), a supplier or customer (vertical integration backward or forward), or some other stronger entity or group in an unrelated line of business (conglomerate). In certain countries, depending on the stage of development of their economic systems, stronger private groups take over weaker companies in the same industry or in related areas. This has been occurring in the private sector in the synthetic fiber, textile, and garment industry in Taiwan during the last several years, for example. In Mexico, Spain, and Italy, as other examples, state holding companies often take over failing enterprises. This has been true particularly for the steel, chemical, and shipbuilding industries, among others, in recent years. In international lending, it is not unusual for companies to move from the private to the government sector or from the government to the private sector.

Outside the United States and other selected developed nations, many heavy industries are nationalized totally or partially, since it is not possible to obtain sufficient concentrations of capital in nations with underdeveloped capital markets except from government sources or foreign investors. To assure a continued flow of foreign investment, protect jobs, and prevent social unrest, foreign bank lenders and other foreign creditors may be saved from loss by nationalization or merger of failing enterprises with existing government-owned or -controlled institutions. Nationalization requires government action, which may or may not involve new or special legislation. In democratic nations, this process may take time and considerable political effort before results can be effected.

7. *Bankruptcy/Liquidation.* Voluntary liquidation by agreement among creditors and the debtor or by court-enforced action, through either voluntary or involuntary bankruptcy proceedings, is almost always time consuming and expensive. In liquidation, all government claims for taxes, Social Security, and similar payments take a priority ahead of other lenders under the laws of most jurisdictions around the world. Only assets remaining after these payments are available to bank and unsecured creditors, and secured creditors generally come ahead of bank or unsecured creditors. Legal and related expenses are high in most jurisdictions. Furthermore, in accordance with the bankruptcy laws in most foreign jurisdictions, the debt of foreign currency lenders is established in local currency on the date of bankruptcy. If the local currency is continually devalued against the currency of the international banker's loan, little of the original debt may ever be recovered by the international banker, even if the bankrupt's assets are liquidated on a reasonable timetable.

8. *Litigation.* The effectiveness of bringing lawsuits in most foreign jurisdictions is almost always in doubt. If war is diplomacy by other means, then litigation in many nations is debt collecting by other means. Accordingly, litigation should be resorted to only after all other collection efforts and methods have failed. Litigation in most developing and some developed nations is not effective to bring pressure against borrowers, even when they clearly owe the money and the facts and documentation are not in doubt. Most legal systems in the world now work extremely slowly and provide results only at great expense (in time, effort, and money) in relation to the objectives sought.

Moreover, some societies have extensive safeguards to provide significant protection to debtors. Even if a judgment can be obtained against the debtor so as to increase pressure for a period of time, appeals on almost limitless issues in some jurisdictions may remove any pressure for settlement and further increase legal expense. In some nations, judges and key court officials can be influenced by considerations other than those related to the merits of the case. Under such circumstances, results are not only surprising but totally unpredictable. Moreover, even the best lawyers in various legal systems do not operate in accordance with uniform standards of ethics. Neither are lawyers in some foreign nations held in high regard within their societies, although this is changing rapidly, especially in parts of Asia. For these reasons, litigation in most locations should be initiated only after all other avenues of collection or settlement have been closed and after determining exactly what results are desired and reasonably possible.

These considerations should not bar litigation, however, in those jurisdictions where the law is clear and legal remedies effective. In some societies, the courts are effective and may be inclined to protect creditors, on balance. If some international commercial banks are more comfortable taking real estate or other forms of tangible assets to settle nonperforming loans, others with extensive legal expertise and a vast network of law firm alliances throughout the world are more comfortable and successful doing battle in the courts or finding other legal remedies. For a complicated international case, especially if fraud or some other dishonesty is involved, it may be necessary to engage many attorneys simultaneously in different cities and on different continents throughout the world to marshal facts, provide complete understanding of international transactions, search for far-flung assets, and then pursue the best remedies after considering a number of different possible solutions.

Nor should criminal laws be overlooked for those cases involving fraud or other dishonesty. United States banking laws, for instance, require reporting of suspected wrongdoing to bank regulatory agencies. Reporting to authorities of other nations where their nationals have violated local laws can sometimes be useful. Although the Federal Bureau of Investigation is more interested in pursuing white collar crime where U.S. nationals are involved in alleged wrongdoing, the U.S. Comptroller of the Currency is interested to some extent in cases that could indicate weakness or patterns in the laws and practices of other nations that could be harmful to U.S. banks doing business in such countries. In Switzerland, bankers as well as others accused of financial mismanagement may be put in jail before trial or without formal proceedings. Finally, recovery may be available under a bank's bonding policy in those rare cases where one of the bank's own employees has been a party to a fraud or other wrongdoing and sufficient evidence exists to prove the case. If many other banks have been involved in a particular situation, legal and related expenses may be minimized by sharing the same law firm or firms and dividing expenses.

Upon formulating a plan short of legal action for handling a nonperforming credit, it is generally advisable to inform the borrower both in person and in writing of the details. In the case of most problem loans, the borrower's cooperation will be needed to resolve the matter and, in any event, the bank wishes to salvage the bank-customer relationship. In many problem credits, the solution may be largely in the borrower's hands. Hence, close monitoring and frequent progress reports are needed by the bank. Usually copies of reports used by the borrower's own management suffice for this purpose and avoid unnecessary duplication of effort by the borrower. If the bank intends to recover out-of-pocket expenses, especially any legal and related expenses, the borrower should be advised in writing of this. The bank should promptly pay all legal and other invoices and forward those to the borrower to obtain reimbursement.

NONACCRUAL, RECOVERY, OR WRITE-OFF

After considering all reasonable alternatives and selecting the most appropriate plan for maximizing recovery or solving credit problems, many bankers find the most difficult job is to stay with any plan long enough and be forceful enough to obtain results. Unfortunately, problem and workout credits often take years to resolve. If real estate is obtained in settlement of a debt, U.S. banking regulations allow a bank up to five years for settlement before requiring write-off. With this timetable, quite extensive properties can be developed and marketed to obtain recovery of bad debts. This factor alone causes U. S. banks in appropriate situations involving realty to tend toward opting for exchange of loan assets on their books for real estate.

Regardless of whether recovery is likely or not, all banks should have consistently applied rules for placing loans on nonaccrual. The most widely accepted standard is ninety days of nonperformance. When loans are placed on nonaccrual, no interest is taken as income until it is actually received, and previously accrued interest generally is reversed and written off. Write-off of a loan or charge against the bank's reserve for loan losses varies from loan to loan and bank to bank. Local banking laws and regulations must be consulted in each jurisdiction for the criteria to be applied for handling interest and writing off all or any part of a bad loan. In addition, the bank should have its own written general policies with regard to write-offs. Needless to say, a great amount of business judgment is involved in any decision to write off or not write off a nonperforming loan. However, most banks lean toward writing off nonperforming loans, even when some ultimate recovery is anticipated, since any recoveries in effect flow back into the loan loss reserve and reduce charges against earnings from subsequent periods.

All nonperforming credits should be reported regularly, at least monthly, to the international unit head, international division managers, and senior bank management, as well as the bank's board of directors. Such reports would be in addition to any daily reports or other information used within the international division. The reports to senior management should include for each credit a synopsis covering the origin of the credit, brief facts about the borrower, the original amount of the credit, any reductions, and efforts or planned measures to collect the balance owed. Any quality classifications used within the bank and by bank regulatory agencies also may be indicated in these reports.

After a bank deals with each bad credit for a period of some months starting from the implementation stage of the planned solution, trends usually emerge to help in predicting likely results with greater accuracy, barring litigation as part of the planned solution. When litigation is involved, up to a year or more may be required even to determine any trend. During this period, management at all levels has time to prepare for the expected outcome. Problem credits, when properly defined, generally involve no ultimate loss of principal or interest to the bank. Workout credits, unfortunately, more often involve loss.

Whenever possible, principal, interest, interest on past due interest, and all reasonable out-of-pocket expenses, especially lawyers' fees, should be collected on nonperforming credits. The bank should apply any recovery first to interest on interest, then to interest, and last to principal. In many jurisdictions, interest on interest is forbidden by law, but it is important to determine whether this rule is part of a nation's general legal system or merely of specialized regulations, usually applied by the central bank or separate foreign exchange regime in connection with remittance of foreign exchange. If only part of foreign exchange regulations, then amounts representing interest on interest or special expenses may be recovered in local currency and put to good use to defray local legal costs, travel, or other expenses in connection with bank activities. Unremittable principal in some situations may be used by the bank locally or loaned in local currency to other entities, pending revisions in the foreign exchange laws or regulations in future years.

Finally, experiences with nonperforming credits should afford all personnel involved, and especially newer lenders, an opportunity for learning to avoid future mistakes. During the last several years, many international banks and banking associations have collected past experiences and developed case studies for use in training programs to teach future international lenders and improve the skills of existing lending officers. Although credit losses represent an expensive form of gaining experience, such experience may be the most valuable and sometimes the only result from certain extensions of credit. Unfortunately, most bankers understandably wish to quickly forget painful experiences and turn to more pleasant and profitable tasks. Yet, to forget the lessons of the past and not make some effort to spare others through educational means only dooms other bankers to repeat the same mistakes.

Appendixes

Appendix A

DEGREES OF RISK
IN INTERNATIONAL
CREDIT EXTENSION

(From lowest to highest degree of risk)

Category of Credit Extension	Period of Risk Exposure for the Bank	Funds Usage and Other Characteristics
Foreign Exchange Contracts		
Spot	One to a few days; three-day maximum in markets for most currencies.	Funds exchanged almost simultaneously, but exposure could be for one day or overnight.
Future (Forward)	Any time period agreed contractually by parties beyond spot period; seldom more than one year; most activity in 30, 60-, or 90-day periods for most currencies.	Funds exchanged almost simultaneously, but exposure upon liquidation could be for one day or overnight.
		In event of failure by bank's customer prior to settlement date, bank may make a new contract with another party.

Category of Credit Extension	Period of Risk Exposure for the Bank	Funds Usage and Other Characteristics

Letters of Credit

Commercial	Most common period of exposure is three months; maximum period usually is six months. Longer periods or renewals are possible by agreement of parties in special situations.	Use of bank's name but generally not bank funds, since same account (of party or correspondent) is charged upon settlement. Usually for financing (exports or imports).
Standby	Maximum period usually is less than one year, although longer periods are possible for special situations.	Use of bank's name rather than funds. Generally used in lieu of a guarantee. Applicable for a variety of activities, not always international, but generally administered in international division.

Bank Deposits

Demand	Amounts on deposit with correspondents fluctuate daily on the basis of individual transactions.	Use of bank's funds for working account balances, most often in foreign currencies. Generally do not earn interest in most countries since subject to immediate withdrawal.
Time (Euro-currencies)	Maximum periods may range up to a year, but most common placements are three or six months. Shorter periods possible in most markets.	Use of bank's funds, which are invested to earn interest on excess funds. May or may not involve foreign currency risk (no foreign currency risk for U.S. banks placing Eurodollars).

Category of Credit Extension	Period of Risk Exposure for the Bank	Funds Usage and Other Characteristics
Bankers' Acceptances	Maximum period is usually 180 days under U.S. laws, which set pattern, although 270 days or longer possible under certain circumstances.	Use of bank's name or bank's funds, depending upon decision of the creating bank. Use of bank's funds until decision to sell in market. If not paid by customer upon maturity, bank must make a loan to customer. Finance international trade, especially readily marketable commodities.
Trade Acceptances	Maximum period is usually 180 days in keeping with terms for short-term trade transactions.	Use of bank's funds, since bank purchases these instruments, drawn by sellers on buyers.
Loans		
Temporary Overdrafts	No set maturity period, but generally not more than a few days. As a rule, 15-day maximum at most banks.	Use of bank's funds, usually for interim financing, pending movement of customer's funds from account at one institution to account at bank extending credit; interest earned.
Short-Term (also called Advances in some cases)	Maturity period of not more than one year, including grace period, as agreed in advance by parties.	Use of bank's funds, most often for purpose of financing trade (exports or imports) or for working capital requirements. As a rule and by custom documentation does not permit resale to participants.

Category of Credit Extension	Period of Risk Exposure for the Bank	Funds Usage and Other Characteristics
Medium-Term	Maturity period usually defined as more than one year but not more than five years, including grace period. (Sometimes Euromarket moves to six- or seven-year periods which may still be considered medium term).	Use of bank's funds, usually for purposes involving acquisition of capital goods or investment for projects that will generate funds to repay loans. Loan documentation most often permits resale to participants at beginning of transaction and increasingly afterward.
Long-Term	Maturity periods of more than five years (or six or seven years, depending on market conditions), but usually not more than ten or twelve years, including grace periods.	Use of bank's funds; same purposes as for medium-term loans. Loan documentation most often permits resale to participants at outset and increasingly afterward.

Appendix B

SEQUENCES IN SEVEN-STEP
BANKWIDE PLANNING PROCESS

(Identifying preliminary and final plan documents)

Preliminary Planning Documents:

Preparation of Documents:

1. Bank Description.
   Bank, unit, and individual
     strengths
   Existing markets
   Current services
   Competitive positions

   Under direction of planning unit
   with input from line and other
   units that write first drafts and
   comment on revisions.

2. World Outlook.
   Country studies for
     Major world powers
     Major market countries
   Dynamic/strategic factors

   Under direction of economics unit
   with input from international division for country studies and other
   information.

3. Money Market Developments.
   Major market nations.
   International bodies and
     arrangements.

   Under direction of economics unit
   with input from international division units.

4. Industrial Surveys, based
   upon particular key markets
   for individual banks,
   such as
     Energy (oil, gas, coal, etc.)
     Steel and shipbuilding, etc.

   Under direction of economics unit
   with input from international and
   domestic commercial lending units.

5a. Market Strategy Alternatives.   By line units, both domestic and
     Markets by industrial and   international, and harmonized by
        geographic sectors   groups or larger units.
     Services, including pos-
        sible new additions
     Financial projections with
        ranges of income and costs

6a. Management Objectives.   By staff and line units and
     All other goals except   coordinated by planning unit with
        market strategies,   input from group executives.
        including projects
        necessary to create
        and supply services
        to implement market
        strategies.

Final Planning Documents:

5b. Market Strategies (final).   By planning unit with participation
     Same as 5a, except that   of line and staff units, group heads,
        only one alternative   and, perhaps, president and chair-
        exists for areas with   man.
        several possibilities
        in earlier versions

6b. Management Objectives   By planning unit with comments
        (final).   from line and staff units, group
     Same as 6a, except that   heads, and president and chairman,
        only objectives to ac-   if necessary.
        company final market
        strategies are necessary

7.   Budget Numbers.   By line and staff units with
     Assets   assistance from planning unit and
     Liabilities   direction from group heads and
     Income   senior executives as needed.
     Expenses
     Staff count

Appendix C

SELECTED INTERNATIONAL
BANKING SCHOOLS,
CONFERENCES, SEMINARS, AND OTHER
POLICY AND TRAINING PROGRAMS

GENERAL SCHOOLS AND PROGRAMS

FOR OFFICERS

School for International Banking, Boulder, Colorado.

Sponsored each July by the International Banking Division of the American Bankers Association with the cooperation of the University of Colorado. Two weeks' duration. The 1980 cost, $700 for members of the American Bankers Association, $875 for nonmembers, excluding transportation.

Started in 1971 for international and domestic banking officers and staff of national and state banking regulatory agencies. Limited to around 200 persons, mainly from U.S. banks, but also some staff from non-U.S. banks. Most students are from international units of their banks, but the number of domestic officers responsible for selling international services is increasing. Most officers have some credit experience or training, but not all, nor is credit experience a requirement, although basic knowledge of financial statement analysis and credit principles is helpful, especially for case studies.

Instructors are almost totally practicing international bankers, many of whom return to teach each year, and teaching methods include lectures, discussion, and case studies. Completion of assignments and preparation for case studies outside of class are necessary. Instructors are rated by students each year.

361

Subject matter includes international bank organization, services, and regulation, as well as general banking, with emphasis on international monetary systems and capital markets. Services discussed are lending, credit, and related fee services, including letters of credit and collections, international payments, and foreign exchange from both operations and marketing standpoints. Lectures in credit extension cover general principles of international lending with emphasis on country risk and trade financing. Cases concentrate on credit extension.

For further information, contact School for International Banking, International Banking Division, American Bankers Association, 1120 Connecticut Avenue, N.W., Washington, D.C. 20036. Telephone (202) 467-4071. Class usually filled early each spring; therefore early application is recommended.

International Banking Program, New York, N.Y., and other selected U.S. cities.

Sponsored at least once a year, usually in October or November, by the American Management Associations. Two days' duration. The 1980 cost, $420 for members of the American Management Associations, $480 for nonmembers, excluding transportation, room, and meals.

For senior executives, including treasurers, controllers, international lending officers, and all managers who want to know more about international banking, both lending and operations. No course limit, but usually 30 to 50 people attend each session. Most students are from international units or senior management of their banks, but domestic officers involved in marketing international services, as well as operations and auditing staff, usually are represented. Most students have several, and some many, years of banking experience. Credit background is not necessarily required.

Instructors are generally practicing international bankers and corporate treasury officers. Some return to lecture each year. Teaching method is basically lecture and discussion with extensive question-and-answer sessions. Outside preparation is not generally necessary. Instructors are rated by students for each course.

Subject matter covered can vary but generally includes international organization and services, including lending as well as fee services. Key topics are collections and letters of credit documentation, sources and techniques of international financing, foreign exchange management, international project financing, and political risk management.

For further information, contact Registrar, American Management Associations, 135 West 50th Street, New York, N.Y. 10020. Telephone (212) 246-0800.

Several dozen other courses of interest to international bankers at roughly the same general cost are available for one- to three-day sessions on such topics as country briefings (Andean Common Market, Argentina, ASEAN, Brazil, Chile, People's Republic of China, Egypt, Israel, Japan, Mexico, Nigeria, and Saudi Arabia), exporting (basic exporting, DISCs, export documentation, and export sales financing), finance (barter and counter-trade, dealing with foreign investors, international credit and collections), human resources (international compensation, international employee benefits, and international personnel management, and tax aspects of these subjects), law (customs laws, Foreign Corrupt Practices Act, international commercial law, and legal aspects of international lending), marketing (international marketing planning), international management (foreign exchange management, international business regulations, international leasing, international risk management, and managing international projects). Ask for International Management Development Programs catalog.

Using International Banking Services Effectively seminar, New York, N.Y., and other selected U.S. cities.

Sponsored at least once a year, usually in July or October, by the World Trade Institute (The Port Authority of New York and New Jersey). Two days' duration. The 1980 cost, $425 for first registrant, $390 for each additional registrant from same company. Cost excludes transportation, room, and meals.

For international bankers, international corporate financial personnel, and banking consultants. No course limit.

Instructors are practicing international bankers, corporate treasury officers, and bank regulatory agency officials.

Courses covered are international services from the corporate viewpoint, role of foreign banks, wholesale banking concept, services of Edge Act banks, international payments services, cash management services, foreign exchange, project finance, and Federal Reserve regulatory changes.

For further information, contact the Registrar, the World Trade Institute, One World Trade Center, 55W, New York, N.Y. 10048. Telephone (212) 466-3162.

About a dozen other courses of potential interest to international bankers are offered at roughly comparable prices on such topics as tax problems in compensating overseas employees, U.S. customs law, introduction to international business law, essentials of international financing and accounting, international cash management, export/import letters of credit, and international taxation. Ask for descriptive brochure.

International Banking Summer School, various cities of the world.

Sponsored by the banking association of each host country with ultimate sponsorship by the London Institute of Bankers. Three weeks' duration each year. Costs vary, but generally in $2,000 – $2,500 range, excluding transportation.

Started in 1948 for bankers from all types of banks from various nations throughout the world, but most participants are usually from Europe, Canada, the United States, Japan, Australia, New Zealand, and South Africa, with occasional students from Asian, African, Middle Eastern, and Latin American nations. Attendance is limited to approximately 200 per year, and national quotas exist to maintain a balanced student body. Participants must have managerial status, be likely to advance in general management, and be between 30 and 45 years of age. Fluency in English is also required. The International Banking Division of the American Bankers Association (ABA) acts as secretariat for the U.S. representatives (quota of 17 out of 200 for 1981), mailing announcements, program details and soliciting U.S. applications. Over the years the ABA has further qualified admission for U.S. bankers to require domicile in the United States, thereby excluding U.S. bank foreign-office representatives. Each national banking association, however, makes it own rates for its nationals. Thus, ABA requirements do not necessarily apply for non-U.S. nationals.

Instructors are practicing bankers from respective host countries each year, although outside speakers and lecturers include national leaders, central bankers, corporate executives, and university professors and experts on international monetary systems. Some outside preparation for group discussion is necessary, but ample time usually is provided for sports and activities.

Subject matter varies from year to year but generally deals with broad policy questions, such as international monetary systems, development of financing and capital markets, regulation of banking, and future issues for all phases of the banking industry, including specialized savings and development banks, as well as commercial banks. Some specialized topics such as project finance and technological developments are also included in some programs.

For further information, bankers should contact the national banking association of their country, since each national association controls participation of its nationals. As indicated above, the American Bankers Association handles selection of candidates from U.S. member banks.

International Banking Institute: Strategic Planning for International Banking, Monterey, California (March 1–11, 1981).

Sponsored by the International Banking Division of the American Bankers Association (ABA) in cooperation with the Federación Latinoamericana de Bancos. Ten days' duration. Fee of $2,300 covers full room and board; transportation excluded.

First program in March 1981 designed for middle to senior middle management international banking officers of Canadian, American, and Latin American banking institutions. Limited to 100 participants to insure effective discussion sessions and encourage a balanced geographic representation. Nominations made to the ABA with review and acceptance handled by the Advisory Board of the Institute. All participants must be fluent in English in order to contribute in discussions.

Participants assigned to seven sections, approximately fifteen per section, with each section headed by a group of Canadian, American, and Latin American banking officers with extensive international experience. Each section has task of developing a strategic plan for expansion of the international banking function of a hypothetical, but realistically described bank in a specific institutional setting. Settings differ in each section in order to promote exchange of information on factors affecting the development of international banking activities in the countries of the Western Hemisphere.

Subject matter covered by leading authorities deals with long-term outlook for growth and development in the world economy, the outlook for world trade and investment, competition in international banking, money and capital markets, and the evolving roles of government programs and international institutions. Other topics include risk and instabilities affecting international banking, the means of coping with these risks, the international banking function from the view of senior management, the impact of technology on international banking, government regulation, financing trade and investment in developing countries, regional cooperation and especially strategic planning, and organizing the international banking function and developing marketing strategies for profitable growth.

For further information, contact the International Banking Division, American Bankers Association, 1120 Connecticut Avenue, N.W., Washington, D.C. 20036. Telephone (202) 467-4071.

FOR NONOFFICERS

American Institute of Banking, International Banking Course, various U.S. cities.

Sponsored by local chapters of the American Bankers Association. Usually offered once a week in evenings for several months. (Generally 10– 15 sessions.) Costs vary, but generally are in $100 – $200 range for course instruction only.

For international division clerical staff and potential officers, with emphasis in most courses on international operations.

Instructors generally are practicing international bankers. Usually, one instructor covers the entire course, but sessions in some cities may involve numerous lecturers or guest speakers.

Subject matter covers international banking organization, international payment services, foreign exchange, collections, and letters of credit, with emphasis on various types of documents used in international trade, such as invoices, packing lists, inspection certifications, marine insurance policies, bills of lading, airway bills, consular certifications, and various negotiable instruments.

For further information, contact local American Institute of Banking chapters in various cities, or International Banking Division, American Bankers Association, 1120 Connecticut Avenue, N.W., Washington, D.C. 20036. Telephone (202) 467-4071.

POLICY-LEVEL CONFERENCES AND SPECIALIZED PROGRAMS

FOR CHIEF EXECUTIVE OFFICERS AND OTHER SENIOR MANAGEMENT
International Banking Conference, New York, N.Y.

Sponsored each January by the international banking division of the American Bankers Association. Three days' duration. The 1980 cost, $425 for members of the American Bankers Association, $525 for nonmembers, excluding transportation, room, and meals.

Started in 1977 for senior bank management involved with international banking, both U.S. and foreign; banking, regulatory, and central bank officials from around the world; and international banking management consultants, among others. Attendance usually in area of 400 to 500. Most participants are from U.S. and foreign commercial banks, especially from New York City, London, and other major European money centers. Most executives are international division heads or those responsible for international functions, among other activities, with many chairmen and bank presidents.

Speakers include central bankers, bank regulatory agency officials, commercial bankers, investment bankers, management consultants, international attorneys, academicians, corporate officers, and others. Speakers address attendees in plenary sessions and in workshops involving small panels and individual discussion leaders. Different speakers participate each year, but many attendees are the same, as program content is redesigned each year.

Subject matter deals with the most timely policy-level issues in international commercial banking each year. Accordingly, over the years, conference programs have covered managing foreign exchange risk, international lending, international management strategies, and managing political risk.

For further information, contact International Banking Division, American Bankers Association, 1120 Connecticut Avenue, N.W., Washington, D.C. 20036. Telephone (202) 467-4071.

For Senior International Unit Managers

International Banking Seminars, London, U.K.

Series of seminars sponsored by the City University Business School in association with Steven Davis. Two days' duration. The 1980 cost, £300 excluding transportation, room, and meals.

For senior international commercial and merchant banking executives involved with topics such as strategy, planning, and marketing for international banking functions. Most participants are from England or other European nations. Each seminar is limited to 40 persons.

Seminar faculty includes management consultants, public accountants, and corporate executives, as well as international bankers. Seminar materials include books written by Steven I. Davis and cases on various specialized problems appropriate for particular seminar topics.

Subject matter for strategy and planning seminar covers strategic planning, operational planning, impact of planning on organization, management information systems and financial structure, and strategic options for different-size and individual banks in light of banking environment for 1980s. Subjects for marketing seminar include developing and implementing marketing plans, identifying markets and market segmentation, risk taking, pricing, and sample marketing strategies.

For further information, contact Course Organizer, The City University Business School, Gresham College, Basinghall Street, London EC2V 50H, United Kingdom. Telephone 01-606 1807/8.

International Department Head Conference, Charlottesville, Virginia.

Sponsored from time to time by the Center for International Banking Studies, affiliated with the Colgate Darden Graduate School of Business Administration of the University of Virginia (under the auspices of the Bankers' Association for Foreign Trade). Three days' duration. The 1980 cost, $650, excluding transportation, room, and meals. Preference given to members of the Bankers' Association for Foreign Trade (BAFT), which includes larger U.S. banks and some foreign banks with U.S. offices.

For international department managers from major regional banks with significant international activity but not necessarily extensive worldwide branch networks. Attendance is limited to 30 with no substitutions permitted for the international department head.

Speakers include practicing international bankers from BAFT and professors from the Darden School.

Subject matter includes such topics as international department strategies, profitability, control of the credit function, sources of country risk problems, and asset/liability management, as well as broader issues mainly relating to cross-border lending.

For further information, contact the Executive Director, Center for International Banking Studies, University of Virginia, Box 6550, Charlottesville, Virginia 22906. Telephone (804) 924-3044.

For Senior Credit and Lending Officers

International Credit Symposium, various U.S. cities (New Orleans in 1980).

Sponsored from time to time by Robert Morris Associates (RMA). Three days' duration. The 1980 cost, $335 for RMA members only. Price excludes transportation and room.

For domestic corporate loan officers who are involved in the international credit approval process or who are about to assume such responsibilities.

Case-study material is used to simulate real-life situations in certain problem loan situations and countries. The planned, yet informal, format of the program affords an opportunity for participants to exchange views with senior international credit banking officers who will present lectures and case-study materials.

For further details, contact Registrar, Robert Morris Associates, National Office, 1616 Philadelphia National Bank Building, Philadelphia, Pennsylvania 19107. Telephone (215) 665-2880.

International Lending Policy Seminar, Charlottesville, Virginia.

Sponsored from time to time by the Center for International Banking Studies. See comments under International Department Head Conference for further details on sponsorship. Three days' duration. The 1980 cost, $475, excluding transportation, room, and board. Preference given to BAFT member bank personnel.

For senior credit officers of BAFT member banks and friends of the Center for International Banking Studies. Registrants must have policy responsibility in international departmental management and should be vice-president to department head. Domestic division participants should be senior officers or international loan committee members.

Speakers are practicing international bankers from BAFT member banks and professors from the Darden School.

Subject matter includes topics such as developing loan policy, legal trends, international loan reviews procedures, country portfolio management, market strategies, profitability, funding international department assets, and handling workout credits.

For further details, contact Executive Director, Center for International Banking Studies, University of Virginia, Box 6550, Charlottesville, Virginia 22906. Telephone (804) 924-3044.

Managing International Lending Risks Workshop, various U.S. cities (Houston and Washington, D.C. during 1981).

Sponsored annually by Robert Morris Associates (RMA). Two days' duration. The 1981 cost, $275 for RMA members, $345 for nonmembers, excluding transportation, room, and meals.

For domestic line account officers with frequent involvement in foreign loans and international credits, international loan and credit officers, and credit officers and others engaged in international loan and credit review or administration.

Intensive work schedule with extensive use of case materials.

Subject matter delineates all pertinent factors involved in credit risk management for foreign government borrowers, for foreign companies, for foreign subsidiaries of domestic companies, and in situations where loan is granted and repaid in a foreign currency. Workshop also covers evaluation of risk and credit criteria, including country risk assessment, risk rating systems, and exposure management and its application in a regional bank setting. (Special program dealing with credit risk in foreign exchange transactions is scheduled for 1981.)

For further details, contact Registrar, Robert Morris Associates, National Office, 1616 Philadelphia National Bank Building, Philadelphia, Pennsylvania 19107. Telephone (215) 665-2880.

Analyzing Foreign Banks and Companies Workshop, various U.S. cities (Dallas in 1980).

Sponsored from time to time by Robert Morris Associates (RMA). Two days' duration. The 1980 cost, $275 for RMA members, $345 for nonmembers, excluding transportation, room, and meals.

For international credit analysts and international loan and credit officers, who need to interpret and utilize statements from overseas correspondent banks and foreign corporations, and for domestic loan and credit officers involved in international credit decisions.

Case-study materials and workshop discussion techniques are used extensively as opposed to formal lectures.

For further details, contact Registrar, Robert Morris Associates, National Office, 1616 Philadelphia National Bank Building, Philadelphia, Pennsylvania 19107. Telephone (215) 665-2880.

Lending in Latin America Workshop, various U.S. cities (Miami in 1981).

Sponsored from time to time by Robert Morris Associates (RMA). Two days' duration. The 1981 cost, $275 for RMA members, $345 for nonmembers, excluding transportation, room, and meals.

For lending officers dealing with Latin American borrowers, especially at regional banks, domestic line account officers with frequent involvement in foreign loans and international credits, credit officers and others engaged in international loan and credit eview or administration, and international loan and credit officers associated with Edge Act corporations and banks. (Similar program scheduled during 1981 for lending in Southeast Asia.)

Case study material is used extensively.

Subject matter is designed to provide a basic familiarity with changes in factors affecting external and internal liquidity in key lending areas in Latin America and with various indicators of near-term structural vulnerability. Four or five countries are treated in a comprehensive manner and topics cover loan documentation, all forms of international lending, country risk considerations, and political risk evaluation.

For further details, contact Registrar, Robert Morris Associates, National Office, 1616 Philadelphia National Bank Building, Philadelphia, Pennsylvania 19107. Telephone (215) 665-2880.

FOR SENIOR MANAGEMENT AND SYSTEMS DEVELOPMENT OFFICERS

International Systems Symposium, Chicago, Illinois.

Sponsored by the International Banking and Operations and Automation Divisions of the American Bankers Association. Two days' duration. The 1980 cost, $280 for members of the American Bankers Association, $350 for nonmembers, excluding transportation, room, and meals.

Started in 1979 for senior management involved with international banking, operations, and systems, both U.S. and foreign. Attendance is usually about 150 to 200. Most participants are from U.S. banks with substantial international operations, mainly major money center banks and more active regionals, but personnel from foreign banks also attend.

Speakers include commercial bankers with responsibility for international planning and systems functions, management consultants, corporate executives, international lawyers, and executives from organizations such as SWIFT. Presentations include panel discussions as well as individual speeches with opportunities for questions and discussion.

Subject matter deals with the impact of technology on international banking, the role of SWIFT, costing and pricing international services, laws concerning information flows, and various technical innovations in computers, fiberoptics, and communications.

For further information, contact International Banking Division, American Bankers Association, 1120 Connecticut Avenue, N.W., Washington, D.C. 20036. Telephone (202) 467-4071.

Appendix D

REPRESENTATIVE TOPICS FOR AN
INTERNATIONAL DIVISION
PROCEDURES MANUAL INDEX

1.00 Accounts
1.01   Index of Accounts (chart of accounts)*
1.02   Account Descriptions (chart of accounts)*
1.15   Reconcilement of Due-From Accounts
1.27   Reconcilement of Other Charges Receivable

2.00 Audits and Examinations
2.10   Internal Audits
2.20   Independent Accountant Audits
2.30   Federal Bank Examination

3.00 Country Analysis and Limits
3.10   Country Risk Analysis Preparation
3.16   Country Limit Setting
3.17   Country Limit Committee Function
3.30   Central Liability Ledger Controls (Also see Section 4.15)

4.00 Credit Extension
4.10   Rules for Extension of Credit
4.15   Central Liability Ledger (Also see Section 3.30)
4.20   Credit Package Preparation
4.21   Credit Committee

*Every account used in the international division would be listed by
  number and title.

Appendix E

SOME COMMON FORMS OF CREDIT EXTENSION TO BANK CUSTOMERS

$5,000,000 *Eurocurrency Deposit Line (Guidance/Unadvised)* –
(or equiv.) (For international division use at London branch).
For placement of Eurocurrency deposits with
maturities not to exceed 180 days from date of
deposit at market rates.

$3,000,000 *Foreign Exchange Line (Guidance/Unadvised)* – (For
(or equiv.) international division use at head office). For
spot or future purchases or sales of foreign
exchange at market rates with *sublimit not to exceed*
$1,000,000 for total exchange contracts maturing on
any one day.

$5,000,000 *Fed Funds and/or CD Line (Guidance/Unadvised)* – *(For*
investment department use at head office). For sale
of fed funds and/or purchases of subject's U.S. dollar
certificates of deposit with maturities not to exceed
180 days at market rates.

$200,000 *Due-from Account (Guidance/Unadvised)* — (For inter-
(or equiv.) national division use at head office). Maximum balance; target balance (average monthly) $50,000.

$1,500,000 *Short-term Line of Credit (Advised)* — (For inter-
national division use at head office). For the
usual international transactions consisting of:

Confirmations of letters of credit at ¼ of 1%
(Negotiation ¼ of 1%);
Financing by acceptances up to 180 days at New
York Bankers Acceptance Discount Rate plus 2%
commission;
Advances up to 180 days at bank's prime rate plus
2.5% per annum; and
Sublimit not to exceed $500,000 for
temporary overdrafts up to 15 days at
bank's prime rate plus 3% p.a.

$1,000,000   *Medium-term Line of Credit (Advised)* — (For inter-
national division use at head office). For U.S.
commercial bank financing under Eximbank's
cooperative financing facility with semiannual
repayment up to five years' final maturity at bank's
prime rate plus 2% p.a. net of taxes, adjusted
semiannually.

Advances under this line will be guaranteed by
Eximbank with guaranty fees for the account of
the bank (or customer).

$4,000,000   *Standby Eurodollar Line (Advised)* — (For inter-
national division use at London branch). For providing Eurodollars for periods of up to 180 days in
event of subject's inability to obtain Eurodollar deposits. Availability until June 30, 1983
at a fee of ½ of 1% p.a. with drawings at
1.5% over LIBO rate or 1.5% over prime rate at
customer's option.

Appendix F

SOME COMMON FORMS OF CREDIT EXTENSION TO CUSTOMERS OTHER THAN BANKS

$3,000,000 (or equiv.) — *Foreign Exchange Line (Guidance/Unadvised)* — (For international division use at head office). For spot or future purchases or sales of foreign exchange at market rates with *sublimit not to exceed $1,000,000* for total exchange contracts maturing on any one day.

$1,000,000 — *Short-term Line of Credit (Advised)* — (For international division use at head office). For the usual international transactions consisting of:
Issuance of letters of credit at ½ of 1% for up to six months or any fraction thereof;
Financing by trade acceptances to 180 days at rate equal to New York Bankers Acceptance Discount Rate offered to the bank plus 1.5% commission;
Advances up to 180 days at the bank's prime rate plus 2% p.a.
Sublimit not to exceed $200,000 for temporary overdrafts up to 15 days at bank's prime rate plus 2.5% p.a.

$5,000,000 — *Revolving Trade Finance Line (Advised)* — (For international division use at head office). For accepting and discounting drafts drawn on bank by The General Company to a maximum of 180 days at a discount rate equal to New York Bankers Acceptance

Discount Rate offered to us, plus a commission of
2% per annum. Line will be available on a
revolving basis from January 1, 1982, for a period
of 24 months and will be repaid in full on January
1, 1985. The purpose of the credit line is to
finance General Company's imports of crude oil
and/or its by-products.

$3,000,000   *Short-term Line of Credit (Guidance/Unadvised)* — (For
international division use at head office). For
purchasing trade drafts with (or without) recourse
drawn by The General Corporation and accepted by
Company Blank for up to 90 days' maturity from
respective shipping dates, discounted at a rate to
yield not less than the bank's prime plus 2.0% p.a.
net, fixed as of each rate setting date.

$2,000,000   *Term Loan (Advised)* — (For international division use
at London branch). For a five-year-term loan with six
consecutive semiannual repayments of principal,
commencing 30 months after funding; with joint and
several guarantees of X and Y.

    Interest — six-month LIBOR plus 2% p.a. (net of
taxes), payable and adjusted every six months.

    Commitment fee — ¾% p.a. on undrawn portion,
payable on each interest date.

    Commission — 1% p.a. flat, payable within 90 days
of initial drawdown; legal fees payable by borrower
upon submission of lawyer's invoice.

Appendix G

REPRESENTATIVE BASIC REFERENCE
MATERIALS
ON INTERNATIONAL BANKING

GENERAL INTERNATIONAL BANKING

Baughn, William H., and Charles E. Walker, Eds. *The Bankers' Handbook*, rev. ed. Homewood, Ill.: Dow Jones-Irwin, 1978.

Hardcover book of about 1,200 pages including four chapters on international banking by five different contributors, all experienced international bankers. Topics covered include the development of U.S. international banking in an international banking organization, meeting the needs of multinational companies, the role of commercial banks in the Eurocurrency markets, and various aspects of international credits, including country risk, international liquidity, and funding.

Fraser, Robert D. *International Banking and Finance*, 3rd ed. Washington, D.C.: R & H Publishers, 1977.

Loose-leaf volume of approximately 500 mimeographed pages with extensive exhibits and appendixes detailing various instruments and specialized activities in the field, with heavy emphasis on international economic issues and international banking operations techniques. Useful for reference or as text for a semester-long university course or the equivalent. Updates available by subscription.

Oppenheim, Peter K. *International Banking,* 3rd ed. Washington, D.C.: American Institute of Banking, The American Bankers Association, 1978.

Hardcover book of about 200 pages introducing the field of international banking, with emphasis on basic international operations techniques and some reference to lending functions. Mainly used as a text for clerical personnel in operations areas and others new to international banking. Used extensively in courses for the American Institute of Banking (educational unit of the American Bankers Association) throughout the United States for introductory international banking courses.

TRADE FINANCING AND FOREIGN EXCHANGE TECHNIQUES

Harfield, Henry. *Bank Credits and Acceptances,* 5th ed. New York: The Ronald Press, 1974.

Hardcover book of about 300 pages describing the functions of letters of credit and acceptances in the context of laws and rules governing the use of these instruments of trade finance, with numerous citations to legal cases and materials. Essential reference and training book for any bank handling letters of credit and acceptances or law firms which advise such banks.

Harfield, Henry. *Letters of Credit.* Philadelphia: American Law Institute — American Bar Association Committee on Continuing Professional Education, 1979.

Paperback book of about 150 pages dealing with the subject of letters of credit from a legal perspective, covering general principles, parties, definitions, classifications, establishment, performance, judicial intervention, and transfer and assignment of letters of credit. Part of the Uniform Commercial Code Practice Handbook series. Appendixes contain Article 5 of the Uniform Commercial Code, Uniform Customs and Practice for Documentary Credits (1975), and a table of cases cited in the book.

Mandich, D.R., Editor, *Foreign Exchange Trading Techniques and Controls*. Washington, D.C.: American Bankers Association, 1976.

Hardcover book of about 200 pages divided into ten chapters with an appendix illustrating an actual transaction in detail and a glossary of terms. Each chapter is written by a different author, each of whom is experienced in foreign exchange activities based upon either banking, public accounting, or corporate work. Subject matter ranges from the mechanics of foreign exchange markets, foreign exchange risks, creating positions, reporting, revaluation, and profitability analysis to establishing trading policy, dealing with tax issues, and auditing the foreign exchange function.

Schneider, Gerhard W. *Export-Import Financing: A Practical Guide.* New York: The Ronald Press, 1974.

Hardcover book of approximately 400 pages covering various institutions engaged in trade financing, mechanics of executing trade transactions (sales contracts, foreign exchange, and various documents), and the financing techniques for trade financing, including collections and letters of credit. Useful both as reference work and textbook for formal course or self-instruction for officers, potential officers, and specialized clerical personnel in international operations areas.

Shaterian, William S. *Export-Import Banking: The Documents and Financial Operations of Foreign Trade*, 2nd ed. New York: The Ronald Press, 1956.

Hardcover book of about 500 pages describing in detail, with extensive use of sample forms, exhibits, and appendixes, the work of the international department and the documents and financial operations of foreign trade. Extremely useful as reference and textbook for specialized courses or in-house training programs on international trade financing.

CROSS-BORDER LENDING TECHNIQUES AND INSTITUTIONS

Bhagavatula, Ramachandra, and Harold van B. Cleveland, *Global Financial Intermediation: Economic Analysis and Policy Issues,* 1st ed., New York, N.Y.: Citibank, 1980.

Paperbound booklet of approximately 50 pages with numerous tables and figures dealing with cross-border banking, how Eurocurrency markets work, and Euromarkets and public policies. In spite of its rather formidable title this slim volume presents a concise and practical explanation of the Eurocurrency markets in the context of history, uses, and probable future developments.

Davis, Steven I. *The Euro-Bank: Its Origins, Management, and Outlook.* London: The Macmillan Press, Ltd., 1976.

Hardcover book of about 100 pages dealing with the history, definition, and evolution of the Eurobank, asset and liability management, capital adequacy, funding, fee-producing activities, and financial performance of Eurobanks. Useful especially for London bankers or others engaged in or considering entry into merchant banking.

Donoghue, Michael F., and E. Paul Dunn, Jr., *International Lending Cases 1979.* Charlottesville, Va.: Center for International Banking Studies, The Colgate Darden Graduate School of Business Administration, University of Virginia, 1980.

Paperback book of approximately 250 pages containing nine case studies, with financial statements and actual materials used in the lending process, including conducting credit analysis, interpreting foreign accounting statements, dealing with devaluations, establishing international credit policies, and analyzing international profitability. Cases cover the world geographically and deal with loans to foreign banks, corporations, and governments. Several cases are presented under actual borrower names; in other cases, although based on actual facts, borrowers' names are disguised. Short-term credit, trade finance, term lending, and project finance are represented by the situations selected. Requires extensive preparation and experienced teachers or leaders for discussion or group sessions.

Mathis, F. John, Ed. *Offshore Lending by U.S. Commercial Banks,* 1st ed. Washington, D.C.: The Bankers' Association for Foreign Trade and Robert Morris Associates, 1975.

Hardcover book of approximately 300 pages with essays by different authors, mainly practicing international commercial bankers, on topics related to cross-border lending, including country analysis, legal aspects of lending, foreign accounting practices, loan syndication, and different types of international lending, such as trade financing, lending to governments, foreign banks, and private foreign companies. Essential tool for all bankers engaged in cross-border lending, although emphasis is on U.S. approach.

COUNTRY ANALYSIS AND COUNTRY RISK EVALUATION

Friedman, Dr. Irving S. *The Emerging Role of Private Banks in the Developing World,* 1st ed. New York: Citicorp, 1977.

Paperbound booklet of about 100 pages analyzing the debt burden of less developed countries (LDCs) and presenting arguments and statistical support for the reasonableness and soundness of commercial bank lending to LDCs. Excellent for answering criticism about commercial banking activities and thinking through the cross-border lending function of international commercial banks based on facts and experience.

Melville, Richard A., introducing others. *Country Risk and Country Evaluation.* New York: Allied Bank International, 1978.

Paperbound booklet of about 50 pages with text of five speeches given by Chandra S. Hardy (The World Bank), Thibaut de Saint Phalle (Export-Import Bank of the United States), Pedro-Pablo Kuczynski (Halco Mining Inc.), Robert R. Bench (Office of Comptroller of the Currency), and Augustus L. Putnam (Allied

Bank International), at May 1978 meeting of International Advisory Committee of Allied Bank International. Useful study of different perspectives of country risk evaluation, especially for banks starting or revising country study techniques.

INTERNATIONAL MONETARY SYSTEM

Solomon, Robert. *The International Monetary System, 1945-1976: An Insider's View.* New York: Harper & Row, Publishers, 1977.

Hardcover book of approximately 300 pages documenting the history of changes in the postwar international monetary system, with detailed descriptions of the pressures, politics, and personalities causing the changes and developments. Excellent background reading for senior international banking executives and management concerned with issues related to capital markets, foreign exchange, and the world money system.

SPECIFIC COUNTRIES — GENERAL REFERENCE

Price Waterhouse & Co. *Information Guides for Doing Business Abroad.* New York: Price Waterhouse & Co., 1981 and preceding years.

These paperback booklets, generally from about 30 to 100 pages in length, contain current information on general business conditions, accounting principles, and taxes in selected countries of the world, including various specialized booklets on the United States and U.S. activities abroad.

Note: Other major international accounting firms, including Arthur Andersen & Co., Authur Young & Co., Coopers and Lybrand, Deloitte, Haskins & Sells, Ernst & Whinney, Peat, Marwick, Mitchell & Co., and Touche Ross & Co., publish similar information on individual nations.

A series from one of these firms is indispensable to the international banker for reference and staying current with changing laws, accounting rules, and business environments around the world.

Appendix H

CHECKLIST WITH BRIEF EXPLANATIONS OF FACTORS USED IN COUNTRY ANALYSIS

ECONOMIC FACTORS

Introduction. Economic statistics and ratios are collected and analyzed to study a nation's (1) size and level of development, (2) balance of payments condition, (3) foreign debt structure, and (4) international liquidity position. The following listing of statistics and ratios, which is representative rather then exhaustive, generally breaks down into performance indicators that help analyze size and level of national economic development and those that indicate direction and trends for measuring economic strength and resiliency. For international banks that are still developing their country analysis capabilities, economic analysis might consist in first studying separately the various statistics and ratios to determine national size and development level and prepare for further analysis. This further analysis then would deal with factors and policies that are usually interconnected and relate to balance of payments condition, debt structure, and liquidity position. Hence, the two subsections that follow are headed "Statistics and Ratios" and "Economic Analysis Factors." All line references are to *International Financial Statistics,* published monthly by the International Monetary Fund (IMF). Most statistics must be collected for at least five years to be useful. However, unfortunately, there is some time lag before the IMF statistics become available for certain countries. Analysis of IMF statistics is the starting point for work with other materials and discussions with various government officials in each nation.

STATISTICS AND RATIOS

1. *Population* (line 99z) is useful for ranking a nation's size and noting any significant changes in demographic patterns.

2. *Gross National Product* (line 99a), which represents the value of all measurable goods and services produced each year, helps in determining absolute size and, when calculated in constant currency units, indicates the direction of economic activity. It is also important to measure agricultural and industrial output as percentages of GNP to determine a nation's level of development and study savings and investment in relation to GNP to measure the rate of internally generated capital formation.

3. *Gross National Product per Capita* (Item 2 above divided by 1) measures the ability of the nation's economy to outpace inflation and population growth and thus improve the position of each individual in a nation. When per capita gains are widely distributed and not concentrated within any one group of the population, social tensions usually are decreased and political stability improved.

4. *Exchange rate* (line a.e.) provides a rough indication of a country's general economic direction and trend of economic performance in relation to the economies of other nations.

5. *Exports* (line 70) represents the value of all goods and services exported. Growth trends and diversity of commodities and other products, along with changes in type of export mix, help predict a nation's foreign exchange earnings. Diversity of trading partners by individual nation and regions of the world also is important to analyze.

6. *Imports* (line 71) represents the cost (CIF basis) of all goods and services acquired from outside the country. Growth trends and the diversity of imports, along with the mix of items imported, measure

the foreign exchange needs of a nation. The import mix is especially important with regard to decreasing or compressing imports in times of foreign exchange shortfalls. If a high percentage of imports consists of luxury goods, then imports are said to be highly compressible. If a high percentage represents foodstuffs or energy products not available domestically, then the economy is more vulnerable to foreign exchange shortages.

7. *Trade balance* (Item 6 subtracted from Item 5), when positive, indicates that exports earn enough to pay for imports. However, a negative figure is not necessarily bad; tourism or workers' remittances may help pay for imports, and imports of capital goods may eventually help increase exports. Continued negative trends without other offsetting factors, however, could indicate potential problems.

8. *Current account/Balance of payments* (lines 77 a.a.d. through 77 a.g.d.) items consist of merchandise export revenues minus merchandise import expenditures plus (or minus) other goods and services items, net private transfers and net official transfers. A country which requires capital inflows or foreign investment in order to balance its current account items must maintain national economic and political policies that foster such flows.

9. *Direct investment/Balance of payments* (lines 77 b.a.d. through 77 d.d) items consist of net direct investment, portfolio investment, other long-term and short-term capital items, and net errors and omissions for a particular period. They can thus often be used to measure the level of confidence by foreign investors in the country.

10. *International reserves plus gold* (lines l.l.d. through l.d.d. and line l.a.n.d.) items measure a nation's liquid assets for settling foreign obligations. These assets are usually composed of gold, foreign exchange reserves, and credit available from the International Monetary Fund in the form of Special Drawing Rights (SDRs) plus gold.

11. *Debt service ratio* (obtainable from World Bank annual reports for most nations) is obtained by dividing total external public debt

payments (principal and interest for one year) by annual export revenues from goods and services. Ratios of more than 25 percent generally are considered to indicate potential problems. However, low ratios could indicate low foreign debt caused by inability to borrow. Moreover, private foreign borrowing is not included in the World Bank statistics. Thus, this ratio must be used carefully in context with other factors.

12. *Reserves to imports* (calculated by dividing international reserves by imports, items 10 and 6 above, respectively) provides an indication of the extent to which imports are covered by existing reserves. A ratio of about 40 percent, or enough to cover imports for approximately five months, generally is considered to be a minimum for most nations, but each country must be studied in its own context.

13. *Money supply (M1 only)* (line 34) is important in connection with the inflation rate and indicates government policies in this regard.

14. *Inflation rate* (line 64) or the consumer price index measures the success of government policies. Excessive rates of inflation over relatively long periods of time generally discourage savings and investment and may cause devaluation of a nation's currency in relation to stronger currencies. Thus, the ability to repay foreign loans in such currencies may be impaired. In addition, accelerating rates of inflation, and especially accelerating high rates of inflation, often warn that countries with such rates may be facing future payments difficulties. This close correlation has been evidenced by various statistical studies.

ECONOMIC ANALYSIS FACTORS

1. *National size and development level.* On the basis of the various statistics and ratios, some conclusion can be reached about whether the international commercial bank should be involved with a particular nation. Obviously, some nations are not of sufficient size or economic level to merit credit without excessive risks. However, this determination is almost always related to the study of other factors.

2. *Balance of payments.* The study of a nation's balance of payments starts with current account transactions, including exports and imports of goods and services, and moves from the balance of trade to transfer payments, such as remittances from nationals residing or working outside the country, and foreign government grants. Buildup of the current account study leads next to analysis of capital account transactions, such as direct investment, foreign borrowings, and, finally, use of reserve assets, including borrowing from the IMF.

3. *Debt structure.* Analysis of debt should include government borrowing, both direct and guaranteed, and private sector indebtedness, from foreign lenders. The balance of payments must be analyzed in relation to trends and likely future developments within the country and with the nation's major trading and investment partners, as must foreign borrowing. Other factors relevant in debt analysis include maturity schedules and diversification of credit sources.

4. *International liquidity position.* In addition to analysis of reserve assets with emphasis for developing countries on dealings with the International Monetary Fund, study of this topic involves the relationship between domestic and foreign assets and liabilities, as shown on the balance sheet of a nation's central bank. Furthermore, the alternatives and changes in government policies, including monetary policy, based upon these balance sheet changes, and the resulting consequences must be considered again in the context of the other related factors. For this reason, it is useful for most bankers to study first certain statistics and ratios separately before moving to the broader and more interrelated topics, which are more closely related to government policies. Moreover, such a pattern is a logical bridge to considering more purely political and social issues.

POLITICAL AND SOCIAL FACTORS

Introduction. Although the economic factors used in country analysis are easy to quantify, political and social factors are not. Nor is the overall approach to analysis in this area as uniform within the international banking industry. The goal of political and social analysis is quite clear, however, and that is to determine the likelihood of political change so severe and disruptive as to impair the ability of the economy to perform and hence generate sufficient foreign exchange to repay foreign borrowings. For this purpose, political analysis is usually divided into factors dealing with government leadership, change of government, social trends, and external relationships. Again, the factors listed here are meant to be representative rather than exhaustive, as some banks use various other measures, as well as those listed.

Government leadership. Within this area, emphasis is placed on the stability of the ruler, ruling faction, or political party, the existence and role of opposition groups or other political parties, and the process for change in government leadership and policies. Moreover, some judgment must be made about the quality or effectiveness of the leadership in power, as contrasted to the bureaucracy or permanent government structure that continues in spite of changes in the leadership.

Social factors. The absence or presence of fragmentation or "nations within nations" historically has had a bearing on the suddenness and degree of change in governing groups in many countries. This aspect is sometimes referred to as measuring the degree of cultural homogeneity and is a useful concept for many nations. In other countries, trends related to religion, the role of women, and the availability of education may be more important. In almost all countries, an important factor is the degree to which social mobility or movement upward in the society is based upon merit and individual effort.

External factors. In an increasingly interrelated world, especially for nations which depend upon foreign trade and investment, the pattern of relationships with other nations and international institutions is crucial. This would include relationships with neighboring nations and those within larger regional blocks, as well as more distant trading and investment partners. Political, economic, and military or strategic groupings and alliances; nations with diplomatic relationships; membership in the International Monetary Fund and in other U.N.-related bodies; and similar linkings must be considered in this regard.

Index